TOWARD AN EXEGETICAL THEOLOGY

BIBLICAL EXEGESIS FOR PREACHING AND TEACHING

TOWARD AN EXEGETICAL THEOLOGY

BIBLICAL EXEGESIS FOR PREACHING AND TEACHING

WALTER C. KAISER, JR.

BAKER BOOK HOUSE
Grand Rapids, Michigan 49506

To all God's choice servants
who minister His Word to His Church
and who, under God, pledge themselves
to end the famine of the hearing
of the whole counsel of God

And especially to
Dr. Merrill C. Tenney
the one under whom I first learned
the analytical method of exegesis
and who instilled in me
an insatiable love for the Scriptures
and the idea of applying
the rudiments of this method to Hebrew

Preface

In 1742 John Albert Bengel observed: "Scripture is the foundation of the Church: the Church is the guardian of Scripture. When the Church is in strong health, the light of Scripture shines bright; when the Church is sick, Scripture is corroded by neglect; and thus it happens, that the outward form of Scripture and that of the Church, usually seem to exhibit simultaneously either health or else sickness; and as a rule the way in which Scripture is being treated is in exact correspondence with the condition of the Church."[1] After more than two centuries we can affirm the validity of Bengel's warning. The Church and the Scripture stand or fall together. Either the Church will be nourished and strengthened by the bold proclamation of her Biblical texts or her health will be severely impaired.

It is no secret that Christ's Church is not at all in good health in many places of the world. She has been languishing because she has been fed, as the current line has it, "junk food"; all kinds of artificial preservatives and all sorts of unnatural substitutes

---

1. John Albert Bengel, *Gnomon of the New Testament*, ed. Andrew R. Fausset, 5 vols. (Edinburgh: Clark, 1857–1858), 1:7. The English translation has been modernized at one or two points.

7

have been served up to her. As a result, theological and Biblical malnutrition has afflicted the very generation that has taken such giant steps to make sure its physical health is not damaged by using foods or products that are carcinogenic or otherwise harmful to their physical bodies. Simultaneously a worldwide spiritual famine resulting from the absence of any genuine publication of the Word of God (Amos 8:11) continues to run wild and almost unabated in most quarters of the Church.

Not all the causes or solutions may be offered in this volume. But as one who is charged under the same Lord who is Head of the Church to prepare undershepherds for the ministry in Christ's Church at large, I feel there is one place where I have a special debt to the Church which I must discharge. I have been aware for some time now of a gap that has existed in academic preparation for the ministry. It is the gap that exists between the study of the Biblical text (most frequently in the original languages of Hebrew, Aramaic, and Greek) and the actual delivery of messages to God's people. Very few centers of Biblical and homiletical training have ever taken the time or effort to show the student how one moves from analyzing the text over to constructing a sermon that accurately reflects that same analysis and is directly dependent on it.

This volume will not solve every problem even in this one selected area. One reason it will not, I must say in all candor, is that there are no complete guides in this area. As far as this writer has been able to discover, no one has ever attempted to author an exegetical theology in English or any modern European language. This discovery in itself was startling. Here is a discipline which is at the very heart of what theological education is all about. In short, it is at once the "proof" and the finishing touch of the whole process. Should the ministry of the pulpit fail, one might just as well conclude that all the supporting ministries of Christian education, counseling, community involvement, yes, even missionary and society outreach, will likewise soon dwindle, if not collapse. Bengel is most accurate and very much to the point here as well.

Therefore something had to be done. Whatever is done here reflects my own attempts to rectify a difficult situation. I have been developing the syntactical-theological method of exegesis and sermon building for several decades now. However, I am also very much aware of the fact that this volume can be regarded only as an exploratory and provisional type of firstfruits. If I do not miss my guess, one positive effect of *Toward an Exegetical Theology* will be a spawning (here used in a positive sense) of many similar exegetical theologies—this is all to the good.

One thing is certain: almost everyone in the field now recognizes the need for such a tool. Many others have been poised with pen in hand ready to take up the challenge and to write just such a volume. I trust that this volume may be the final encouragement for them to press on to completion what they have planned to do, for the need is as large as the fields of the earth. Perhaps after I have read all of these fine projected works, I may be able to remove the "toward" from my title and produce an enlarged exegetical theology, *Deo volente*.

I have tried to write with as large a spectrum of the body of Christ in mind as possible. Obviously, not everyone is going to find everything equally helpful since abilities and past achievements will markedly differ. The reader is urged to skip to those parts that he can more easily digest. At one or two points I have deliberately engaged in some rather technical discussions, for I wish to carry on a conversation not only with those whose orientation is more practical, but also with those who are acquainted with some of the more technical aspects and with some who may not share our own theological convictions but who are, nevertheless, also diligently seeking for answers to some of the same questions.

In my own view, I cannot see how the person who wishes to be totally prepared could hope to begin unless and until he is able to translate the text from Greek or Hebrew. However, I also know that many of God's choice pastors, Bible teachers, missionaries, and third-world preachers and teachers, have not been so favored by circumstances and educational opportunities thus far. But their degree of accountability (and perhaps the generation they serve)

will be different before the Lord than that of others who have had
great privileges, but have failed to use them. Therefore, I have
shown that the method expounded in this book can be profitably
employed even if one has access only to a translated version of
the Scriptures. True, it may require that these persons should also
buy a paperback textbook to review their own grammar, certain
grammatical terms, and key syntactical forms. But after all, that
is what public elementary education (not to mention the secondary level of education, which is usually grades 9–12) is all about.
In the American Colonies, people were taught to read and write,
not primarily so that they could get a better job and improve their
financial situation, but, in the colonists' view at least, so that they
could better their spiritual health by reading God's Word for themselves. Consequently, if putting the suggestions of this book into
practice means relearning a few basic facts like the definitions of
nouns, verbs, adjectives, adverbs, prepositions, and the like, then
so be it. Let us relearn these definitions and the basic rules of
grammar and syntax, for the lives of men and women depend
upon it.

I must express my gratitude to our Lord for His help and pro-
vision of strength as I composed these chapters while maintaining
an extremely heavy schedule of speaking and teaching. I trust
that the seasoned veteran pastor, the diligent Bible-study leader,
the hungry churchman who wishes to dig into God's Word on his
own, and the aspiring theological student who is just beginning
to get involved in this aspect of the ministry, will all profit im-
mensely from what is written here. But I also pray that, even
more significantly, they may all sense this writer's own response
and willingness to stand under the Word of God so that it will be
obvious that more is involved here than just a mere academic
discipline.

Many other friends faithfully ministered to bring this project
to completion. Among those who deserve special mention are:
Cornelius Zylstra from Baker Book House, who has constantly
urged me on and given repeated encouragement for this project
since 1973; my wife Margaret Ruth Kaiser, Renae Grams, Marty
Irwin, and my secretary Lois Armstrong, who have typed the

manuscript with such care; and finally my graduate assistant, Timothy Addington, who helped with proofreading this manuscript at several stages of its composition.

Contents

PART I

Introduction

Chapter 1

Current Crises in Exegetical Theology

In a world that has been treated almost daily to one crisis after another in almost every aspect of its life, it will come as no shock to have another crisis announced: a crisis in exegetical theology. Already we have been warned about crises in systematic theology and Biblical theology, and about ignorance of the contents of Scripture.[1]

But we cannot help agreeing with Professor George M. Landes that the most "basic crisis in biblical studies" must be placed in the discipline of exegesis.[2] In many ways, it is this crisis that has precipitated the other theological crises.

---

1. Respectively: Tom F. Driver, "Review of Langdon Gilkey's *Naming the Whirlwind: The Renewal of God Language*," *Union Seminary Quarterly Review* 25 (1970): 361; Brevard S. Childs, *Biblical Theology in Crisis* (Philadelphia: Westminster, 1970); James D. Smart, *The Strange Silence of the Bible in the Church: A Study in Hermeneutics* (Philadelphia: Westminster, 1970), p. 10.

2. George M. Landes, "Biblical Exegesis in Crisis: What Is the Exegetical Task in a Theological Context?" p. 274. (When a book or article appears in the bibliography at the end of this volume as does this article, bibliographic information is not given in full in the footnotes.)

17

The Crisis in Exegetical Theology

A gap of crisis proportions exists between the steps generally outlined in most seminary or Biblical training classes in exegesis and the hard realities most pastors face every week as they prepare their sermons. Nowhere in the total curriculum of theological studies has the student been more deserted and left to his own devices than in bridging the yawning chasm between understanding the content of Scripture as it was given in the past and proclaiming it with such relevance in the present as to produce faith, life, and bona fide works. Both ends of this bridge have at various times received detailed and even exhaustive treatments: (1) the historical, grammatical, cultural, and critical analysis of the text forms one end of the spectrum; and (2) the practical, devotional, homiletical, and pastoral theology (along with various techniques of delivery, organization, and persuasion) reflected in collections of sermonic outlines for all occasions forms the other. But who has mapped out the route between these two points?[3] The number of books and articles worth mentioning which provide both faithfulness to the text of Scripture and spiritual nourishment to contemporary men and women is so sparse and hidden in such remote journals or languages as to be of very little aid for our needs today. To the best of my knowledge, no one has even produced in English or in any modern European language what we would call an exegetical theology that maps out this most difficult route of moving from the text of Scripture over into the proclamation of that text.

To be sure, the Church has had more than her rightful share of "meditations" or "topical sermons" which are more or less loosely connected with a Biblical phrase, clause, sentence, verse, or scattered assortment thereof. But where are the textbooks or articles that have attempted to seriously treat a legitimate unit of the Scriptures (e.g., a paragraph or group of paragraphs) *in its present canonical shape* and to instruct the aspiring or present proclaimer of God's Word how to move from the text to the ser-

---

3. This concern is well expressed in Manfred Mezger, "Preparation for Preaching: The Route from Exegesis to Proclamation," pp. 159–79.

mon without losing sight of either the Biblical shape of his source or the crying needs of modern men who await a meaningful word for their lives?

Those sermons whose alleged strength is that they speak to contemporary issues, needs, and aspirations often exhibit the weakness of a subjective approach. In the hands of many practitioners, the Biblical text has been of no real help either in clarifying the questions posed by modern man or in offering solutions. The listener is often not sure whether the word of hope being proclaimed is precisely that same Biblical word which should be connected with the modern situation or issue being addressed in the sermon since the Biblical text often is no more than a slogan or refrain in the message. What is so lacking in this case is exactly what needs to be kept in mind with respect to every sermon which aspires to be at once both Biblical and practical: it must be derived from an honest exegesis of the text and it must constantly be kept close to the text.

So strong is this writer's aversion to the methodological abuse he has repeatedly witnessed—especially in topical messages— that he has been advising his students for some years now to preach a topical sermon only once every five years—and then immediately to repent and ask God's forgiveness! In case the reader does not recognize the hyperbole in that statement, then let me plainly acknowledge it as such. However, the serious note that lies behind this playfulness is a loud call for preaching that is totally Biblical in that it is guided by God's Word in its origins, production, and proclamation.

On the other hand, let it also be acknowledged just as quickly that nothing can be more dreary and grind the soul and spirit of the Church more than can a dry, lifeless recounting of Biblical episodes apparently unrelated to the present. The pastor who delivers this type of sermon, reflecting his seminary exegesis class, bombards his bewildered audience with a maze of historical, philological, and critical detail so that the text drops lifeless in front of the listener. The message is so centered on a mere description of detail that it remains basically a B.C. or first-century A.D.

word far removed from the interests and needs of twentieth-century men and women.

Therein lies the dilemma. The strength of one method tends to be totally lacking in the other. Both approaches exhibit serious problems. And the tragedy is that, more often than not, this situation has been the chief cause for the current famine of the Word of God which, in the view of many contemporary observers, continues to exist among the Lord's people. The proof of this blanket charge can be found among scores of American parishioners who continue to travel all over the land searching for a seminar, a Bible conference, a church or a home Bible study that will fill their famished spiritual needs. Alas, however, they are often rewarded with more or less of the same treatment: repetitious arrangements of the most elementary truths of the faith, constant harangues which are popular with local audiences, or witty and clever messages on the widest-ranging topics interspersed with catchy and humorous anecdotes geared to cater to the interests of those who are spiritually lazy and do not wish to be stirred beyond the pleasantries of hearing another good joke or story. Where has the prophetic note in preaching gone? Where is that sense of authority and mission previously associated with the Biblical Word?

No one element has been so responsible for this whole process of deterioration in Biblical preaching as has been the discipline of Biblical exegesis. Certainly, it has taught its students how to parse the verbs; to identify grammatical forms in Hebrew, Aramaic, and Greek; to translate the text into idiomatic English; and to analyze the passage historically and critically according to the legitimate canons of lower and higher criticism. But has its job been completed at this point?

In our view, the very discipline that should have mapped out the route from exegesis to proclamation has traditionally narrowed its concerns too severely. As a result, exegesis has been the one subject most quickly jettisoned by pastors in the pulpit. They have found the discipline, as currently practiced by most departments of theology, to be too deadening, dry, irrelevant to contemporary needs, and therefore otiose. This is not to impose a pragmatic test for truth, but it is to observe that exegetical theology has not found its proper niche in the divinity curriculum in that, with its imposition of strictures and limitations, it has failed to serve the needs of the Church.

One cannot help strongly concurring with Landes's analysis of this problem. It was his opinion that "the seminary Bible teacher does a gross injustice to the biblical documents if he interprets them only in their historical setting. Though that is indeed where he must begin, if he does not go on to articulate their theology and the way they continue to address him theologically in the present, he ignores not only an important part of their intentionality for being preserved but also their role and function. . . ."[4]

Likewise, Professor James D. Smart offered the identical assessment in his 1970 book significantly entitled *The Strange Silence of the Bible in the Church*: "The predicament of the preacher has been created to a large extent by the hiatus between the biblical and the practical departments in our theological seminaries."[5] He continued by charging that "the Biblical departments in [the] seminary rightly make the student labor with care to discern what the text meant when it was first written or spoken. But frequently the assumption is made that, without any further research or assistance or extension of his methodology, he can move from the original meaning to the contemporary meaning, as though there were no serious problems in making that transition."[6]

Published sermons and sermon outlines can show only the final product, but the route which has been traversed from the start in exegesis to the result in a sermon has not been laid out. These steps are the ingredients that many have sensed are missing. But whose job is it to map out this route: the Biblical department of exegesis or the homiletical department of practical and pastoral theology?

In a real sense, neither department can be completely absolved from filling this hiatus. Yet, if primary and preliminary responsibility for preparing a Biblical text for preaching is to be assigned,

4. Landes, "Biblical Exegesis in Crisis," p. 275. Our discussion will also develop his point about theology in a later chapter.

5. Smart, *Strange Silence*, p. 29.

6. Ibid., p. 34.

then we believe Biblical exegesis must take the initiative in developing such extensions of its methodology that the interpreter can move safely and confidently from the original meaning of the Biblical author to the contemporaneous significances of that text for modern listeners. This is but a consistent extension and furthering of exegesis. Surely in the act of proclamation all the various preliminary preparations in working with the text—including specifying the focal point or central point of reference; the theology that "informed" that text; the historical, cultural, and theological context of the text; and its application—are brought to their most condensed and intended form. In the other direction, preaching will not only reflect the results of exegesis, but it will also assess the validity of the content and focus of its proclamation in terms of the Biblical text it proposes to exegete. Competence in the technical aspects of homiletics and the art of persuasion is not enough. In effect, the proclaimer must exhibit in his own person the professional unity of the exegetical professor and the practical preacher. Whether this professional person ever has been or ever will be exposed to such modeling in the classroom should now be beside the main point. It is current practice that should receive immediate attention.

It is hoped, then, that this volume will be useful to those who are already in the pastorate and who are struggling week after week to resolve just this problem. But the main object of our work must be the scores of those men and women who are currently enrolled in Biblical and theological studies at the collegiate or seminary level. It is for them and their professors that we have ventured to break new ground and tread where no one else has labored. As we do so, we are especially aware of incompleteness and built-in traps in attempting an exegetical theology.

But let this work serve as a kind of offering of a type of firstfruits to the Church at large with the express wish and hope that many others will join in a conversation with this author so that we can help each other to complete one of the central aims of Biblical and theological education. We have tolerated various forms of mediocrity in preaching and exegesis for too long now. It is time either to rectify the situation with a good theory of exegesis and a corresponding announcement of a series of valid steps in the route of moving from exegesis to preaching or to drop all professional pretensions from our Biblical and theological departments and offer only research-oriented degrees leading to teaching and writing posts in academia. Already an underground movement has arisen in the form of what I would call "house-seminaries" (where various local churches offer a two- or three-year course of studies and a practical internship for two to twenty students at a time, taught by the professional staffs of those same local churches). These house-seminaries are often a protest against the lack of professional integration with the courses of study. Seldom are these schools a revolt against the requirement of learning Greek and Hebrew. Instead they almost always require at least Greek and often both languages, but they work most diligently at attempting to relate language studies to developing what are often called truly expository or textual sermons. Alas, they too, on this point, struggle along with the existing seminaries to cut the Gordian knot. Therefore, in the bonds of Christian compassion toward and fellowship with many of these house-seminaries, we pass on our results for their inspection and interaction as well.

The Crisis in Hermeneutics

How ironical it is that just as our generation is beginning to show signs of facing up to the hiatus between the departments of exegesis and homiletics that the whole area of general hermeneutics should also suddenly show such tremendous convulsions that the old landmarks cannot be lightly assumed any more. Yet, on a closer inspection, even this crisis is not unrelated to the root crisis in exegetical theology presented above. For at the heart of much of the debate here is (to use the popular words now in use) the problem of how the interpreter can relate "what the text *meant* in its historical context" to "what that same text *means* to me." When the issue is put in these terms, there can be no denying the fact that this is the very hiatus which is troubling interpreters in all the humanities; it is not an issue unique to the Biblical interpreter.

The Single Meaning of the Text

The issue must be put bluntly: Is the meaning of a text to be defined solely in terms of the *verbal* meaning of that text as those words were used by the Scriptural author? Or should the meaning of a text be partly understood in terms of "what it *now* means to me," the reader and interpreter? There hangs one of the great dilemmas of our age. And there also hang the fortunes of the authority of Scripture.

William Ames. Perhaps the best place to begin is with the view of William Ames (1576–1633), whose book served as the standard text at Harvard for decades after the founding of that institution in the seventeenth century. The answer to our question was clear and unequivocal for Ames's day: ". . . there is only one meaning for every place in Scripture. Otherwise the meaning of Scripture would not only be unclear and uncertain, but there would be no meaning at all—for anything which does not mean one thing surely means nothing."[7]

But the question would not rest there. Did that one meaning also include the application of the text to contemporaries and the expansion of that meaning to the subject matter it partially introduced? The modern basis for this debate can already be seen in the eighteenth-century debate between J. A. Ernesti and J. S. Semler as it has been so skillfully traced by Hans W. Frei.[8] For Ernesti, exegesis (which is designed, of course, to determine meaning) consisted of discovering (1) the use of words, (2) the historical circumstances controlling their usage, and (3) the intention of the author strictly governed by his own words.

Johann August Ernesti. The scope of hermeneutics in Ernesti (1707–1781) was confined to and identical with the words used by the author. Theological interpretation and application of the Biblical text were to be attempted only on the basis of and in strict

7. William Ames, *The Marrow of Theology*, ed. and trans. John D. Eusden (Boston: Pilgrim, 1968), p. 188. This textbook (*Medulla theologica* in Latin) continued to be widely read and greatly appreciated by seventeenth-century American Puritans. I am grateful to my student William Glass for pointing out this reference to me.

8. Hans W. Frei, *The Eclipse of Biblical Narrative: A Study in Eighteenth and Nineteenth Century Hermeneutics* (New Haven, Conn.: Yale University, 1974), pp. 245–60.

reliance on the prior determination of the verbal meaning found in the text.[9]

A sample of some of Ernesti's key affirmations would include:

[1.] *The act of interpretation:*
The act of interpretation implies two things: viz, a right perception of the meaning of words, and a proper explanation of that meaning.[10]

[2.] *The art of interpretation:*
The art of interpretation is the art of teaching what is the meaning of another's language; or that faculty, which enables us to attach to another's language the same meaning that the author himself attached to it.[11]

[3.] *Skill in explanation (Subtilitas explicandi):*
This is exhibited by expressing the sense of an author, either in words of the same language which are more perspicuous than his, or by translating into another language, and explaining by argument and illustration.[12]

[4.] *Definition of hermeneutics:*
Hermeneutics is the science which teaches [us] to find, in an accurate and judicious manner, the meaning of an author, and appropriately to explain it to others.[13]

[5.] *Single meaning theory:*
Although a word can have but one meaning at the same time and in the same place, usage has gradually assigned many meanings to the same word. . . . *How can the meaning in each case be*

9. Ibid., p. 248.

10. J. A. Ernesti, *Elements of Interpretation*, 2d ed., ed. and trans. Moses Stuart (Andover: Flagg and Gould, 1824), § 4, p. 2. This translation, made from the fifth Latin edition of *Institutio interpretis Novi Testamenti*, ed. C. F. Ammon (Leipzig, 1809) is the best despite its incompleteness. A complete translation was made by Charles H. Terrot and titled *Principles of Biblical Interpretation*, 2 vols. (Edinburgh: Clark, 1832–1833). See Frei for a slightly improved translation of this phrase. *Eclipse*, p. 330, n. 1. The italicized words are Stuart's brief notices of the contents of the section.

11. Ibid., § 3.

12. Ibid., § 9.

13. Ibid., § 10.

found? (1) From the general manner of speaking, i.e. common usage [*usus loquendi*]. (2) From the proximate words or context.[14]

[6.] *The error of assigning many meanings to the same word
at the same time and in the same place:*
Such an opinion is to be rejected; although the practice is very old, as Augustine testifies, Confess XII. 30, 31. . . . A principle of this nature, however, must introduce very great uncertainty into exegesis; than which nothing can be more pernicious.[15]

[7.] *The error of those who affirm that the words of Scripture
mean all that they possibly can mean:*
This sprung from the Rabbinical schools, and passed from them, in early times, to Christians. . . .[16]

[8.] *The grammatical sense the only true one:*
Those who make one sense *grammatical*, and another *logical*, do not comprehend the full meaning of *grammatical sense*. We are not to look, therefore, for a sense of words, which varies (in its nature or simply considered as the sense) with every departure of learning, or with every diverse object. For if this were the case, words would have as many kinds of sense, as objects are multifarious.[17]

[9.] *Any method of interpretation not philological, is fallacious:*
Moreover, the method of gathering the sense of words from *things* is altogether deceptive and fallacious; since things are rather to be known from pointing out the sense of words in a proper way. It is by *words* of the Holy Spirit only, that we are led to understand what we ought to think respecting *things*. Said Melanch-

14. Ibid., §§ 18-19.
15. Ibid., § 22.
16. Ibid., § 23. Stuart commented further: "The Rabbinic maxim is: On every point of Scripture, hang suspended mountains of sense. The Talmud says, God so gave the Law to Moses, that a thing can be shown to be clean and unclean in 49 different ways. Most of the fathers, and a multitude of commentators in later times, were infected with these principles. Little more than a century ago, the celebrated Cocceius of Leyden maintained the sentiment, that all the possible meanings of a word in the Scripture are to be united. By his learning and influence a powerful party were [sic] raised up, in the Protestant Church, in favor of such a principle. The mischiefs resulting from it have not yet ceased to operate." To this we add: Nor has it ceased even at this late date as we go into the twenty-first century.
17. Ibid., § 30.

thon very truly: The Scripture cannot be understood *theologically*, until it is understood *grammatically*. Luther also avers, that a *certain* knowledge of the sense of Scripture, depends solely on a knowledge of the words.[18]

[10.] *Subject matter, doctrine, applications and preunderstandings must not control interpretation:*
The meaning, which according to grammatical principles should be assigned to any word of Scripture, is not to be rejected then on account of reasons derived from things or previously conceived opinions; for in this way, interpretation would become uncertain.[19]

Johann Salomo Semler. On the other hand, J. S. Semler (1725–1791) gave priority to a grasp of the general subject matter which the words of the text in part represented. And he carried the day, for the majority followed him. Semler's point was this: "The most important thing, in short, in hermeneutical skill depends upon [1] one's knowing the Bible's use of language properly and precisely, as well as distinguishing and representing to oneself the historical circumstances of a biblical discourse; and [2] one's being able to speak today of these matters in such a way as the changed times and circumstances of our fellow men demand. . . . All the rest of hermeneutics can be reduced to these two things."[20]
Apart from Semler's preemptive and negative historical criticism in which he judged certain supernatural features of the historical circumstances of the first century A.D. to be impossible (all of which is unacceptable to this writer if for no other reasons than Semler's methodology), it is clear he was already in 1760

18. Ibid., § 33. Likewise in § 34 and § 37 Ernesti goes on to deny that the analogy of faith or doctrine (*regula fidei*) is a guide to interpreting passages. But cf. his § 142. My own hesitations in the use of the analogy of faith as an exegetical tool have been expressed in Walter C. Kaiser, Jr., *Toward an Old Testament Theology* (Grand Rapids: Zondervan, 1978), pp. 16, 18–19; and idem, "The Single Intent of Scripture," pp. 139–40. See also idem, "Meanings from God's Message: Matters for Interpretation," *Christianity Today*, 5 October 1979, pp. 30–33.

19. Ernesti, *Elements*, § 36. This italicized heading is my own.

20. J. S. Semler, *Vorbereitung zur theologischen Hermeneutik, zu weiterer Beförderung des Fleisses angehender Gottesgelehrten*, 2 vols. (Magdeburg: Hammerde, 1761), 1:160f. Translated by Frei in *Eclipse*, p. 247.

assigning to hermeneutics in step [2] above the task of bridging the chasm modern interpreters are worried about. But he fails to connect this step with the words and truth-intentions of the author. In this respect, Ernesti is to be followed when he declares: "It is by *words* of the Holy Spirit only, that we are led to understand what we are to think respecting *things*."[21] Semler, of course, did point to the need for a grammatical and textual understanding, but this was, in Frei's words, a "merely chronological or procedural matter."[22] Actually for Semler the words remained somewhat inert and dead until the subject matter they represented was grasped and became the basis for understanding them.

Friedrich Ernst Daniel Schleiermacher. Ernesti and Ames, as two representatives of earlier scholars, had been confident that the text of Scripture was directly accessible. For Ernesti, the act of interpretation included two parts: (1) *subtilitas intelligendi*, that is, exactness of understanding; and (2) *subtilitas explicandi*, that is, exactness of explication. To put it in more current terms, Ernesti argued that the hermeneutical procedure of using grammatical analysis to get at (1) the single *meaning* of the words as used by an author should not be abstracted from the process of (2) the *application* or the pointing out of the *significance* of this meaning.[23]

But in the thought of Friedrich Schleiermacher (1768–1834) these two parts became separated and the term *hermeneutics* was reserved for the first part. Hermeneutics dealt only with grammar and the members of sentences. And whereas for Ernesti every word had only one *Sinn* (*sensus*) which unfolded in various *Bedeutungen* (*significationes*), Schleiermacher taught that the process of grammatical understanding (*subtilitas intelligendi*) of an author's words must be distinct and separate from the "psycho-

21. See Ernesti's point [9.] above.
22. Frei, *Eclipse*, p. 248.
23. Ernesti, *Elements*, § 4; see n. 10 above. *Subtilitas* refers to a capacity or power. Richard E. Palmer pointed to J. J. Rambach's distinctions, published in 1723, between three powers: *subtilitas intelligendi* (understanding), *subtilitas explicandi* (explication), and *subtilitas applicandi* (application). *Hermeneutics: Interpretation Theory in Schleiermacher, Dilthey, Heidegger and Gadamer*, p. 187. Ernesti seems to blend the last two powers under the term *subtilitas explicandi*.

logical" or "technical" interpretation.[24] Grammatical interpretation, he assured us, focuses only on the objective side of interpretation while the "technical" deals with the subjective. Therefore, as such, grammatical interpretation can never function as a source for universal principles and significations for all men and times. It has purely a "negative role" in that it merely "mark[s out] the boundaries."[25] But for Schleiermacher, his technical and psychological interpretation (Ernesti's *subtilitas explicandi*) involved the additional step of personally assimilating the subject by determining or attempting to reconstruct the *mental process* of the author—an altogether impossible task.

For our limited purposes here, the most significant point is that Schleiermacher produced his whole conception of language in opposition to Ernesti's point that there is a single meaning (German, *Sinn*, sense) for an author's words which may then unfold in numerous significances or applications insofar as they still reflect that single meaning. Schleiermacher countered by saying instead that every word has a general sphere of meaning which is not to be found in itself, but is to be worked out from the total given value of language brought to the text and the heritage common to the author and his reader.[26]

Hans Georg Gadamer. In the later years of Schleiermacher's life he began, in the view of many, to stress the technical and psychological part of understanding. This aspect of his thought was developed by Wilhelm Dilthey (1833–1911), Martin Heidegger (1889–1976), and Rudolf Bultmann (1884–1976). Hans Georg Gadamer (b. 1900) extended and codified this tradition in what is now generally referred to in theological circles as "The New Hermeneutic."[27]

---

24. Friedrich Schleiermacher, *Hermeneutics: The Handwritten Manuscripts*, ed. Heinz Kimmerle, trans. James Duke and H. Jackson Forstman, American Academy of Religion Text and Translations Series, 1 (Missoula, Mont.: Scholars, 1977), p. 41. From "The Aphorisms of 1805 and 1809–10."

25. Ibid., p. 42.

26. Ibid., pp. 76–77.

27. James M. Robinson, "Hermeneutic Since Barth," in *The New Hermeneutic*, ed. James M. Robinson and John B. Cobb, Jr., New Frontiers in Theology, 2 (New York: Harper & Row, 1964), pp. 1–77.

In Gadamer, the hermeneutics of Ames and Ernesti has turned 180 degrees. The fullest statement of his thought appeared in 1960.[28] In his view, not only is the recognition of an author's meaning an impossibility, but so is the association of what a text now means with what it once meant to its author. Instead, the meaning of a text lies in the subject matter, the thing meant, which is independent of both the author and reader; yet it also is some-how shared by both. Thus the meaning of a text *always* goes beyond what its author intended, and the true sense is an unend-ing process which is never exhausted or captured by an infinite line of interpreters! Thus there remains no yardstick for deter-mining which interpreter is more nearly correct if both happen to hit upon conflicting interpretations at the same moment in time. There is neither anyone nor anything that can validate the inter-pretation in this sad state of affairs: not the author, not his words as he intended them—not even what the text meant in the past!

One method of escape from this totally unacceptable situation has been invented. It is the idea of tradition: a kind of history of the different ways a particular text has been interpreted in the past all rolled together in one. However, there is nothing that can be appealed to in this tradition, for it does not have any normative status or validating power. What is to be done then? As E. D. Hirsch, Jr., so incisively comments, there is very little for Gada-mer to do but to involve himself in a few self-contradictions about a repeatable, yet unrepeatable written sign of the text which still abides.[29] But in the last analysis, an interpretation is the fusion of the original outlook of the text and the interpreter's own view of it in what Gadamer calls a "fusion of horizons."

For our study of Biblical texts, the interesting aspect of Gad-amer, the new hermeneutic, and many who attach themselves in one degree or another to this school, is that application (*subtilitas applicandi*) finally receives the attention it deserves as an impor-tant step in the interpretive process. But the necessary grounding

---

28. Hans Georg Gadamer, *Wahrheit und Methode: Grundzüge einer philosophischen Hermeneutik* (Tübingen: Mohr, 1960). For this assessment I am dependent, in the main, on E. D. Hirsch, Jr., *Validity in Interpretation*, pp. 245–64.

29. Hirsch, *Validity*, pp. 251–52.

of application in understanding what the author meant by his use of his words is now swallowed up. The process of exegeting a text is declared to be circular (the hermeneutical circle) and not linear. While we are assured that the circle is not a vicious circle, the point usually made is that the interpreter affects his text (by his own culture, beliefs [ontology], and methods for discovering meanings) as much as the text affects the interpreter!

Emilio Betti and E. D. Hirsch, Jr. If Gadamer is the most prominent representative of what could be called the later Heideggerian version of hermeneutics, then Emilio Betti and E. D. Hirsch, Jr., stand almost alone in attempting to return hermeneutics and exegesis to a more objective version of interpretation. Indeed, Heidegger and Gadamer (not to mention Rudolf Bultmann[30] and his two disciples Gerhard Ebeling and Ernst Fuchs) began by denying the possibility of objective historical knowledge. The result has been to thrust the integrity of knowledge of the past out on a sea of relativity and subjectivism (a charge which many in this school often complain about, but never wholly extricate themselves from, for in the attempt they invariably give additional evidence for the substantial truth of the claim).

In a heroic attempt to reinstate what he called the "venerable older form of hermeneutics," which he feared was now "fading out of modern German [and we would add Western] consciousness," Betti, an Italian historian of law, wrote to counterbalance the German preoccupation with *Sinngebung* (the interpreter's assignment of meaning to an object) and the false equation of this meaning with the interpretation of an author's text.[31] Distinguishing between *Auslegung* (interpretation) and *Sinngebung* is essential.

---

30. Though Rudolf Bultmann's popularity began in 1941 with the publication of his essay "Jesus Christ and Mythology," it was not until the second half of his Gifford Lectures of 1955 that he answered the question, How are we to understand historical documents delivered by tradition? These lectures were published in English as *History and Eschatology* (Edinburgh: Edinburgh University, 1957). All interpretation, he claimed, is guided by the interpreter's "pre-understanding" (p. 113), and "the question of meaning in history has become meaningless" since meaning arises only out of the interpreter's relation to the future, which is unknowable (p. 120).

31. Emilio Betti, *Die Hermeneutik als allgemeine Methodik der Geisteswissenschaften* (Tübingen: Mohr, 1962), p. 1. Translated by Palmer in *Hermeneutics*, p. 55. See Palmer's excellent description of Betti's thought on pages 54–60.

This is exactly the point made by Hirsch, professor of English at the University of Virginia, in 1967.[32] We must draw that crucial distinction between "meaning" and "significance": "meaning" is that which is represented by a text, its grammar, and the author's truth-intentions as indicated by his use of words, while "significance" merely denotes a relationship *between* (note well, it must be linked) that meaning and another person, time, situation, or idea. "Meaning" according to Hirsch (and this writer also) is unchanging once the Biblical writer commits himself to words, while "significance," of course, does and must change since interests, questions, and the times in which the interpreter lives also change. But an author's original meaning *cannot* change—not even for himself! Should the author subsequently modify his views or totally reverse himself, he must go through the painful process of repudiating and disassociating himself from his previously printed views, for they continue to stand as a testimony against his present meaning.[33]

Betti does acknowledge that in the interpretive process the interpreter does involve his own subjectivity. But if that subjectivity does not penetrate into the meaning (foreign to and different from the style, ideas, word usage, and questions of the interpreter as it may be), then the interpreter has succeeded in doing nothing more than projecting his own ideas and preferences (=subjectivity) on the text he *thinks* he is interpreting. Betti's acknowledgment does not concede the case to Bultmann, for Betti continues to raise against all existentialists the objection that they deny the possibility of attaining any real objective knowledge about the past.

Gadamer had contended that every interpretation involves an application to the present. Betti agreed that this was true of law (and we would add Biblical exegesis), but unfortunately he disallowed it for history. Furthermore, since Betti and Hirsch grounded their *Sinngebung* or significance in the discovered grammatical meaning of the text, even this supposed agreement on the *need* for application was no agreement in actuality.

32. Hirsch, *Validity*, pp. xi, 8.
33. Ibid., p. 9.

There have been several rejoinders and incisive criticisms of Hirsch which have sought to undercut his major argument that a text means what its author meant as he used his words. Usually the essence of these criticisms has been that textual meaning is independent of an author's meaning. These criticisms include: (1) Hirsch has failed to establish and give the grounds for the possibility and the content of a criterion for testing the validity of a text.[34] (2) There is a lack of consistence in his definition of meaning.[35] (3) He has uncritically adopted Aristotelian definitions which separate meaning from significance not in a mechanical way, as Hirsch thinks, but by engaging in a type of disguised criticism which constructs this distinction after the act of understanding has been completed.[36]

In our view, Hirsch did give a criterion for testing validity of meaning: the *author's* intended meaning is what a text means. This, of course, is unacceptable to Barrie A. Wilson and most of our contemporaries. There is a point worth noting here, a refinement we have to make with respect to Hirsch. Hirsch steadfastly refuses to locate meaning in the text, though it should be carefully noticed that the text is still, nevertheless, important for him, for the written text represents the author's truth-intention. Thus Hirsch does relate meaning to the text, but it is always secondarily the text and primarily the intention of its author. Hirsch's reluctance to fully relate "meaning" to the *text* of the author makes him vulnerable to the charge of using "preferential criteria."

Elsewhere we have attempted to develop another argument that would ground man's ability to communicate and to understand communication in the gift of the image of God.[37] The general rules for interpreting do not appear to be formally learned, nor

34. Barrie A. Wilson, "Hirsch's Hermeneutics: A Critical Examination," esp. pp. 27–28.

35. William E. Cain, "Authority, 'Cognitive Atheism,' and the Aims of Interpretation: The Literary Theory of E. D. Hirsch," p. 339. He also points to Susan Suleiman, "Interpreting Ironies," *Diacritics* 6 (1976): 15–21. It is true that Hirsch does wrongly expand the definition of *meaning* to "simply meaning-for-an-interpreter" in E. D. Hirsch, Jr., *The Aims of Interpretation* (Chicago: University of Chicago, 1976), pp. 79–80.

36. Palmer, *Hermeneutics*, pp. 63–65. In Palmer's view hermeneutics has been changed in Hirsch from the "theory of understanding" into the "logic of validation."

37. Walter C. Kaiser, Jr., "Legitimate Hermeneutics," in *Inerrancy*, ed. Norman L. Geisler (Grand Rapids: Zondervan, 1979), pp. 117–47.

abstractly invented or discovered by man; rather they appear as part and parcel of his nature as an individual made in the image of God. The art of speaking and understanding has been in use from the moment God spoke to Adam in the garden until now. Thus as soon as children learn to speak they are also involved in interpreting whether they formally know the principles of hermeneutics or not—and we think not.

The major problem we sense in Hirsch's thought is that he has not treated with any depth at all the problem of contemporary application and significance. We cannot agree with Richard E. Palmer's criticisms that Hirsch's division between meaning and significance is either unwarranted or a type of disguised retrospective criticism once the act of interpreting has been completed. If Hirsch is guilty of anything, it is that he, like Schleiermacher, has, in effect, limited hermeneutics to *subtilitas intelligendi* (the act of understanding); the changing significances (presumably *subtilitas applicandi*) are included only insofar as they participate in the unchanging and testable single meaning of the author's intention as known through his grammar and syntax.

What, then, is the authority status of the *Sinngebung* (Betti) or "significance" (Hirsch) which the interpreter finds in these texts? As far as I can see, this question has received no answer. This, of course, introduces the question that has become the entry for many interpreters on the road we have just traced: Can we as interpreters understand a writer better than he understood himself?

The Multiple "Meanings" of the Interpreter

One way to break this Gordian knot is to fall back on the formula, "Interpreters often can understand authors better than they understand themselves."[38] The promise that this saying ap-

---

38. The history of this formula has been traced in Otto Friedrich Bollnow, "What Does It Mean to Understand a Writer Better Than He Understood Himself?" pp. 17–19. Bollnow traces the formula through Immanuel Kant, Johann G. Fichte, Friedrich Schleiermacher, August Böckh, and Wilhelm Dilthey. See also Hirsch, *Validity*, pp. 19–23 and n. 16; and Frei, *Eclipse*, p. 299. Frei counts only four times in Schleiermacher where this formula appears, and it is always in balance between the psychological-technical and grammatical sides of interpretation.

pears to hold is that there is a stratum of thought, an "inner form of the work" (Dilthey), which in the creative process bypassed the author's consciousness, but is now left for the interpreter to uncover.

But what do we refer to when we speak of understanding a writer better? It is best, with Otto Friedrich Bollnow, to exclude the question of the author's psychic experience and to refer only to understanding his text. Thus in the formula under consideration the word *authors* should be understood as the "works" they composed.

With a masterful touch, Bollnow pauses to first ask the question whether it is possible to understand a writer *as well as* he understood himself before going on to ask if we can know a work better than its author could. If understanding is merely the elucidating of the inherent logic in events as in nature,[39] then understanding may be illustrated by the way we grasp the inner coherence of a mathematical proposition. Bollnow found another illustration of this same process in the relationship of fitting means to ends as extrapolated from a human action, a tool, or the working parts in a machine. Due to this inner logic, it is possible to say that understanding has a closely defined "completeness" and "conclusiveness" about it which allows neither approximation nor improvement beyond what is contained in itself.[40] "Conclusiveness," as used here, means that all the parts are finished, formed, and everything willed has come to its full definition. It is the condition of the possibility of certain knowledge. Thus a text is understandable when the author has expressed himself in a clear and sensible way. Given fulfillment of these conditions, Bollnow answers: Yes, it is possible to know a text as well as the author knew it.

---

39. This argument rests on Friedrich von Gottl-Ottlilienfeld's *Die Grenzen der Geschichte* [*The Limits of History*] (Leipzig: Duncker & Humblot, 1904). Also consider Fichte's comment, "What has been thought with complete clarity is understandable."

40. This is a bold step indeed. Even though Bollnow cannot prescribe this process that leads step by step to knowledge, he believes it does break the "hermeneutical circle" in the humanities. The multiplicity of parts can be united in a unified whole, for example, in the understanding of a Latin sentence.

But what about knowing a work *better* than its author did? Bollnow acknowledges that "total conclusiveness" or what we might refer to as comprehensive knowledge is seldom if ever achieved. Usually we reserve this privileged status for God alone. Thus we may say better understanding is possible because there is a potential (1) for completing what is unfinished in the subject,[41] and (2) for clarifying the self-evident background, assumptions, and fundamental concepts or guiding convictions.[42] But there is a limit; in Bollnow's judgment the concept of better understanding cannot be stretched to the production of new meaning.[43] It can only make a further contribution to the same subject, ferret out the underlying presuppositions, fundamental concepts, or guiding convictions, or (and this Bollnow doesn't mention) it can point to possible significance a work could have for humanity in another setting, time, or culture.

Accordingly, such "better understanding" is not different from the writer's meaning; for at the points at which it improves or criticizes a work of a writer, one always begins by first understanding what the writer said as separate from the so-called "better understanding," which occurs in areas that do not affect meaning. Therefore, it can hardly be claimed that this is the way to determine the contemporary relevance, application, or significance of a text.

Rather, the interpretive act must proceed along the lines set for it by Hirsch. Significance will need to be a secondary and subjective determination which will derive legitimacy only to the extent that it has already accurately assessed the author's single meaning in that text. To this basic meaning the interpreter and reader may then bring their questions, criticisms, and suggested modern analogues.

The Crisis in Homiletics

One more crisis must be faced before we begin to suggest some solutions of our own: the crisis in the pulpit. For large segments

41. Bollnow, "What Does It Mean?" pp. 22–23.
42. Ibid., pp. 23–25.
43. Ibid., p. 27.

of the Christian Church it is a truism to say that Biblical exposition has become a lost art in contemporary preaching. The most neglected of all Biblical sections is the Old Testament—over three-fourths of divine revelation!

This state of affairs can be charged, in part, to Marcion, Julius Wellhausen, and a galaxy of others. Yet, overriding all of the reasons for neglect of the Old Testament (and there would be an extremely long list if we stopped to collect them all) is the issue of the Bible's historical particularity; that is, its words are most frequently, if not always in the Old Testament, directed to a *specific* people in a *specific* situation at a *specific* time and in a *specific* culture. That is the real difficulty. How could Christian interpreters keep from avoiding those passages, not only in the Old Testament, but also in the New Testament, that appear to be so very specifically addressed and dated? There seems to be no way to escape this problem.

One of our contemporaries has struggled most diligently to get out of this trap. He has endeavored to make the Bible available to all and especially useful to pastors for a modern word of proclamation. Lawrence E. Toombs has attempted to make the Old Testament relevant for our times by stressing the fact that both Testaments invite us to participate in the past events of history where God approached men like ourselves.[44] The key for Toombs is our common humanity. Thus the task of the preacher is to raise this question for his audience: to what facet of the human condition am I being directed in this Old Testament text? What are the contemporary equivalents of this shared human condition? Can I contextualize, transform, and rebaptize that ancient Old Testament word, now that I know that I am a man like those men and face similar situations? Can I put that word into a new form and an authentic message for my day?

However, as Elizabeth Achtemeier pointed out, the difficulty with Toombs's suggestion is that he has not realized just how *specific* that Old Testament historical particularity is. The Word

44. See these works by Lawrence E. Toombs: *The Old Testament in Christian Preaching*; "The Old Testament in the Christian Pulpit," *Hartford Quarterly* 8 (1968): 7–14; and "The Problematic of Preaching from the Old Testament," pp. 302–14.

was not addressed to humanity in general, but to a very specific people in a specific relationship to God with a very specific mission. Here arises the "offense" of the Bible.[45]

The question of the relevance of the Old Testament for contemporary homiletics will rest on the answer to another question, observes Achtemeier with excellent insight; namely, what is the Church's relationship to Israel? Do we in any way share in Israel's blessing as well as in her judgments? The question is proper and it calls for a penetrating involvement in exegetical and Biblical theology. This question gives more promise of a resolution and shape to a potential solution than does Toombs's analogical methodology.

Bultmann also wrestled with the same problem, but his solution differed from Toombs's. Bultmann concluded that God's dealings with Israel were terminated; thus the Old Testament with its specific history is no longer a revelation from God to us.[46] The only things in the Old Testament relevant to us are general moral demands rooted not in divine revelation as such, but rather in a human relationship. Thus the offense of Old Testament specificity means that we must abandon the Old Testament. The Old Testament, in Bultmann's hands, becomes *a*historical, and valuable only as a pedagogical tool as it is *re*actualized in the life of each individual who hears it entirely apart from anything said to Israel. It now has a present history and a present address to the contemporary individual—but totally apart from anything ever said in Israel's history.

Bultmann has acknowledged the specificity of the Old Testament and in the process has had to yield its normative authority for the Church. The Old Testament functions only as a propaedeutic to the gospel. Even then, the gospel is transformed into an

45. Elizabeth Achtemeier, "The Relevance of the Old Testament for Christian Preaching," in *A Light unto My Path: Old Testament Studies in Honor of Jacob M. Myers*, ed. Howard N. Bream et al., Gettysburg Theological Studies, 4 (Philadelphia: Temple University, 1974), pp. 5–6. In this section I am indebted to Achtemeier for her general approach.

46. Rudolf Bultmann, "The Significance of the Old Testament for Christian Faith," in *The Old Testament and Christian Faith: A Theological Discussion*, ed. Bernard W. Anderson (New York: Harper & Row, 1963), pp. 8–35.

existential, eschatological, nonhistorical, individualistic framework.

A new attempt to solve this problem of the particularism of the Bible came in 1952. On the basis of Israel's contemporizing the past in her three great annual festivals Martin Noth urged that the Church also preach the past history of the Old Testament as a re-presentation" (*Vergegenwärtigung*) to the Church. In the festivals of Passover, Unleavened Bread, and the Feast of Tabernacles, God's gracious acts in the past (such as His deliverance of Israel from Egypt, His giving the Law on Sinai, His help to Israel in the wilderness) were annually presented as present, contemporary happenings which called for a corresponding action of love and service to the God of Israel.[47]

The point is extremely helpful. Not only were the festivals treated as if they were still relevant, but note also the strong emphasis on "this day" in Deuteronomy 29:10–15: "All of you are standing *this day* before the Lord your God . . . that you may enter into the sworn covenant of the Lord your God, which the Lord is making with you *this day*; that He may establish you *this day* as His people, and that He may be your God, as He promised you, and as He swore to your fathers, to Abraham, to Isaac, and to Jacob. Nor is it only with you that I make this sworn covenant, but with him who is not here with us *this day* as well as with him who is standing here with us *this day* before the Lord our God."[48]

This is a graphic illustration of the Scriptural phenomenon of contemporizing past events. It is very similar to what the Church does when it partakes of the Lord's Supper or Communion: "This is my body which is broken for you."

Another example of the Bible's own direct application of earlier historical events to later generations can be found in the frequent use of "we," "us," and "you" when these events are retold. Thus, Deuteronomy 6:20–21 teaches later generations to answer when they are asked the meaning of the ordinances God has com-

---

47. Martin Noth, "The 'Re-presentation' of the Old Testament in Proclamation," trans. James Luther Mays, in *Essays on Old Testament Hermeneutics*, ed. Claus Westermann and James Luther Mays (Richmond: John Knox, 1963), pp. 76–88 (chap. 4).

48. Translation and italics are mine.

manded: "*We* were Pharaoh's slaves in Egypt and Yahweh brought *us* out of Egypt with a strong hand." Or consider the confession of Deuteronomy 26:6–7: "The Egyptians dealt ill with *us* . . . but Yahweh heard *our* voice. . . ."

Yet for all the solid advantages of this method of "re-presentation," the crisis in homiletics still persists. C. Trimp has found some weaknesses in Noth's method of making the Bible "kerygmatically" relevant: the sermon obtains a sacramental character in which the historical event, whether it happened or not (unfortunately this school usually says it did not), is actualized once again just as the Roman mass re-actualizes the great sacrifice of Christ.[49] Thus instead of the *sola Scriptura* principle, we have a living tradition of re-interpretation which stands on a par with or even supersedes the written form of Scripture. This re-presentation has a liberating power and it sets the message free from the boundaries of the text as written. Inspiration, then, is shifted from the Scriptures to the work of interpreters and proclaimers.

Trimp offers another view, while continuing to complain about views like those of Noth and Toombs: "The historical distance between the first hearers of the Word and later generations is bridged by God in the power of His faithfulness to Himself. Nothing is bridged by distilling timeless truths of a rational or moral nature from the historically determined text, nor by constructing analogies with situations of those who are addressed. . . . The Lord did not allow the meaning of His revealed Word to become fixed within the narrow confines of the mind-set of the first speakers or hearers, but in the dated work and word of His revelation He also thought of us living in these last days."[50]

Clearly homiletics has a real problem which also must be faced by the exegete if our work is to result in any meaningful application or contemporary significance.

---

49. C. Trimp, "The Relevance of Preaching (in the Light of the Reformation's 'Sola Scriptura' Principle)," p. 8.
    50. Ibid., pp. 27–28.

Chapter 2

The Definition and History of Exegesis

It is still difficult to find a good working definition of Biblical exegesis even though our generation has at its finger tips a wide assortment of Biblical handbooks, dictionaries, and journal articles. Since this branch of study is so basic to the whole curriculum of divinity, one could hope for at least an intensive chapter or two specifically defining the term and its task—especially since there are no handbooks available which detail exegetical methodology for the beginning interpreter, much less for the more seasoned practitioners!

At the request of the Association of German Evangelical Theological Students, Otto Kaiser and Werner Georg Kümmel produced a slender volume in 1963.[1] This volume, excellent as it is in its rich bibliography in the various fields of lower and higher criticism,[2] still leaves much to be desired. In our judgment, except for the commentaries on Romans 5:1–11 and Matthew 12:22–37,

---

1. Otto Kaiser and Werner Georg Kümmel, *Exegetical Method: A Student's Handbook.*
2. Lower criticism is that area of Biblical study dealing with questions of which books belong to our Bible (canon) and which reading represents the original text (textual criticism). Higher criticism deals with questions of date, authorship, addressees, distinctive style, literary forms, etc.

which briefly interrupt the major points of discussion, this volume focuses more on what resources are available to help the exegete in the areas of textual criticism, literary criticism, analysis of Hebrew meter, form criticism, tradition criticism, and finally subject, concept, and content exegesis.[3]

The problem is that this general outline and approach tend to be followed by almost all of those brave individuals who have ever made an attempt to describe the nature and task of exegesis. For example, in 1973 Victor Paul Furnish contributed to the *Perkins School of Theology Journal* a major article which followed this outline: A) Textual Analysis, B) Literary Analysis, C) Historical Analysis, and D) Theological Analysis. He concluded with a word about the issue of translations and five rules for exegetes. Only on the last page of this rather extensive article did he come to the matter of "Working on the Passage Itself."[4]

In our view, his last page is the heart of the matter—at least 75 percent of what exegesis should be about. Too frequently teachers of exegesis have allowed their enthusiasm over and personal interest in the latest developments in the fields of historiography, lexicology, literary parallels, archeological and epigraphical materials or the like to consume so much of the time in the overall task and mission of exegesis that the primary goals of the discipline have been threatened with extinction. If this keeps up, exegesis will function only as a synonym for what is technically known as the field of isagogics—general and special introduction to the Bible.

Of course it is necessary to set the passage that is to be exegeted in its proper context. But we are here calling for balance and proportion. In our judgment, there is an absolutely fundamental and essential work in background studies which must precede the in-depth study of the selected passage. And that is the strength of Kaiser and Kümmel. But in no case should these concerns become so overwhelming that they become a substitute for a direct confrontation with the passage itself.

3. These topics are the basic outline of Kaiser's chapter and, in a more abbreviated form, of Kümmel's chapter.

4. Victor Paul Furnish, "Some Practical Guidelines for New Testament Exegesis."

Even when Furnish finally did turn to giving us seven steps by which we can engage the primary text under consideration, his suggestions tended to range more on the side of subject or topical study than on the side of any direct analysis of specific points of grammar or syntax. In his list he urged that the exegete: (1) formulate the main points of the passage (But according to what principles or procedures? Furnish merely advised: "As you see them."); (2) either note what is problematical in the passage or compare various translations to see if there is any major disagreement (But is exegesis limited only to problem areas?); (3) identify key words or concepts (But how?); (4) list all other historical, literary, and theological problems in the text (This, however, appears to be a return to the concerns of background studies); (5) prepare a tentative outline for the passage in keeping with the "overall context" (I would want to see the outline tied in even more closely with the paragraph development); (6) refer to Biblical passages or "related literature" where ideas similar to those found in this text appear (But then the exegete must first pay attention to the passages which preceded it in time); and (7) record in a set of notes "any wider implications" the text may have.

Certainly, I for one am pleased with this list *as far as it goes*. Very few other exegetes have even attempted in print to aid the student even to this degree. But as can be seen from my editorial comments on the list, it does not show how one derives a teaching or preaching outline from the given phrases, clauses, sentences, and paragraphs of the chosen passage. And that is the job that still needs to be done. Thus, we still must attempt to define and state what the task of exegesis is.

The Definition of Exegesis

The term *exegesis* is derived from a transliteration of the Greek word ἐξήγησις, meaning a "narration" or "explanation" (this noun form, however, does not occur in the New Testament, and only once in the Vaticanus form of the Septuagint [Greek translation of the Old Testament]—Judg. 7:15). The Greek verbal form is ἐξηγέομαι, which literally rendered means "to lead out of" (note the prefix ἐξ). In the Septuagint ἐξηγέομαι mainly translates the Hebrew verb סָפַר, which in the intensive stem means "to recount, tell, or declare." In the New Testament this verb occurs only once in John and five times in Luke–Acts.[5] In John 1:18, we read that it is the "only Son, who is in the bosom of the Father, who has *exegeted* [the Father to us]." Luke recorded that famous walk on the road to Emmaus, after which Cleopas and his companion "explained," "exegeted," or just simply "related" these events to the others later that evening (Luke 24:35). Likewise, Cornelius "explained" to the others his vision (Acts 10:8); Paul and Barnabas "exegeted" what the "signs and wonders God had done through them among the Gentiles" meant (Acts 15:12); Peter "exegeted" how God first visited the Gentiles (Acts 15:14); and Paul "exegeted in detail" what God had accomplished through his ministry to the Gentiles (Acts 21:19).

It is quite clear from even this limited New Testament usage that the term *exegesis* is closely related to hermeneutics, the science of interpretation. There are about twenty occurrences of ἑρμηνεύω and related words in the New Testament, half of which mean "to translate." Thus Matthew 1:23 "translates" the Hebrew word *Emmanuel* to mean "God with us," while Mark 5:41 "translates" the Aramaic expression *talitha qum*, "Little girl, get up." But the related word διερμηνεύω meant "to expound" or "to interpret," as when an Old Testament passage was selected and its meaning was set forth to an audience other than that of the original authors; for example, when Jesus began with Moses and all the prophets to "*expound*" all the things concerning His own person and mission (Luke 24:27). Traditionally, then, exegesis and hermeneutics focused on the text itself in an effort to determine what that text said and meant in its own original objective. Unfortunately, this emphasis was not maintained in all periods of Church history.

Under the strong impetus of the Reformation there was a renewed emphasis that there is only *one sense* or meaning to be

---

5. Anthony C. Thiselton, "Explain, Interpret, Tell, Narrative," in *The New International Dictionary of New Testament Theology*, ed. Colin Brown, 3 vols. (Grand Rapids: Zondervan, 1975–1978), 1:573–84.

gleaned from every passage if the interpreter is true to his mission. The sole object of the expositor is to explain as clearly as possible what the writer meant when he wrote the text under examination. It is the interpreter's job to *represent the text*, not the prejudices, feelings, judgments, or concerns of the exegete. To indulge in the latter is to engage in *eisegesis*, "a reading *into*" a text what the reader wants it to say. In adopting this stance the Reformers sided with the earlier Antiochian school against Origen's school at Alexandria.

It is precisely at this point that the issue gets sticky for modern interpreters. While all would, to some degree or another, disparage *eisegesis* as a poor substitute for exegesis, not all are convinced that the discipline can be defined in such objective terms. Meaning for many moderns has become *plural*—they see various levels of meaning.[6]

Vern S. Poythress places the question in its sharpest form: "Is it indeed true that there is always only one meaning which is *the* meaning of a text?"[7] The answer had, up until this last decade, been, "Yes, there is only *one* meaning which is always *the* meaning of a text."

Poythress is very unhappy with that answer. Instead of limiting himself either to the meaning intended by the speaker (what many have unwisely called "the intentional fallacy") or the meaning garnered from audience reaction (which, in this writer's view, should be called the "affective fallacy"),[8] Poythress suggests that there is also discourse meaning which will be established by those who are competent judges and have adequate knowledge in linguistics and historical background.[9] Even if we are willing to grant that only "competent judges" will be allowed to set the discourse

6. See, for example, Susan W. Wittig, "A Theory of Multiple Meanings," *Semeia* 9 (1977): 75–103; Gerald Downing, "Meanings," in *What About the New Testament? Essays in Honour of Christopher Evans*, ed. Morna Hooker and Colin Hickling (London: SCM, 1975), pp. 127–42.

7. Vern S. Poythress, "Analysing a Biblical Text: Some Important Linguistic Distinctions," *Scottish Journal of Theology* 32 (1979): 113.

8. W. K. Wimsatt, Jr., *The Verbal Icon: Studies in the Meaning of Poetry* (Lexington: University of Kentucky, 1954), pp. 3–18, 19–39.

9. Poythress, "Analysing a Biblical Text," p. 126.

meaning (this odd view simultaneously argues that there are also a speaker's meaning and an audience meaning), Poythress's conclusion is disappointing: "Distinguishing different types of meaning can therefore be useful. But by itself, it will not tell us *which* meaning or meanings are to be treated as 'canonical.' "[10] And that is the real catch in all this business of establishing *many* meanings. Who will arbitrate for us between the various meanings?

Such a system of polyvalence invariably must finally resort to a "metacommunicative" dimension. This new system would have us understand a text not in terms of its syntactical or semantic structures, but in the variety of ways in which that text is "actualized" in our minds.

To state it briefly, we are instructed that we should be reading ourselves as much as the text. Thus, all efforts to find the "real or single meaning" are considered fruitless for most moderns, since in their view, texts generate a variety of meaning structures. Some of these meaning structures may be Jungian, Freudian, Structuralist, deep-structure, or what have you, advises Susan W. Wittig.[11]

Another recent author has contended that there are indeed "various layers of meaning" which can be divided into two categories: the ontological (the true and authoritative) and the aesthetic (a meaning or significance beyond the literal meaning of a text).[12] In this view, interpretation proceeds in a circle[13] instead of the traditional linear movement from explanation to meditation to application.

All of this introduces difficulties not only for interpreting Scripture, but even for interpreting all the articles currently being writ-

10. Ibid., p. 137.

11. Wittig, "A Theory of Multiple Meanings," pp. 96–97.

12. John Sandys-Wunsch, "On the Theory and Practice of Biblical Interpretation," *Journal for the Study of the Old Testament* 3 (1977): 66–74. The quoted phrase is from p. 67.

13. The "hermeneutical circle" refers to the interrelationship of the text, the human psyche that produced it, and the interpreter, so that text and interpretation together make up a larger whole. See Richard N. Soulen, *Handbook of Biblical Criticism* (Atlanta: John Knox, 1976), p. 75.

ten on hermeneutics. Why should those writers waste so much time trying to communicate the key idea that there is a plurality of meanings which are locked into a hermeneutical circle? It would seem that these contemporary authors would like to borrow the single meaning and the traditional linear-movement hermeneutic just long enough to establish their own theses. Then they would like to invalidate the further use of the single-meaning procedure in interpreting other documents such as Scripture, for they regard application of the single-meaning procedure as a hopelessly antiquated approach to interpretation.

The best argument for a single-meaning hermeneutic is to be found in observing what happens when it is removed from current conversation or writing. Communication itself is severely handicapped if not made impossible. If individual speakers or writers are not sovereign over the use of their own words, and if meaning is not a return to how they intended their own words to be regarded, then we are in a most difficult situation—everyone communicating, but no one in particular ever receiving (or knowing if he has adequately received) the message.

This is not to argue that the interpreter is able to gather all the special nuances that a speaker or writer may have intended. It is to contend only that there is enough that is jointly shared to make it possible to speak of *adequate* knowledge of what the sender intended to communicate. Few, if any, would argue that what has been received by the listener or interpreter is a *comprehensive* knowledge of the sender's thoughts with all of its nuances, much less a *comprehensive* knowledge of the total subject.

Therefore, while hermeneutics will seek to describe the general and special principles and rules which are useful in approaching the Biblical text, exegesis will seek to identify the single truth-intention of individual phrases, clauses, and sentences as they make up the thought of paragraphs, sections, and, ultimately, entire books. Accordingly, hermeneutics may be regarded as the *theory* that guides exegesis; exegesis may be understood in this work to be the *practice* of and the set of *procedures* for discovering the author's intended meaning.

The Practice of Exegesis

The pastor, theological student, and serious interpreter of Scripture are shocked to learn that virtually no one has mapped out the actual route that the interpreter is to take as he enters the practice of exegesis. Instead, what the fledgling exegete learns is that both ends of this route have been exhaustively examined in (1) preparatory studies in the source from which preaching originates and (2) detailed treatments of what the finished product should look like when one arrives at his destination of preaching a sermon. But in between these two points? Unfortunately we are all left to work it out as best we can! It is this task, more than any other, that we wish to address in the chapters ahead of us.

To begin with, let it be stated as a sort of first principle that preparation for preaching is always a movement which must begin with the text of Scripture and have as its goal the proclamation of that Word in such a way that it can be heard with all its poignancy and relevancy to the modern situation without dismissing one iota of its original normativeness.

Yet even if we state the principle this way, it may seem as if the text is important only at the start of the exegete's work. The fact is that if any other concern begins to rival the text in importance or place, the process of exegesis has already been sidetracked. There are many other errors that the exegete may commit, but this one is the most devastating methodological mistake of all. If the text of Scripture is the central concern, then a mastery of Hebrew, Aramaic, and Greek is a basic requirement. But this mastery of the Biblical languages must be properly aimed. There must be more to this admittedly arduous study than the assemblage of a laborious English translation and the correct parsing of the verbal forms. Whenever this type of linguistic study is regarded as the main function of exegesis, the yield is so low that it is unconscionable.

If the theological student is being taught no more expertise in the languages than this, then it would be better to give an introductory lecture on the basic nature of the verb structure in Greek and Hebrew with some help in using a Greek or Hebrew analyt-ical lexicon which conveniently parses every verb in an alphabet-ical listing. In this way, the student would be able to parse every verb instantaneously. Another lecture giving hints on the use of translations (perhaps including something like *Young's Literal Translation of the Bible* or one of the interlinear translations) and the use of concordances with their transliterated lists of Greek and Hebrew words at the back could complete this minimal introduction.

I have seen all of these tools introduced to laymen, and they have been able to produce acceptable exegetical papers, if that is all that is needed. After all, the verbs were parsed, and the general morphological range of many of these words was pointed out with some parroted comments from introductory studies on the prob-lems of date, authorship, and literary styles and types.

But we contend that the original languages serve best when we become aware of the syntax and grammar involved in phrases, clauses, and sentences. The bonding material between these oth-erwise isolated words or groups of words is what all the sweat and tears are about in language study. If this latter aspect is not the goal of our linguistic studies, then we should indeed switch to the simplified, but heavily dependent and secondarily derived method sketched in the above alternative.

We contend, however, that the serious exegete should learn to master the basic principles of Greek and Hebrew grammar and syntax; otherwise most of one's exegetical insights will necessar-ily be dependent on the statements of others who profess abilities in these languages. While very few theological students, their pro-fessors, or established pastors can be expected to retain in their minds every grammatical or syntactical detail, well-marked gram-mars within handy reach are of tremendous assistance. Obviously, the wider our experience in translation, the more finesse we will acquire in dealing with some of the more sophisticated questions.

Facility with grammatical and syntactical structures requires more than rote memorization or even the ability to locate discus-sions of these items in grammars and handbooks. Eduard Haller referred to the "faculty of discernment,"[14] the ability of lovingly staying with each sentence until we can discern the finer points of its style, structure, beauty, and the special nuance of meaning the author had in mind. Haste, superficiality, and an unreceptive heart and mind are dangerous enemies to sound exegesis, warns Haller. They can be even more detrimental to a sound exegesis than can a lack of linguistic facility—and that is bad enough!

Haller also urges the aspiring exegete to have a patient persistence, a disciplined mind and methodology, a confidence motivated by a personal faith and born of a hunger to experience firsthand the transforming impact of what is discovered in the text. Rewarding results will come only if the search is sustained by an enthusiastic joy of discovery through the long hours of hard and patient work. And in all, it must be tempered by the experience of prayer and suffering, cautions Haller. The exegetical route is not easy; it requires a lot of work, but in the end it is just as rewarding as it is awesome in its initial demands.

Lest it be said that we are advocating the abandonment of all introductory studies, let it be announced in bold relief that it is exceedingly important that the interpreter complete a thorough investigation of the Biblical book's author, date, cultural and historical background. It is virtually impossible to locate the book's message in space and time without this essential material.

Thus background studies about the author, culture, time, literary genre, and organizing principles of the Biblical book are exceedingly helpful and necessary as a proper *preparation* for approaching a Biblical text. But finally we must come to the *text itself*. It must consume the majority of our interest and attention. It must be to that text's phrases, clauses, sentences, paragraphs, or strophes that we devote our most detailed examination and searching analysis.

Improper teaching of exegesis will be the result when it is believed that the main, if not the only, function of exegesis is to explore the *Sitz im Leben* (setting or situation in life—most schol-

14. Eduard Haller, "On the Interpretive Task." This article first appeared as "Ad virtutes exegendi" ("On the Virtues of Exegesis") in *Evangelische Theologie* 25 (1965): 388–95.

ars will focus on repeated patterns rather than the unique historical happening) and the *Sitz im Buch* (situation or setting in the book of Scripture as determined by an investigation into the alleged prehistory of the literary unit). As proper as many of these studies are, if they are made to be the all-consuming interest of exegesis, then the discipline becomes a mere lackey for doing the legwork that is really the proper concern of isagogics (Biblical introduction which involves higher criticism, i.e., date, author, times, audience, literary genre; and lower criticism, i.e., text and canon). Again, let it be stressed that Biblical isagogics is extremely necessary and indeed helpful to the interpreter, but it is merely preparatory.

One other preparatory task would be most helpful. The exegete should prepare a translation of the text that is being examined. One helpful way of doing this is as follows:

After you have translated the text for yourself and are sure you understand all the words and their function in their sentence, then quickly read through five other translations. If there are any significant differences between these translations, record just the problem clauses or phrases as they are found in each version (on separate lines to facilitate study) and then give your own translation with a brief statement as to why you would opt for that rendering (see fig. 2.1).

RSV: _____

NEB: _____

NAB: _____

NASB: _____

NIV: _____

Mine: _____

Reason: _____

Fig. 2.1   A form for the comparison of translations

The History of Exegesis

There is a special value in studying the various theories of interpretation and periods in the history of exegesis. The most obvious benefit is that the interpreter can avoid some of the excesses that have been associated with certain exegetical traditions. But by the same token, the reverse is also true: such study can be a guide to those methods that have proven their worth and have been tested by fact and time.

For our purposes here, we may divide the history of Christian exegesis into five stages: the Apostolic Age, the Patristic Age, the Middle Ages, the Reformation, and the Post-Reformation Age.

The Apostolic Age

By the Apostolic Age, we mean generally the first century of the Christian Era. What we have in mind here is basically the New Testament writer's use of the Old Testament. But it is also necessary to say something about sectarian exegesis, such as that of the Essenes from the Qumran community, and what may be broadly called Rabbinic exegesis (which included material antedating the apostles and eventually both Talmudic and medieval Jewish exegetical literature). This arrangement is extremely schematized, but helpful for our purposes here.

When the traditional Jew approaches the exegetical task, he has before him, as it were, two Torahs: the written Law found in the Old Testament and the oral Law as preserved, for example, in the Talmud. In his view, both have equal claim on him since the oral Law contains the past expositions and interpretations which some argue were also received by Moses and therefore likewise possess Sinaitic roots!

One of the primary categories in this oral Law may be defined as "rules whereby the Torah is expounded." Through the use of these rules or *Middot*, the Biblical text of the Old Testament was extended, limited, provided with analogies, parallels, and logical inferences, as well as clarified and explained.

Three principal systems of hermeneutics were developed in Rabbinic literature: the famous seven basic rules of Hillel (c. 30 B.C.–A.D. 9); the thirteen rules of Rabbi Ishmael (c. A.D. 60–121), which served as the chief instruments in developing the Midrashic method of expounding Halachic texts (religious and civil law); and the thirty-two rules of Rabbi Eliezer (2nd c. A.D.), which were used in interpreting Haggadic texts (popular homilies).[15]

The Midrashic method of exegesis had its genesis in public lectures and homilies. The lecturer would set forth the theme of his homily by reading from a passage of Scripture which enunciated the truth on which he wished to speak. He would then illustrate that truth with a parable and enforce it with a saying that was already popular with the people. This rule was given in the Midrash on the Song of Solomon (1.a).

In order to make these lectures more aesthetically attractive and a pleasant experience for the listener, the speaker would often resort to interspersing his lecture with plays on words, reducing words to their numerical value to make certain points clearer, and finding analogies between numbers and persons that were said to be related to one another in some way. Such pleasantries had a tendency to pass over into the mystical or allegorical sense, called the *Sod*, meaning "secret." This form of interpretation tended to be found more frequently in the Haggadah, the Jewish collection of popular lectures, tales, and legends.

The more sober, "plain," or "simple" method of interpreting the Biblical text was called the *Peshat*. This form was found more frequently in the *Halachah*, a word derived from the Hebrew verb "to go," meaning here the traditional law or practice. Hillel's seven rules are the best representation of this approach. They may be briefly stated and illustrated here:

1. *Qol weḥomer*, קַל וְחֹמֶר ("Light and heavy"). This rule, which uses Scripture to interpret Scripture (as is true of all seven of Hillel's rules), moves *a fortiori* from the less stringent or less important to that which is of greater *Halachic* weight, more im-

---

15. Consult the following excellent summaries: Bernard Rosensweig, "The Hermeneutic Principles and Their Application"; J. Weingreen, "The Rabbinic Approach to the Study of the Old Testament"; Brevard S. Childs, "Midrash and the Old Testament," in *Understanding the Sacred Text: Essays in Honor of Morton S. Enslin on the Hebrew Bible and Christian Beginnings*, ed. John Reumann (Valley Forge, Pa.: Judson, 1972), pp. 45–59; Richard Longenecker, *Biblical Exegesis in the Apostolic Period* (Grand Rapids: Eerdmans, 1975), pp. 32–45.

portant, and more stringent. An example of this rule (and logic) can be found in Jeremiah 12:5: "If you have raced with men on foot, and they have wearied you, [now the inference] how then can you compete with horses?" See also Genesis 44:8; Exodus 6:12; Deuteronomy 31:27.

2. *Gezerah shawah*, גְּזֵירָה שָׁוָה ("Equivalence [or Analogy] of expressions"). An analogy is made between two separate texts on the basis of a similar phrase or word or even root of a word. As an example, the angel of the Lord told Samson's mother that no *razor* was to come on Samson's head, for he was to be a Nazirite (Judg. 13:5); it may be deduced from Hannah's vow that no *razor* would touch Samuel's head (I Sam. 1:11) that he also was a Nazirite.

3. *Binyan ab mikathub 'ehad*, בִּנְיָן אַב מִכָּתוּב אֶחָד ("Building of the father [or a family] from a single text"). One explicit Biblical passage serves as a foundation, a starting-point, so as to constitute a rule (*ab*, "a father") for all similar passages or cases. This is very close to what Protestants would later call the "law of first reference." Thus, since God addressed Moses from the bush, "Moses, Moses" (Exod. 3:4), it is concluded that whenever God spoke to Moses, He addressed him in the same manner.

4. *Binyan ab mishene kethubim*, בִּנְיָן אַב מִשְּׁנֵי כְתוּבִים ("Building of the father [or a family] from two texts"). This is in effect an extension of the preceding rule. Two texts or two provisions in a text serve as a foundation for a general conclusion. Thus, while Exodus 21:26–27 specifies only two parts of the body (the eye and the tooth), each and every part of the body is in mind. In the event of the mutilation of any part of a slave's body, he was given his freedom.

5. *Kelal upherat*, כְּלָל וּפְרָט ("The general and the particular"). A general statement is first made and is followed by a single remark which particularizes the general principle. For example, Genesis 1:27 speaks of man's creation in general terms—"Male and female created he them"; but Genesis 2:7 and 2:21 tell of the material God used and how woman was also made. These latter two references are not another record or story of creation nor are

they contradictory to 1:27; they only particularize the initial general statement.

6. *Kayoṣē' bo' mimeqom 'aḥar*, כַּיּוֹצֵא בּוֹ מִמָּקוֹם אַחֵר ("Analogy made from another passage"). A third passage can be used to explain two others. Thus the apparent contradiction that the Lord spoke to Moses from "out of the tent of meeting" (Lev. 1:1) and "from above the ark of the covenant between the cherubim" (Exod. 25:22) is resolved in Numbers 7:89, where it is recorded that Moses had to enter the tent in order to hear God speaking "from between the cherubim." Also compare II Samuel 24:9 and I Chronicles 21:5 with I Chronicles 27:1; the last-mentioned verse has been used to explain the apparent numerical discrepancy between the other two.

7. *Dabar hilmad me'anino*, דָּבָר הַלְמֵד מֵעֲנִינוֹ ("Explanation obtained from the context"). The total context, not the isolated statement, must be considered for an accurate exegesis. For example, Exodus 16:29 ("Let no man go out of his place on the seventh day") is not to be understood absolutely, but as restricted to leaving for the purposes of gathering manna in the wilderness on the Sabbath day.

This Rabbinic system of exegesis is a mixed blessing for the Church. In many of its rules (*Middot*) it offers the *Peshat*—plain, simple, or literal—method of exegesis. But its playfulness and search (*Derash*) for the deeper or more exotic meaning tended to work at cross-purposes with the more sober and literal approach to the text. Eventually the *Sod* overtook the concerns of *Peshat*.

The Essenes of the Qumran community were an eschatological sect that believed they were living in the last days. They were also convinced that predictive prophecies could and should be directly applied to their times and to the history of their sect.

Their method of exegesis was simply to quote a brief passage of from one to three verses, the "word," and then to follow that word with its *pesher* ("interpretation"). The tendency was arbitrarily to equate individuals, movements, and situations in their own times *directly* with individuals, movements, and situations in the Biblical text. Thus, the "righteous" of Habakkuk 1:4 became the founder of their sect, "The Teacher of Righteousness." The "wicked [who] surround the righteous" (Hab. 1:4) was that "wicked priest" and "Man of lies" who persecuted and perhaps eventually killed the sect's founder. The "Chaldeans" of Habakkuk 1:6 became the Romans, whom the sect bitterly hated and for whose speedy removal from Palestine they fervently hoped.

The other great source of hermeneutical principles for what we are calling here the Apostolic Age is the New Testament writers' use of the Old Testament. A great number of contemporary scholars argue most vigorously that, in the main, the New Testament writers adopted the somewhat looser rules which, as has been pointed out above, were already in practice in the Jewish community.[16]

This conclusion is most improbable, however. If the New Testament writers were trying to convince a somewhat hostile audience that their own Old Testament had predicted in detail many of the features of Jesus' life and ministry, then they would certainly have used a *Peshat* type of exegesis and not a *Midrashic*, *pesher*, or *Sod* type of exegesis. Any sort of New Testament ad hoc contemporization of the Old Testament in order to make it apply to the new situation would have been readily recognized for what it really was.

For example, Paul is alleged to have used a type of *pesher* exegesis in I Corinthians 9:9–10 and Galatians 4:21–23, but these conclusions rest on an inadequate view of Paul's use of Deuteronomy 25:4 and of Genesis 16 and 21.[17] Likewise, when Paul is alleged to have used *Midrashic* or *pesher* exegesis in Romans

16. E. Earle Ellis, "How the New Testament Uses the Old," in *New Testament Interpretation: Essays on Principles and Methods*, ed. I. Howard Marshall, pp. 199–219; and D. Moody Smith, Jr., "The Use of the Old Testament in the New," in *The Use of the Old Testament in the New and Other Essays: Studies in Honor of William Franklin Stinespring*, ed. James M. Efird (Durham, N.C.: Duke University, 1972), pp. 3–65. However, cf. Frederic Gardiner, *The Old and New Testaments in Their Mutual Relations* (New York: Pott, 1885), pp. 310–31 ("The New Testament Use of the Old").

17. For full argumentation of this point, see Walter C. Kaiser, Jr., "The Current Crisis in Exegesis and the Apostolic Use of Deuteronomy 25:4 in 1 Corinthians 9:8–10," *Journal of the Evangelical Theological Society* 21 (1978): 3–18. Also Robert J. Kepple, "An Analysis of Antiochene Exegesis of Galatians 4:24–26," *Westminster Theological Journal* 39 (1976–77): 239–49.

10:5–10;[18] I Corinthians 10:1–6; II Corinthians 3:12–18;[19] Galatians 3:16; and Ephesians 4:8,[20] we beg to differ most decidedly. Rather, we would contend that in all passages where the New Testament writers quote the Old to establish a fact or doctrine and use the Old Testament passage argumentatively, they have understood the passage in its natural and straightforward sense. This is not to say they did not cite the Old Testament for other purposes. They did; for example, they at times borrowed its language without appealing to its argument, they used it for illustrative purposes, and they drew on its word pictures. But such practices were avoided when the New Testament writers were engaged in serious exegesis and where the point rested on the fact that the Old Testament had foreseen a feature that had explicitly come to pass in New Testament times or where the Old Testament was the basis for the principle or teaching now being urged in the New Testament.

The Patristic Age

The history of exegesis in the early Church is basically a history of the struggle between the two schools of Alexandria and Antioch.[21] But even before the tension took these classic shapes, the early Church fathers exhibited a decided tendency toward the allegorization of Scripture.

For example, Irenaeus, a student of Polycarp, who in turn was a disciple of the apostle John, wrote in A.D. 185 in his work *Against Heresies* (V.8.4) that the Old Testament description of

18. See Walter C. Kaiser, Jr., "Leviticus 18:5 and Paul: 'Do This and You Shall Live (Eternally?),' " *Journal of the Evangelical Theological Society* 14 (1971): 19–28.

19. See Walter C. Kaiser, Jr., "The Weightier and Lighter Matters of the Law: Moses, Jesus, and Paul," in *Current Issues in Biblical and Patristic Interpretation: Studies in Honor of Merrill C. Tenney Presented by His Former Students*, ed. Gerald F. Hawthorne (Grand Rapids: Eerdmans, 1975), pp. 176–92.

20. See Gary V. Smith, "Paul's Use of Psalm 68:18 in Ephesians 4:8," *Journal of the Evangelical Theological Society* 18 (1975): 181–89.

21. See James N. S. Alexander, "The Interpretation of Scripture in the Ante-Nicene Period: A Brief Conspectus," *Interpretation* 12 (1958): 272–80; Allan E. Johnson, "The Methods and Presuppositions of Patristic Exegesis in the Formation of Christian Personality," *Dialog* 16 (1977): 186–90.

clean and unclean animals is symbolic of the classes of mankind. Old Testament Law had designated as clean those animals which have divided hooves and chew the cud (Lev. 11:3). Irenaeus regarded animals with divided hooves as symbolic of men who make their way toward the Father and the Son, and he regarded animals that chew the cud as symbolic of men who meditate on the Law day and night. Animals whose hoof is not cloven and which do not chew the cud represent Gentiles, and those animals which chew the cud but do not have the double hoof represent the Jews. There are even more exasperating examples of this type of "exegesis" in the Epistle of Barnabas (written in c. A.D. 130).

But it was Clement of Alexandria and Origen who in effect institutionalized this allegorical method in the late second century and early part of the third century. Origen explained his approach in his work *De principiis* (*On First Principles*). It was his contention that every passage potentially has a threefold meaning; he later saw possibilities of a fourfold meaning (4.1). These allegorists, being heavily influenced by Philo, resorted to this exegetical expediency whenever: (1) there appeared anything in the text which in their judgment was unworthy of being attributed to God, (2) the text presented an insoluble difficulty, or (3) an expression made no sense or contained what appeared to be a contradiction.

But the Alexandrian school's theory of multiple meanings did not stop members of the exegetical school of Antioch from suggesting that, while the Old Testament author may himself have foreseen by means of a vision granted him by God the future fulfillment of his prophetic word, yet this sense was inherently *one* with the historical sense in which that word would have been understood in the prophet's own day.[22] With this strong emphasis on the single meaning of the text, the Antiochian school set an example worth emulating and steered a tricky course between the overly rigorous literalism of the Ebionites and the arbitrary allegorization of the Hellenists, Gnostics, and Alexandrian school.

---

22. See A. Vaccari, "La *Theōria* nella scuola esegetica di Antiochia," *Biblica* 1 (1920): 3–36.

The Middle Ages

The key figures in exegesis during the long years of A.D. 600 to 1500 were the Victorines from the Abbey of St. Victor in Paris.[23] Hugh of St. Victor (1096?–1141) still used the threefold principle of interpreting Scripture allegorically but he did, somewhat enigmatically, also distinguish himself by his emphasis on the literal sense. Hugh believed that the literal sense as intended by the author is *the* meaning of the text. Thus he prepared the way for the distinguished theologian Thomas Aquinas.

In the twelfth century, Andrew of St. Victor, one of Hugh's students, furthered this emphasis on the literal meaning even though he continued to use a twofold exegetical method for controversial passages: on the one hand, he utilized the Vulgate text and gave a Christian interpretation, while on the other, he gave a Jewish explanation based on the Hebrew text. Thus, for example, Isaiah 7:14 was given both a Jewish and a Christian explanation.

Another leading light during this period was Stephen Langton (1150–1228), Archbishop of Canterbury. He is best known today for his work of dividing the Bible into its present chapter divisions, but he also should be noted for his emphasis on the necessity of having all interpretations conform with the Christian faith. Unfortunately, he, too, like many of the earlier fathers, tended to use this principle with great freedom, even though he did feel that spiritual interpretations should be based squarely on the literal text.

The real symbol of this era, however, is Thomas Aquinas (1225–1274). He made a clear distinction between two orders of facts, which, while being closely connected, nevertheless have different values.[24] The Holy Spirit speaks to us clearly in some texts, for His message is readily apparent in the natural or literal

23. On exegesis in the Middle Ages, see Beryl Smalley, *The Study of the Bible in the Middle Ages* (Notre Dame, Ind.: University of Notre Dame, 1964); Ceslaus Spicq, *Esquisse d'une histoire de l'exégèse latine au moyen âge* (Paris: Vrin, 1944); Robert E. McNally, *The Bible in the Early Middle Ages*, Woodstock Papers: Occasional Essays for Theology, 4 (Westminster, Md.: Newman, 1959).

24. Thomas Aquinas, *Summa Theologica* 1a.1.10; *Quaestiones Quodlibetales* 7.14–16.

sense of the words. By interpreting these words literally, the theologian establishes his conclusions and theology.

But the Bible also has a symbolic meaning, and this for two reasons: (1) heavenly things cannot be explained in earthly terms without some degree of symbolism; (2) the history of Israel was disposed by the divine Master of history in such a way that He could bring in matters relating to the new covenant. Thus it is plain that Thomas still found it hard to shake the old "doctrine of correspondences," even though he had begun to drink heavily of a new stream; namely, that the literal meaning of the text is the basis for all solid teaching.

Meanwhile a Jewish believer, Nicholas of Lyra (1270–1340?), began to press the literal sense as the only reasonable basis for exegesis. What an important role he played in the history of exegesis is apparent in the celebrated aphorism, "If Lyra had not piped, Luther would not have danced."

The Reformation Age

Out of the Renaissance with its new emphasis on a return to the original languages of Scripture come Johann Reuchlin's Hebrew grammar and lexicon and Erasmus's first critical edition of the Greek New Testament (A.D. 1516). In part, they set the groundwork for the arrival of Martin Luther and John Calvin. Erasmus was stimulated by John Colet (1467–1519) to apply to the Scriptures the new humanistic emphasis on the historical and philological approach. Returning from Italy to lecture in England on Romans and I Corinthians, Colet was filled with this new approach and with a total rejection of the allegorical and mystical exegesis of the Scholastics. In 1498 Erasmus attended his lectures and the rest became history.

Luther's clear (was he ever veiled in his thought?) affirmation that the single meaning of the text is the only proper basis for exegesis marked another new impetus in Biblical interpretation. His comments on the allegorical method were just as strong as they were clear. Said he characteristically, "Origen's allegories are not worth so much dirt," for "allegories are empty speculations . . . the scum of Holy Scripture." "Allegories are awkward,

absurd, invented, obsolete, loose rags." Such a method of interpretation, he opined, "degenerates into a mere monkey game."
"Allegory is a sort of beautiful harlot, who proves herself specially
seductive to idle men."[25] For Luther, "The Holy Ghost is the all-
simplest writer that is in heaven or earth; therefore his words can
have no more than one simplest sense, which we call the scriptural or literal meaning."[26]

Calvin was not one whit softer on the allegorizers. Commenting
on Galatians 4:21–26, he blasted every such introduction and
foisting of numerous meanings onto Scripture as "a contrivance
of Satan." And in his commentary on Romans, he inscribed a
dedicatory letter to a friend in which he said: "Since it is almost
his [the interpreter's] only task to unfold the mind of the writer
whom he has undertaken to expound, he misses his mark, or at
least strays outside his limits, by the extent to which he leads his
readers away from the meaning of his author. . . . It is . . . pre-
sumptuous and almost blasphemous to turn the meaning of scripture around without due care, as though it were some game that
we were playing. And yet many scholars have done this at one
time."[27]

More than any others, Calvin and Luther reversed the exegetical tide which had been ebbing and flowing for and against allegorization since before the Christian Era. Not that they
themselves were always successful in their own practice of their
principles, but they had set a course for the Church that was now
most clearly marked for all future days.

The Post-Reformation Age

Two new movements significant for the history of exegesis appeared in the seventeenth century: Pietism and rationalism.

25. See Martin Luther, *Lectures on Genesis*, in *Luther's Works*, vols. 1–3, ed. Jar-
oslav Pelikan (St. Louis: Concordia, 1958–1961), comments on Genesis 3, 15, 20.

26. As quoted in Frederic W. Farrar, *History of Interpretation*, Bampton Lectures,
1885 (Grand Rapids: Baker, 1961), p. 329.

27. John Calvin, *Commentary on the Epistle of Paul to the Galatians and Ephesians*,
trans. William Pringle (Edinburgh: Calvin Translation Society, 1854), p. 135; idem, *The
Epistles of Paul the Apostle to the Romans and to the Thessalonians*, trans. Ross
MacKenzie, Calvin's Commentaries, ed. David W. Torrance and Thomas F. Torrance
(Grand Rapids: Eerdmans, 1961), pp. 1, 4.

✗ Pietism, itself a protest of sorts against institutionalism and doctrinal dogmatism devoid of personal faith, set its highest priority on the personal experience of conversion and all practical works of piety. While one could list such leaders as Philipp Jacob Spener and August Hermann Francke, the most valuable contributor, from our perspective of exegesis, was John Albert Bengel (1687–1752). He was the first to classify the New Testament Greek manuscripts into families on the basis of various similarities. His commentary, the famous *Gnomon of the New Testament* (1742), is a model for its combination of historical roots, explanation of figures of speech (a glossary with explanations of some one hundred figures of speech and related terms appears in the index), and suggestions on practical application.[28]

Philosophical rationalism found its roots in the writings of René Descartes (1596–1650), Thomas Hobbes (1588–1679), Baruch Spinoza (1632–1677), and John Locke (1632–1704). But theological rationalism may be more directly linked with three eminent fountainheads: Christian von Wolff (1679–1754), Hermann Samuel Reimarus (1694–1768), and Gotthold Ephraim Lessing (1729–1781). Wolff tried to tie Biblical revelation in with natural revelation. Reimarus, then, made natural revelation the entire source for Christianity; since faith and reason were irreconcilable for him, he refused to accept the concept of special revelation. For Lessing the contingent truths of history could never be a proof for the necessary truths of reason.[29] To these men can be traced the origins of much of what later developed in liberal theology, including the destructive Biblical criticism of the nineteenth century.

The eighteenth century experienced the continuation of both of these movements; however, Pietism received more visibility, largely through the life and preaching of John Wesley (1703–1791). The Wesleyan revival called men and women back to God and back to individual and group study of the Word of God.

28. John Albert Bengel, *Gnomon of the New Testament*, ed. Andrew R. Fausset, 5 vols. (Edinburgh: Clark, 1857–1858).

29. See the fine analysis in Geoffrey W. Bromiley, "History and Truth: A Study of the Axiom of Lessing," *Evangelical Quarterly* 18 (1946): 191–98.

But the underlying current of protest broke out again, this time in the writings of Immanuel Kant (1724–1804) and Friedrich Schleiermacher (1768–1834). While Kant tried to establish an approach and new evidence for God within the bounds of his "categorical imperative," that "Thou Shalt" which he felt was within the soul of every man, Schleiermacher emphasized *Gefühl*, human feelings, as the seat of man's consciousness of God. Religion no longer had its source in a book, reason, or anything external; its primary source was that feeling of ultimate dependence on someone outside ourselves. Sin was a disruption of this sense or feeling of dependence on God, not a rebellion against what God had revealed of His will or law in a book!

Joining Schleiermacher's rejection of a person-religion as revealed in an event in history and in a book was Albrecht Ritschl (1822–1889). Ritschl argued that Christianity was based on a value judgment and thus he stressed the moral and ethical value of Christianity.

The climax of this line of thought appears to be Adolf von Harnack (1851–1930). He called for a return to the religion of Jesus, but not the religion *about* Jesus. Accordingly, he purged the Gospels of whatever he felt were Hellenistic accretions improperly attached to them.

The basic theological concern of the eighteenth and nineteenth centuries was hardly conducive to the difficult questions of method and approach in Biblical exegesis. The more pressing question which consumed the time and interests of the best of the minds of those centuries, both inside and outside of the Church, was whether the Bible would serve to any degree as a credible source and authority for the Church and Christianity.

Nor has the twentieth century escaped the snares of this bedeviling and, by now, boring harangue. It has taken on a more sophisticated face, but often it has remained just as sterile and unproductive.

This is not the place to outline the very long and complicated history of Biblical criticism during the last two-and-a-quarter centuries. However, the reader is deserving of at least some idea of this author's stance as it bears on the subject of exegesis.

The task of higher criticism is *not* an optional task which evangelicals may drop from their consideration any more than nonevangelicals may claim it as their special province for defeating what they regard as distasteful doctrinal claims in the Bible. The truth is that questions of date, style, authorship, audience, parallels, and claims for sources must be investigated if we are to be honest exegetes and "make full proof of our ministry."

But a good exegete will have nothing to do with *hypothetical* sources which have never materialized in any form. These sources are deductively "authenticated" and then inductively "proven" from the same document in what becomes a most vicious circle. What you put in, you get out! In the meantime, there are scores of *real* sources that must and should be investigated; for example, the sixty to seventy sources explicitly listed in Chronicles. Furthermore, this is not the total mission of higher criticism; there is more.

A new approach called form criticism was inaugurated by Hermann Gunkel (1862–1932). Gunkel's interest was in identifying types or genres of Biblical literature which developed out of an oral preliterary stage and a special *Sitz im Leben* (i.e., a situation in life—such as in a cult, the state, or community—which tended to be repeated in a pattern set by custom or the like and which assumed a certain shape or associated form).

Gunkel's initial observations were refined and applied to the Book of Psalms (Sigmund Mowinckel, 1921–1924), the covenant treaties in the Old Testament (George E. Mendenhall, 1954), and New Testament studies, especially the Gospels (Karl Ludwig Schmidt, Martin Dibelius, and Rudolf Bultmann).

Again, we find ourselves unable to grant the underlying premise: that the literary forms of Scripture first arose in their pristine form as an oral piece associated with a special *Sitz* in Old-Testament Israel or the first century that not only left its mark on the literature, but also in some ways *controlled its substance or content*. This is too speculative for our blood. But where real evidence does exist (such as second- or first-millennium B.C. vassal-treaties with a literary *Gattung* that exhibits a basic outline or structure similar to that of several Biblical covenants and even the whole of Deuteronomy), we are most anxious to include it in our exegesis and to adapt our method accordingly.[30]

Finally, there are the new developments in tradition criticism and redaction criticism. The former discipline is interested in tracing the history of the formation, modification, and new synthesis of the oral and then the written sources in the Bible. The names connected with this school are Ivan Engnell (1906–1964), Martin Noth (1902–1968), and Albrecht Alt (1883–1956). Redaction criticism, on the other hand, is far more interested in the theological motivations for deciding what was to be included, how it was to be arranged, and what shape the material would take. The idea is to show how the theological emphases of the New Testament authors differ from each other. The key scholars connected with redaction criticism are Günther Bornkamm, Hans Conzelmann, and Willi Marxsen.

While both of these disciplines provide some sources of insight into the Scriptures, they also bring liabilities in their wake insofar as they tend to avoid taking the text on its own terms and according to its own claims. Thus, if the author (or, as some would have it, the editor or redactor) claims a revelatory stance and yet is preemptorily declared by these disciplines to be a scissors-and-paste man who assembled or a stenographer who merely took down assorted tales and customs—something is going to have to yield. And surely the evidence of the text itself must take the front seat in that decision until independent and external evidence to the contrary is uncovered.

We truly believe that some forms of a modified redaction criticism can and should be used with respect to both Testaments, for anything that helps us to get at the author's selection and arrangement of materials (of course, as the writers claim, all of this was directed by God) in historical passages according to theological principles will obviously help us in preparing to preach

---

30. See the discussion of some of these points as they relate to Old Testament studies in Walter C. Kaiser, Jr., "The Present State of Old Testament Studies," *Journal of the Evangelical Theological Society* 18 (1975): 78. Here we cite evangelical contributions to form-critical studies from O. T. Allis, Meredith G. Kline, Kenneth Kitchen, and Herbert W. Wolf.

from those texts. Some of the theological differences (e.g., between the Gospel writers), while real, are not so much, in our judgment, contradictory as they are complementary. Though they may aim at different theological goals, in the process they weld the Scriptures into a more complete and unified whole.

⚡Thus Biblical exegesis must use any and all of those tools which it legitimately can, while preserving the autonomy of the text and assuming (until proven otherwise) its integrity. But two-and-a-quarter centuries of work on Biblical criticism must not be substituted for the hard demands of the exegesis that still must follow this preparatory work. Somehow we must return to the major problem with which the Church has wrestled for almost seventeen centuries and which has been dropped in the interest of reacting to the isagogical issues introduced by most of the critical studies.

What has been dropped in exegetical studies in favor of these various critical studies has been continued under the rubric of hermeneutics. We have already, in part, traced this movement in our introductory chapter. It remains for us to plead for a revival of the older program of exegesis involving an enlarged approach with the restricted methodology of analyzing the author's grammar and syntax in a most minute and detailed way as a preparation for discovering the theology and teaching of that word together with a basis for declaring it anew in our generation.

PART II

The Syntactical-Theological Method

Chapter 3

Contextual Analysis

Where must the exegete begin? Shall he begin with the most intricate and smallest components such as phonemes, morphemes, words, and then gradually work up to phrases, clauses, sentences, paragraphs, sections, and books? Or is the reverse order to be followed?

Good exegetical procedure dictates that the details be viewed in light of the total context. Unless the exegete knows where the thought of the text begins and how that pattern develops, all the intricate details may be of little or no worth. This ability—the ability to state what each section of a book is about and how the paragraphs in each section contribute to that argument—is one of the most critical steps. If the exegete falters here, much of what follows will be wasted time and effort.

Samuel Davidson set this forth in the plainest terms:

In considering the connection of parts in a section . . . acuteness and critical tact are much needed. We may be able to tell the significance of single terms and yet be *utterly inadequate to unfold continuous argument*. A capacity for verbal analysis does not impart the talent of expounding an entire paragraph. Ability [1]

to discover the proper causes, [2] the natural sequence, [3] the
pertinency of expressions to the subject discussed, and [4] the
delicate distinctions of thought which characterize particular kinds
of composition is distinct from the habit of carefully tracing out
the various senses of separate terms.[1]

So the problem is not merely the common error of forgetting
or disregarding the immediate context. It is, rather, the more serious error of attempting to atomize or fragment the text and then
presuming that meaning can be attributed to phrases, sentences,
or even paragraphs in isolation from the rest of the context.

Scripture is especially vulnerable to this type of an approach.
Believing (rightfully) that the message of the text in its verbalized
form is the very word which God Himself wanted to be com-
municated through His free, but obedient, writers, many go on
to invest every word and phrase with almost an independent
meaning(s) of its own apart from its context. Without thinking
they allow this to pass over into a quasi-magical use of the words
of Scripture where they may be detached from their context and
used at the pleasure of the exegete—just as long as this is done
for spiritual purposes and is in general harmony with the teaching
of Scripture somewhere else.

But we will have no part of this bad business. If the particular
truth in which we are interested is indeed taught somewhere else
in the Bible, then we must proceed immediately to that context
for the message. We must not make a pretense of exegeting a text
just because the wording is to our liking. That in essence would
be a deliberate misleading of the congregation, for they would
assume we are pointing to that text as authoritative for the matter
under consideration.

No, knowledge of the context is extremely necessary and important. We must, therefore, consider four levels of context: sec-

1. Samuel Davidson, *Sacred Hermeneutics Developed and Applied: Including a History of Biblical Interpretation from the Earliest Fathers to the Reformation* (Edinburgh:
Clark, 1843), p. 240. Cited in Milton S. Terry, *Biblical Hermeneutics: A Treatise on the
Interpretation of the Old and New Testaments* (New York: Phillips & Hunt, 1890; reprint
ed., Grand Rapids: Zondervan, 1964), p. 220.

tional context, book context, canonical context, and the immediate context.

The Sectional Context

The word *context* is composed of two Latin elements, *con* ("together") and *textus* ("woven"). Hence when we speak of the context, we are talking about the connection of thought that runs through a passage, those links that weave it into one piece.

The exegete must feel that his primary obligation is to find this thread of thought which runs like a life stream through the smaller and larger parts of every passage. When this connection is missed or avoided, there is a fair chance that the interpreter may miss the scope, end, purpose, and entire plan by which the author ordered the various parts of his work. Thus the study of scope and plan belong to the study of a work's context.

How then shall we approach the study of context? There must be a preliminary reading of the book. This reading will be an inspection of some of the key vistas and features. One way in which we might accomplish this initial task is simply to note if the author has explicitly stated in his preface, conclusion, and/or constant refrains throughout the book what his intention is. The rest of his work can then be systematically skimmed to note how this explicitly stated purpose and plan have been worked out.

However, if the scope of the work has not been laid out in definite terms, then an x-ray type of approach must be taken. In this approach the interpreter will make use of a variety of clues to locate the slightly exposed seams which mark off specific sections of the book. For example:

1. A repeated term, phrase, clause, or sentence may act as the *heading* to introduce each part or as the *colophon* (tailpiece) to conclude each individual section.
2. Often there may be grammatical clues such as transitional conjunctions or adverbs; for example, "then, therefore, wherefore, but, nevertheless, meanwhile," and the Greek words οὖν, δέ, καί, τότε, διό.

3. A rhetorical question could signal a switch to a new theme and section. It may be that there also will be a series of such questions which carries forward the argument or plan of a whole section.

4. A change in the time, location, or setting is a frequent device, especially in narrative contexts, to indicate a new theme and section.

5. A vocative form of address deliberately showing a shift of attention from one group to another constitutes one of the most important devices. It is often used in the epistolary type of literature.

6. A change in the tense, mood, or aspect of the verb perhaps even with a change in the subject or object may be another clue that a new section is beginning.

7. Repetition of the same key word, proposition, or concept might also indicate the boundaries of a section.

8. In a few cases, the theme of each section will be announced as a heading to that section. In those unusual cases, the interpreter need only make sure that all of the contents of the section are judged in light of the stated purpose of the author.[2]

Now it may seem strange to break in on the matter of the whole context by proceeding to disassemble a book into its major working parts much as an auto mechanic might disassemble a car into its components: a body, motor, front end, electrical system, transmission, rear axle, and so on. But the analogy is proper here, for we wish to discover how this book "works." From the connection and organization of its parts, the unity and overall function are learned and made ready for our use. Thus, while our goal is to learn and to be able to state the unifying theme of the whole book in a single sentence or, if absolutely necessary, in a few sentences, we cannot state what that unifying theme consists of until we have made some preliminary inspections of the total work.

Of course, if the author has flatly declared what his work is all about, either in his preface or conclusion, this task is greatly simplified. The purpose for writing can readily be discovered. In

2. Most of these ideas and some of the examples I owe to John Beekman and John Callow, *Translating the Word of God* (Grand Rapids: Zondervan, 1974), pp. 279–81.

this happy situation, however, the interpreter still needs to identify the various sections. But in this case, it is necessary to learn where the sections come only to find out how the stated plan or purpose has unfolded. In any event, it still seems best to begin at the level of sectional analysis, which immediately embraces both the overall purpose and connections in the unfolding of that plan.

Some Biblical examples of the previously listed principles for discovering sectional divisions will be helpful at this point.✝

The skeleton of Genesis protrudes most visibly in the oft-repeated phrase, "the generations [or histories, happenings] of X." Ten times the phrase appears as a *heading* for the section which follows. Each time a new name is inserted; for example, "the generations of the heavens and earth" (Gen. 2:4), "the generations of Adam" (Gen. 5:1), "the generations of Noah" (Gen. 6:9), "the generations of the sons of Noah" (Gen. 10:1), "the generations of Terah" (Gen. 11:27), and so on.

But this phenomenon of a repeated term, phrase, clause, or sentence can also appear at the *end* of a section. Five times Matthew closed major teaching blocks of material with the refrain, "And it came to pass when Jesus had ended these sayings . . ." (Matt. 7:28; 11:1; 13:53; 19:1; and 26:1).

In a similar way, Solomon used a repeated refrain as a colophon to mark the four sections in Ecclesiastes. His repeated line was, "Eat, drink and find enjoyment in your work, for this is the gift of God" (Eccles. 2:24–26; 5:18–20; and 8:15).[3]

On the other hand, Romans 6:1 uses a rhetorical question to introduce a new section: "What shall we say then? Shall we sin that grace may increase?" In fact the whole section is tied together with Paul's repeated insistence, τί οὖν ("What then?"—Rom. 6:1, 15; 7:7). The Old Testament exhibits a somewhat similar case in the repetition of a slightly rhetorical question. The seminarians at Bethel and Jericho both asked Elisha the same question: "Do you know that today the Lord will take away your master from you?" Each time his response was, "Yes, I know it;

3. See our developments of this plan and our case for Solomonic authorship in Walter C. Kaiser, Jr., *Ecclesiastes: Total Life*, Everyman's Bible Commentary (Chicago: Moody, 1979).

don't pester me about it'' (II Kings 2:3, 5). The question functions to advance the narrative and to close each of the episodes as the moment for Elijah's translation to heaven draws near.

The most celebrated of all cases where the rhetorical question is used to structure a whole book is in Malachi. Repeatedly, in a unique conversational style, Malachi begins each major section with a bold declaration from God only to have the audience reaction be that pretended, innocent, and hurt look which asks rhetorically, "Who, us? We did that?" Literally, the Hebrew reads בַּמֶּה ("With what?"—Mal. 1:2, 6, 7; 2:14, 17; 3:8, 13). To every charge God made against Israel, they responded rhetorically, "Who us? No, not us!" Ironically, their bad manners are a real boon to the interpreter who seeks the proper division of the sections in the Book of Malachi.

Sometimes the repeated material is an imperative with a vocative word of address. Nowhere is this clearer than in the introductory words to the three sections of Micah. In each case, the prophet begins with the shout, שִׁמְעוּ ("Hear"—Micah 1:2; 3:1; and 6:1). In the message found in the first two chapters, his command to "hear" is to the peoples of the earth. In the second section he begins with a summons for the "heads of Jacob, the rulers of the house of Israel," to "hear," and in the last section Micah calls on the mountains to sit in the jury box to "hear" while the Lord states His complaint against the defendant, Israel.

The final section of Isaiah (40–66) is especially well-organized by the use of a colophon: " 'There is no peace,' says the Lord, 'for the wicked' " (Isa. 48:22; 57:21; and an expansion of this concept at the end of the book in 66:24). Thus Isaiah 40–66 is divided into three large teaching blocks, each composed of an ennead (nine addresses roughly corresponding to our present set of nine chapters each).

But the most extensive use of repeated vocabulary to demarcate sections is probably in the Book of Amos. Almost everyone has noticed that Amos 1–2 eight times repeats these phrases: "For three transgressions, yea for four . . . ," "because they have . . . ," "so I will send a fire on . . . and it shall devour. . . ." There is no doubt about how far this section (Amos 1–2) extends.

Before the exegete attempts to discover the divisions of more difficult and less obvious sections, it would be well to take a close look at the characteristics of the other sections of Amos, which are also well marked by stylistics. Amos's middle section, chapters 3–5, uses the imperative שִׁמְעוּ ("Hear") as a heading to mark off what are now three chapters. Each section has its own unique characteristic, theme, and motif.

In Amos 3 there is that series of nine rhetorical questions that lead irrevocably and unmistakably to the cause-and-effect conclusion towards which Amos's argument is aimed: "The Lord has spoken, who can but prophesy?" (3:8). Then again, Amos 4 sets forth one disaster after another until the total reaches five. After each divine judgment is recounted, the sad refrain is repeated, "Yet you did not return to me, says the Lord" (Amos 4:6, 8, 9, 10, 11). All of this builds to the climax—there is an end to the ever so patient, long-suffering goodness of God: "Therefore here is what I will do to you, O Israel; and because I will do this to you, prepare to meet your God, O Israel!" (4:12). Amos 5, which is also introduced by, "Hear this word . . . O house of Israel," repeats the words *Seek* and *live*: "*Seek* me and *live*" (5:4); "*Seek* the Lord and *live*" (5:6); and "*Seek* good, and not evil, that you may *live*" (5:14).

Next Amos has a transitional section composed of several indictments, most of which begin with the words, "Woe to you" (5:18; 6:1, 4; the expression, "I hate, I despise . . . ," in 5:21 is a functional equivalent).

Finally, five visions conclude Amos's work, four of them introduced by "the Lord God showed me" (7:1, 4, 7; 8:1; there is an equivalent expression in 9:1). Two parts of this final section seem to intrude on its unity: a narrative (7:10–17) and still another address introduced by "Hear this" (8:4–14). Here the exegete's job is to discern why the author arranged the material of his book in this peculiar manner. We should try to explain the position and sequence of every immediate context. Failure to grapple with the problem will generally result in our missing the author's total purpose and plan. More will be said on this topic in our discussion of immediate context.

Illustrations other than those we have listed here will occur to the reader. Of course it is always a joy when the theme of the section is explicitly cited, as, for example, in I Corinthians 12:1: "Now concerning spiritual gifts." In fact, almost all of I Corinthians uses the περὶ δὲ ("Now concerning") construction to introduce the next item that Paul wishes to address (e.g., I Cor. 7:1, 25; 8:1; 12:1; 16:1). Paul has apparently organized his material in the form of a series of responses to questions the Corinthians had asked of him in a letter.

Yet, once again, the exegete must be alert for variations even in the midst of what would appear to be unrelieved uniformity. In I Corinthians 6:12 and 10:23 (just to take two obvious examples, without bringing in, for the moment, additional difficulties, such as the probable case of 14:34–35), Paul introduces a quotation from the Corinthians' letter (a quotation which apparently reflected their perspective) without using the introductory formula of "Now concerning."

But in all cases such as these, we know that we are dealing with a quotation and not with the author's own point of view, because these cases are accompanied by one or more of the following characteristics: (1) the quotation is marked by a strong contrast to the immediate context; (2) the writer alludes to the readers' own knowledge of the subject; or (3) a statement is made which is in marked contrast to other passages the author has written. Accordingly, Paul must be quoting the Corinthians' attitudes when he says, "All things are lawful" (6:12; 10:23), for he immediately counters by adding, "But not all things are helpful." Again, by way of rejoinder to the Corinthian point of view that "all things are lawful," Paul adds, "But not all things build up," and "I will not be enslaved by anything."

And could it not be that the debated passage of I Corinthians 14:34–35 is a quote from the Rabbinic law? Surely it is not from the Old Testament, for the Old Testament nowhere states: "Women should keep silence. . . . They are not permitted to speak, but should be in subordination as even the law says. If they desire to know anything, let them ask their husbands at home." Note, too, that Paul had commanded, as a matter of fact, that the Church should teach the women and let them learn (I Tim. 2:11). Furthermore, he had instructed that women be allowed to speak and pray in Church "in like manner as the men" (I Cor. 11:4–5; I Tim. 2:8–9). No wonder then that the immediate context of I Corinthians 14:36 blares out such a strong disclaimer of the Rabbinic restriction: "What! Are you men the only ones [μόνους–masculine; not μόνας–feminine!] the Word of God has reached? Did the Word of God originate with you?"

Regardless of whether you agree with this last example, most will, on the basis of the two earlier examples in I Corinthians, grant the point being made. Close attention to each subtle nuance that may aid us to detect sectional divisions can be as important as recognizing the more obvious connections which bind these sections together.

The Book Context

At this point it should be possible to identify the overall purpose and plan of the book. The parts should add up to the total work.

In some works, such as Ecclesiastes, the writer bluntly tells us his purpose: "Now the conclusion [סוֹף] of the matter is this: Fear God and keep his commandments; for this is *the entirety* [הַכֹּל] of what a person [is all about]" (Eccles. 12:13). Likewise, Luke wrote his Gospel so that Theophilus might "know the certainty" of what he had heard about Jesus (Luke 1:1–4). Again, I John aims at rehearsing the reality of the gospel found in Jesus "that our joy might be complete" (1:1–4). Or even better still, John 20:30–31 asserts that the miracles selected for inclusion in John's Gospel were purposely chosen "that [readers] might believe that Jesus is the Christ, the Son of God, and that in believing [they] might have life in his name." These are examples of books that give us an explicit and stated goal by which to judge their total progress as the sections unfold.

But in those books where the overall purpose must be ascertained by the contents and the transitions from section to section and paragraph to paragraph, our task is much more difficult. One such book is the Book of Hebrews. Since the purpose is not stated in just so many words, it is best to pay special attention here to the hortatory phrases sprinkled throughout the parenetical sections ("Let us . . . ," e.g., Heb. 4:1, 11; 6:1; 10:35–36; 12:1; 13:15). The writer seems to be aiming at rebuking fickleness and the introduction of confusing ideas about the salvation that many in the Jewish community had so recently received. Judged in this light, the doctrinal sections with their emphasis on the advantage of the New Testament order of salvation over that of the admittedly provisional nature of the Old Testament ceremonial institutions begin to reveal a meaningful shape and pattern of purpose.

The most difficult pattern of all to determine is in those cases where the major portion of a book, if not its entire text, is made up of narrative materials. We will develop this topic at greater length in a later chapter, but for now it is important to note that the interpreter must make his decision on the basis of what details were *selected* for inclusion and how were they *arranged* by the writer.

Take as an example the narration found in the brief work of Ruth. It is true, of course, that the writer's interest in Ruth is found in part in the genealogy of David which appears at the conclusion of the book. But even that detail hardly says all that needs to be said, especially if the interpreter is going to be successful in proclaiming the message of the Book of Ruth for our day.

Ronald M. Hals points out that the writer of Ruth introduced God's name into the narrative twenty-five times in eighty-five verses.[4] In nine of these references God's name is used in a prayer asking for blessing on one of the major characters in the book. It is significant that each of the major characters is the object of at least one such prayer. Even more striking is the fact that, without interrupting the flow of the narration, the writer goes on to show by implication that in each case the prayer was answered.

Thus restraint and reticence dominate the author's style in that

4. Ronald M. Hals, *The Theology of the Book of Ruth*, Facet Books: Biblical Series, ed. John Reumann, 23 (Philadelphia: Fortress, 1969), pp. 3–19.

he does not openly moralize or editorialize on what has (or has not) taken place. This makes the conclusion all the more dramatic and powerful. The major and minor incidents in the life of this family are all under the providential care of God and included in the history of salvation. The "thread of God's plan" is woven directly "into the tapestry of everyday events."[5] That He directs even the smallest details of our lives is a motif which recurs throughout the Book of Ruth.

In summation, we may conclude that there are four ways to ascertain the intention of the writer as far as his general scope and plan are concerned:

1. Search first to see if the writer himself clearly sets forth his purpose in the preface, conclusion, or body of the text.

2. Study the parenetical sections (the hortatory aspect), particularly of the New Testament Epistles, in order to determine what applications the author himself has made of the factual and doctrinal portions of the text. Usually an author's exhortations will flow out of his special purpose for writing his book.

3. As a clue to the writer's overall purpose in collecting and editing history or narrative, observe what details he *selected* for inclusion and how he *arranged* them.

4. When no other clues are available, the interpreter must work out his own statement of the author's purpose. The interpreter will begin by studying how the topic sentences of individual paragraphs work together to explicate the theme of a given section. Then he will proceed to study the themes of all the sections and to evaluate the connections between and within sections. Only when this has been completed will the interpreter experience any kind of confidence in stating what the author's implied theme is.

The Canonical Context

Lately there has been in the Church a whole new emphasis on the canon. One name stands out beyond all other recent com-

5. Ibid., p. 19.

mentators in this new emphasis on canon, Brevard S. Childs.[6] Canonical analysis, as he sees it, must focus on the text itself—in the final form which now lies before the Church. Thus the present shape of the text, apart from what he would still regard as the legitimate avenues of historico- and traditio-criticisms, has its own kind of integrity. Someone must explain the Bible that presently is in the hands of the Church; in Childs's view reconstruction of the text is an important, but totally different matter.

Thus, while not attempting to use canonical analysis to stifle authentic isagogical concerns in favor of some externally derived doctrinal categories, this approach urges that the interpreter work within the structure which the Biblical text has received from those who shaped and used it as sacred Scripture. This emphasis has been long overdue in a field that has usually felt content to do everything else but to deal with the text precisely as it was canonically contained in the Church of the living God.

Childs is anxious to make sure that no one confuses the approach of canonical analysis with several other recent critical methods. It is not the so-called New Criticism, Structuralism, or Rhetorical Criticism. In plain fact, the canonical approach aims at understanding the "theological shape"[7] of the text instead of attempting to recover its original literary form or its aesthetic unity.

Again, Childs explains that he is not advocating under the rubric of canonical analysis a form of Gerhard von Rad's "Kerygmatic exegesis" (or that of Hans Walter Wolff, Claus Westermann, or Walter Brueggemann), which is strongly tied with reconstructing the historical context by means of a form-critical method. Nor is his approach a traditio-critical one which merely evaluates the history of the formation of the text.

6. See Brevard S. Childs, "The Old Testament as Scripture of the Church," *Concordia Theological Monthly* 43 (1972): 709–22; idem, *Introduction to the Old Testament as Scripture* (Philadelphia: Fortress, 1979), pp. 69–83; and Gerald T. Sheppard, "Canon Criticism: The Proposal of Brevard Childs and an Assessment for Evangelical Hermeneutics," *Studia Biblica et Theologica* 4 (1974): 3–17.

7. Childs, *Introduction*, p. 74.

What Childs insists upon is that the Scriptures must not be viewed apart from the Church, and vice versa.[8] Each passage of Scripture must be heard, not as a "proof text" in and of itself, but both in the context of the book in which it is found and in the context of the whole canon. Only then can its normative force as a *witness*(!) to divine revelation be understood.[9] While Childs will allow the historian of the ancient Near East to approach these written materials from a documentary and critical position and will agree that one can distinguish between, say, the Yahwistic and priestly source, he still feels that it is only the full, combined text as it has now emerged in the Church (after being indeed redacted from the layers of tradition!) that "continues to exercise an authority on the community of faith."[10]

Two comments may be offered here by way of evaluation. While evangelicals can only applaud the courage of Childs's bold new program which takes the Scripture on its own terms as canon, we regret that this must be a canon severed from the original writer's intention in all of its historical particularity. In Childs's canonical analysis a new historical relevance is forged by the final shape of the canon and its latest (in his view!) context. Of course Childs allows that the canon will confront each new generation as a new Word from God by virtue of its transhistorical capacity, but he pays a high price for this. Ultimately, the tradition will need to be authorized in some way—only the Church is left to do the job. It seems that Childs would ultimately be led back to Rome for authentication of the canon—or are there other options available to authenticate it? We would, instead, point out most vigorously that the writers themselves as well as the early Church insisted that the normativeness of the text was prior to and the very basis for the Church itself.

8. Brevard S. Childs, *Biblical Theology in Crisis* (Philadelphia: Westminster, 1970), p. 103.

9. See Sheppard, "Canon Criticism," p. 6.

10. Childs, *Introduction*, p. 76. I would take exception to his espousal of the documentary theory and to his discovery of layers of textual tradition that allegedly went into the literary shaping. My objections are not in the first instance doctrinal but methodological. See the summary in Walter C. Kaiser, Jr., "The Present State of Old Testament Studies," *Journal of the Evangelical Theological Society* 18 (1975): 69–79.

Our second criticism is that the whole canon must not be used as the context for every exegesis. We do agree that "proof texting," the isolation and use of verses apart from their immediate or sectional context, is reprehensible and should be discontinued immediately. But in our chapter on theological analysis we will argue that the Church at large (since the time of the Reformers especially) is in error when she uses the analogy of faith (*analogia fidei*) *as an exegetical device for extricating meaning from or importing meaning to texts that appeared earlier* than the passage where the teaching is set forth most clearly or perhaps even for the first time. It is a mark of *eis*egesis, not *ex*egesis, to borrow freight that appears chronologically later in the text and to transport it back and unload it on an earlier passage simply because both or all the passages involved share the same canon.

Fortunately, Childs also disavows the philosophical hermeneutics of Paul Ricoeur and his school. They view the Bible as a deposit of metaphors which have contemporary powers to interpret and order our present world.[11] Interestingly enough, Childs's criticism is that, while Ricoeur deals with what is "ahead of" (*devant*), not behind the text, he fails to ground the Biblical metaphors in the context of historic Israel; instead they become free-floating metaphors.

Childs's evaluation is correct! But that is our point with Professor Childs as well. While carefully attempting to ground the canon in the resulting tradition of the Church, he has ripped it from the hands of those writers who claimed to have heard and understood the revelation first. What will we do with their claims? Surely, even if traditio-critical methods were able to be adequately substantiated (even for our own skeptical eyes), could this method ever entirely purge every one of the claims these authors make in the text (unless, of course, another human canon was decided on as a *Vorverständnis* to reading the text; namely, that the author

---

11. See Paul Ricoeur, *Philosophical Hermeneutics and Theological Hermeneutics: Ideology, Utopia, and Faith*, Protocol Series of the Colloquies of the Center for Hermeneutical Studies in Hellenistic and Modern Culture, 17 (Berkeley, Calif.: Center for Hermeneutical Studies in Hellenistic and Modern Culture, 1976). This work also appeared as an article in *Studies in Religion/Sciences Religieuses* 5 (1975–76): 14–33.

must go!)? I don't think it is possible. *Some* of these claims would still remain. Thus, while we sincerely laud and appreciate Childs's new emphasis and find many helpful and hopeful signs in it, we believe that it has a serious flaw: the canon has usurped the place of the author in the exegetical procedure.

There is one place where canonical concerns must be introduced, however. *After* we have finished our exegetical work of establishing what, indeed, the author of the paragraph or text under consideration was trying to say, *then* we must go on to set this teaching in its total Biblical context by way of gathering together what God has continued to say on the topic. We should then compare this material with our findings concerning the passage being investigated. But mind this point well: canonical context must appear only as part of our summation and not as part of our exegesis.

The Immediate Context

There is one more aspect that must be considered here, and that is paragraph analysis (or in poetry, strophe analysis) within the section. Since we will treat poetry in a separate chapter, we will limit our focus here to the prose paragraph.

The investigation of the context of a paragraph can be as illuminating as the discovery of how the various sections of a book relate to one another. Without the benefit of knowing the connection between the paragraph under consideration and the section of the book in which it is found, the exegete will often be at sea in interpreting a passage. Once again the primary work of identifying context is most important.

One good illustration of the help that an exegete can derive from knowing and taking account of the immediate context is found in Exodus 6:14–25. An otherwise dry and lifeless genealogy is dutifully trotted out in the text. Most Christian expositors, feeling that surely nothing worthwhile can be drawn from this text, usually skip it and go on to the next paragraph.

Yet, by skipping this paragraph, exegetes miss several rather interesting and helpful points. The first is that the paragraph is framed by essentially the same material. Thus the paragraph just preceding (vv. 10–12) and the paragraph just following (vv. 28–30) the target passage repeat these words: "Tell Pharaoh king of Egypt. . . . But Moses said to the Lord, I am a man of uncircumcised lips."

Second, the genealogy lists only three of Jacob's sons (Reuben, Simeon, and Levi) instead of the usual twelve sons (!) because the object is to go only as far as needed to get to Moses' and Aaron's appearance on the list. Note verse 26: "This is that Moses and Aaron to whom the Lord said. . . ."

Why was it necessary to say anything about Reuben and Simeon? What was the basis for the inclusion of these two brothers of Levi? I believe it was because every one of these men had, as the expression goes, "skeletons in their closets," that is, they each had committed grievous sin, and yet they had also received God's forgiving grace. So also had Moses. Had he not murdered a man and fled? So the answer to the question, "Why did God choose this Moses and this Aaron in light of what we know about them?" can be found in the same grace that God had extended to the likes of Moses' and Aaron's ancestors. Thus when Moses balks at further confrontations with Pharaoh, God gently reminds the reader not to think as highly about the channel (Moses and Aaron) as about the Caller and Equipper of men. After all, this was just "that Moses and Aaron"—but they were called of God nevertheless.

There are various types of connections between individual paragraphs and immediate context:

1. *Historical.* There may be a connection of facts, events, or happenings in space and time.
2. *Theological.* A doctrine may be dependent on some historical fact and circumstance.
3. *Logical.* A paragraph may connect with an argument or line of thinking that is under development in the whole section.
4. *Psychological.* Something in the preceding line of reasoning may suddenly trigger a related idea. The result is often a parenthetical aside or an anacoluthon; that is, a breaking off from

the argumentation or exposition to present what at first appears to be a totally unrelated idea.[12]

An illustration of the importance of knowing the immediate context when there is a theological connection can be seen in Galatians 5:4: "You have fallen away from grace."[13] If the statement is used by itself as a proof text, it yields a whole new system of theology. But when taken in the context of what Paul was saying to the Galatians, it says something very different. If someone, argues Paul, is going to contend that he is justified by the Law, then he must be prepared to keep the whole Law in all its detail or to be cut off from Christ. For those who would be justified by the Law cut themselves off from the system of grace. In this context, "grace" is not to be understood as the personal experience of God's free, unmerited mercy and life; rather, "grace" is to be understood as the *gospel system of salvation in Christ.*

Only an awareness of and respect for the immediate context will keep the exegete from going off the deep end here. The author has the right to define his own words as he wishes to do so—and context is a key to unlocking part of that meaning.

12. For this list see Terry, *Biblical Hermeneutics*, p. 219.
13. Ibid., p. 218.

Chapter 4

Syntactical Analysis

Ever since Karl A. G. Keil's Latin treatise on historical interpretation (1788) and German textbook on New Testament hermeneutics (1810),[1] exegetes have generally adopted his term as being descriptive of their own approach to the exegetical task: the "grammatico-historical" method of exegesis. The aim of the grammatico-historical method is to determine the sense required by the laws of grammar and the facts of history.

The term *grammatico-*, however, is somewhat misleading since we usually mean by "grammatical" the arrangement of words and construction of sentences. But Keil had in mind the Greek word *gramma,* and his use of the term *grammatico-* approximates what we would understand by the term *literal* (to use a synonym derived from Latin). Thus the grammatical sense, in Keil's under-

---

1. Karl A. G. Keil, *De historica librorum sacrorum interpretatione ejusque necessitate* (Leipzig, 1788); idem, *Lehrbuch der Hermeneutik des neuen Testamentes nach Grundsätzen der grammatisch-historischen Interpretation* (Leipzig: Vogel, 1810). A Latin translation of the latter was made by Emmerling and appeared in 1811. This information we owe to Milton S. Terry, *Biblical Hermeneutics: A Treatise on the Interpretation of the Old and New Testaments* (New York: Phillips & Hunt, 1890; reprint ed., Grand Rapids: Zondervan, 1964), p. 203, n. 1.

standing, is the simple, direct, plain, ordinary, and literal sense of the phrases, clauses, and sentences.

The historical sense is that sense which is demanded by a careful consideration of the time and circumstances in which the author wrote. It is the specific meaning which an author's words require when the historical context and background are taken into account.

The grand object of grammatical and historical interpretation is to ascertain the *usus loquendi,* that is, the specific usage of words as employed by an individual writer and/or as prevalent in a particular age.[2] And the most fundamental principle in grammatico-historical exposition is that words and sentences can have only one signification in one and the same connection.[3]

We find ourselves in perfect sympathy and harmony with the goals of the grammatico-historical method of exegesis. More than ever before the central battle in exegetical methodology remains just where it was for Keil: Is meaning indeed singlefold? Must that single meaning be located solely in the author's truth-intentions and his own usage of his words? Keil's response was unequivocal: "Yes," and the method the exegete must employ is grammatico-historical interpretation. We could not agree more wholeheartedly and enthusiastically with this answer and projected methodology for exegesis.

Nevertheless, while the time-honored method described by this label has helped interpreters to focus their attention on the literal or natural meaning of the text as it was originally intended by the writer and his times, grammatico-historical exegesis has failed to map the route between the actual determination of the authentic meaning and the delivery of that word to modern men and women who ask that that meaning be translated into some kind of normative application or significance for their lives. In other words, moderns have shifted their interest in the hermeneutical quest to the other end of the interpretive spectrum. They are more inter-

2. Terry, *Biblical Hermeneutics*, p. 181.
3. Ibid., p. 205.

ested in "what the text," as they say, "means to me—what I can get out of it."

Therefore, we propose to feature a new name for the task and mission of Biblical interpretation. We propose that this method be called the syntactical-theological method of exegesis. Of course, behind this new label lies the assumption that there is no fault with the term *grammatico-historical exegesis* except that it fails to go far enough in describing the main job of exegesis.

In syntactical-theological exegesis, the accent falls on two key parts of the exegetical process. The first part stresses that syntax is one of the most important avenues for the interpreter to use in reconstructing the thread of the writer's meaning. The way in which words are put together so as to form phrases, clauses, and sentences will aid us in discovering the author's pattern of meaning.

Assuming, as we do, that every word will be affected to some degree (1) by its grammatical function in the phrase, clause, or sentence and (2) by the words, phrases, clauses, sentences, and paragraphs which surround it, the contention of this method is that only as the exegete discovers how this surface structure works (and then, only secondarily and derivatively, the semantic structure) can he successfully begin to distinguish main assertions from supporting assertions in the text. Thus syntactical analysis systematically operates from three basic building blocks: (1) the concept, (2) the proposition, and (3) the paragraph. It is through the precise way in which these three units are organized and arranged that the exegete receives all the data he needs to begin the journey of moving from the text to the destination of using that text in a teaching or preaching situation.

The second part of the new program advocated here picks up another neglected feature (i.e., theological exegesis), with several nuances not explicitly championed in previous literature on exegesis. All too frequently the exegete has had the unpleasant prospect of either delivering a message which, though based on a technically proper analysis, is but a sterile rehearsal of the words and events in a text, or delivering a message which, though based on a methodological nightmare (as judged by any teacher of exegesis), is scintillating and refreshing to the Church of God because the message imports doctrine and theological truth by the carload from all over Scripture without caring in the least whether the practice is legitimate or not.

Neither one of these alternatives contains much help for the present problem. The one is dead, sterile, and boring. The other is entertaining and also didactically suggestive, but only at the expense of sacrificing the prior claims of the Biblical text being expounded. It is methodologically a fraud. What, then, can be done?

In chapter 6 the solution to this problem is framed in terms of an "informing theology" or the analogy of *antecedent* Scripture. The discipline of Biblical theology is missing from many theological curricula. This discipline, if kept in a distinctive diachronic (Greek: "through time, with time") pattern where the accumulating theology is studied and classified by the particular period(s) in which it occurs, will be the chief contributor to the theological exegesis of a passage. The exegete will use Biblical theology whenever a concept, word, citation, or event in the passage being exegeted indicates that there were originally both an awareness of its relation to a preceding core of faith and an intention of making a further contribution to or elaboration on that preceding core. Identification of this lively conversation which the Biblical writers had with those who went before them legitimately introduces the concerns of theology and instructs the exegete on how he can direct his own formulation of significances and applications.[4] Biblical theology, then, is one of the twin tools of exegesis as well as the chief contributor to systematic theology.

Here, then, are the two new foci for exegesis: syntax and theology. If the term were not so awkward and clumsy, the truth of the matter is that the method should be called grammatical-contextual-historical-syntactical-theological-cultural exegesis, for each of these concerns, and more, must participate in the exegetical venture. Our aim in this chapter will be to describe only syntactical analysis.

---

4. See my elaboration in chapter 6 and in Walter C. Kaiser, Jr., *Toward an Old Testament Theology* (Grand Rapids: Zondervan, 1978), pp. 17–19.

The Literary Type

Before in-depth work on the paragraph can begin (which after all is the center of our concern in syntactical analysis), a preliminary step must be taken. It is necessary to decide what type of literary composition is before us.

There are five basic literary forms used by the Biblical writers—if we may be allowed for the moment to paint with a wide brush and to use a somewhat sweeping generalization. These types may be listed as (1) prose, (2) poetry, (3) narrative, (4) wisdom, and (5) apocalyptic. Each of these literary forms has a distinctive shape and style; accordingly, the approach to each form must be modified to meet its particular needs. Further, each of these five categories is capable of being subdivided. We will suggest enough variations here to alert the exegete to the basic nuances involved in most of the patterns.

1. Prose compositions are the basic model of Biblical communication. The word *prose* comes from the Latin adjective *prosus* or the earlier *prorsus*, meaning "direct" or "straight." Prose, then, is the plain speech of mankind which is used without reference to the rules of verse (an awkward definition to say the least, since it defines prose by way of contrast with poetry; it is amazing how difficult it is to define something as basic as prose).

Prose may be divided into four subcategories. There is (a) descriptive prose (narrating directly or plainly about people, places, things, or actions); (b) explanatory or expository prose (on the subjects of law, science, philosophy, theology, politics, etc.); (c) emotive prose (primarily aimed at inducing feelings rather than thoughts); and (d) polemical prose (the trade of fiction writers, journalists, critics, orators, etc.).

A system of classification closer to the needs of the Biblical scholar is to divide prose into (a) speeches (sermons and prose prayers); (b) records (contracts, letters, lists, laws, ritual observances); and (c) historical narratives. Making applications of the material which falls into this last category presents so many important problems for the exegete that we will discuss it as a separate literary form.

2. Poetry, a second form of Biblical compositions, is important enough to occupy about one-third of the Old Testament. Only seven Old Testament books exhibit no poetry: Leviticus, Ruth, Ezra, Nehemiah, Esther, Haggai, Malachi (five of the seven coming from the postexilic period!).

What constitutes Biblical poetry? Since the beginning of the modern study of Biblical poetry in 1753 when Robert Lowth published his Latin treatise *Lectures on the Sacred Poetry of the Hebrews*, semantic parallelism has been considered one of its major devices, if not the chief one. While in classical poetry parallelism has only a marginal significance, in Hebrew poetry it is of major importance both for identifying the literary form and for getting at its meaning.

The basic idea of parallelism is that two or more lines of poetry express either a synonymous idea by use of an equivalent but different word, or an antithetic idea by some type of contrast. The parallelism may be semantic (dealing with meaning) or grammatical (pertaining to the form). Too frequently these two distinct types of parallelism have not been distinguished as carefully as they should have been. The demands that exegesis of poetry make on the interpreter are so unusual that we have decided to treat them in much more detail in chapter 11.

3. Historical narrative is, of course, a type of prose writing; and for purpose of analysis, it does follow most of the rules for prose. However, because of special problems we have decided to analyze this type in more detail in a separate chapter (chapter 10). The difficulty this time is not in understanding what is said, but in bridging the gap from the "then" to the "now" of contemporary audiences. The key problem is relating historical truth and theological teaching.[5] In this special category, we will be greatly aided by Scripture's own later use of earlier narrative forms and its own method of "principlizing" the text.

4. There are two basic types of wisdom writings. The first is a reflective or a philosophical type of wisdom that tends to carry

5. Cf. the discussion in John Goldingay, " 'That You May Know That Yahweh Is God': A Study in the Relationship Between Theology and Historical Truth in the Old Testament," *Tyndale Bulletin* 23 (1972): 58–93.

a sustained argument across a large body of text. It deals with some of the more basic questions of life and tends either to be argumentative and polemical in style (such as Ecclesiastes[6]) or to lean more towards the hortatory pleading of a teacher with his pupil (as in Prov. 1–9). The second type is a prudential type of wisdom writing consisting of smaller units of thought which are disconnected and often isolated contextually (Ps. 1, 37, 49, 112;[7] Prov. 10–31; James).

The most difficult of the wisdom writings to classify are Job, Song of Songs, and the Sermon on the Mount (Matt. 5–7). Yet, a fair case could be gathered for their inclusion in the reflective or philosophical type. Surely, our Lord sustains a single extended argument in His address. And Job in his dialogical style works— though, to be sure, somewhat erratically (as judged by our Western standards)—on the problem of evil. And Solomon, with a heavily disguised narrative involving a Shulamite girl and her hometown shepherd boyfriend winning out over the advances of King Solomon, writes what he has learned about the divine gift of marital love.[8]

5. The last literary type we will discuss here is apocalyptic. Whether the type of writing that deals with the end of this age and the glories of the age to come constitutes an identifiable literary genre is still debatable. But there are some general literary features of this type of writing that we can agree on: (a) rich symbolism involving angels, demons, and mixed features of animals, birds, and men; (b) a formalized phraseology indicating that the revelation came by a vision or dream; (c) frequent conversations between the prophet/seer/apostle and a heavenly being who disclosed God's secret to him; (d) cosmic catastrophes and con-

6. See Walter C. Kaiser, Jr., *Ecclesiastes: Total Life*, Everyman's Bible Commentary (Chicago: Moody, 1979).

7. Other wisdom Psalms are 19b, 32, 34, 78, 111, 119, 127, 128, and 133. For the criteria used to distinguish these, see Kaiser, *Toward an Old Testament Theology*, pp. 165–66.

8. For discussions of Job by E. W. Hengstenberg, Ecclesiastes by J. Stafford Wright, and Song of Songs by Frédéric Godet, see Walter C. Kaiser, Jr., ed., *Classical Evangelical Essays in Old Testament Interpretation* (Grand Rapids: Baker, 1972), pp. 91–112, 133–50, 151–75.

volutions; (e) a radical transformation of all of nature and the nations in the near future of that day; and (f) the imminent end of the present age and the establishment of the eternal kingdom of God (the coming King shares the inauguration of the coming kingdom with the righteous and the remnant).[9]

The unusual exegetical demands of apocalyptic are normally treated in the area of special hermeneutics. As for vocabulary, the interpreter must realize that the seer often projects the future in terms gleaned from the actions of God in past history. Also the art forms and cultural vehicles of past civilization are readily employed to vivify the otherwise prosaic format of the material. Thus, as the exegete treats apocalyptic writings such as Ezekiel, Daniel, Zechariah, the Olivet Discourse in the Synoptics, and the Book of Revelation, as well as smaller sections of almost every prophet (e.g., Isa. 24–27; Joel 2:28—3:21), there will be a need to rely heavily on the informing or antecedent theology (see chapter 6). Once the symbols and antecedent theology are accounted for in the exegesis, the material may be treated as straightforward and direct prose.

Since the Bible is not written in one literary form, careful attention must be paid to each of these five forms. Often the key to the use and function of language is the literary form in which it was cast. The literary form may also reflect the setting in which that particular text was given its shape and to a lesser extent determine some of the stereotyped expressions or vocabulary in its content.

While we do not advocate all the insights of the modern discipline of form criticism which began with the axioms laid down by Hermann Gunkel at the turn of the century, we do feel that form is helpful to the exegete as long as it does not govern and dictate what the content must finally mean.[10]

Form criticism may help us determine the exact limits of the pericope by calling our attention to opening and closing formulae

9. See Leon Morris, *Apocalyptic* (Grand Rapids: Eerdmans, 1972).

10. It would be profitable to examine three or four evangelical contributions to form-critical studies. See Walter C. Kaiser, Jr., "The Present State of Old Testament Studies," *Journal of the Evangelical Theological Society* 18 (1975): 78.

and to some internal structures. Furthermore, the literary form suggests a certain range of purposes, audiences, or effects and responses that were desired by the original author.

The problem with form criticism has been the small measure of agreement among scholars and the resulting temptation of many to save the theory at the expense of the text.[11] This raises fundamental issues: must form govern content or can content break out of our conception of forms? Certainly, the way Rudolf Bultmann applied form criticism to the New Testament made it a dubious and very ineffective tool without external controls. Therefore, for our present purposes, in the absence of greater controls, this book will treat the literary forms as being helpful for defining pericopes, internal structures, audiences, responses, and the broad needs of homiletics. Our emphasis will be on narrative, poetry (both in the Psalms and in Wisdom literature of the Old Testament), and prophecy (a special form which at times combines prose, poetry, and apocalyptic forms), each of which will be developed in a separate chapter. Certainly, a knowledge of these forms is basic to any beginning exegete and for the daily needs of the homiletician.

The Paragraph

Once the exegete has determined the natural divisions and the literary type(s) of the individual book, it is time to get down to examining the passage that has been selected for exegeting. Usually this will be a pericope, or the like, consisting of one, two, or three paragraphs. It becomes evident that at this point the unit of concern must be the paragraph.

How shall we define and delimit the paragraph? Most of the criteria resemble those for marking off a section (see "Sectional Context" in the previous chapter). The list includes the following:

11. For details on this criticism, see Francis I. Andersen and David Noel Freedman, *The Anchor Bible: Hosea* (Garden City, N.Y.: Doubleday, 1980), pp. 315–16. A more positive assessment can be found in Donald E. Gowan, *Reclaiming the Old Testament for the Christian Pulpit* (Atlanta: John Knox, 1980), pp. 11–14.

1. The principal feature of a paragraph is a unifying theme. This is often indicated by the repeated use of the same term or concepts ("love" in I Cor. 13; "wisdom" in I Cor. 2:6ff.).
2. Rhetorical questions will often introduce a new paragraph (cf. Rom. 6:1).
3. A vocative form of address may commence a new paragraph (e.g., Col. 3:18—4:1).
4. Sudden changes in the text are one of the best ways to detect the beginning of a paragraph. For example, there may be an abrupt shift in the key actor or participant; the mood, tense, or voice of the verb; the location of the action; or the topic. The use of a striking introductory connective, be it a conjunction, preposition, or a relative pronoun, can also be an indicator.
5. Frequently what appears at or near the end of one paragraph is taken up and developed more fully in the next paragraph (e.g., "wisdom" in I Cor. 2:5 and 6ff.).[12]

The framework for expressing and developing a single idea, then, is a paragraph. It generally deals with a single topic, or a series of events that relate to one actor or participant in the same time-setting and location. It may be concluded that a paragraph consists of an assertion of a thematic proposition together with supporting propositions.

Analyzing how the supporting propositions in a paragraph are related to one another is the hardest task the exegete faces. Usually the surface structure will supply many of the clues. For example, Greek has a number of introductory particles (Hebrew, on the other hand, is deficient in grammatical units which relate propositions to one another). Aside from the evaluation of independent sentences, which are very difficult to relate to the theme proposition in the absence of subordinating or connecting grammatical units, the exegete will be dealing most frequently with relating clauses and phrases within each sentence. The result of analyzing all this subordinating of sentences, clauses, and phrases will be a block diagram that illustrates how all the elements in the whole paragraph relate to the theme proposition (see pp. 166–81).

12. I am indebted for these observations to John Beekman and John Callow, *Translating the Word of God* (Grand Rapids: Zondervan, 1974), pp. 279–81.

Let us consider the clause first. A clause is a group of words which has a subject and a verb/predicate and which forms part of a sentence. Clauses may be classified according to (1) type and (2) grammatical function.

There are three types of clauses: (1) independent, main, or principal clause (i.e., any clause that expresses a complete idea and that can stand alone); (2) coordinate clause (i.e., any clause that forms one part of a compound sentence); and (3) dependent or subordinate clause (i.e., any clause which does not express a complete thought and which cannot stand alone or by itself). It is important not only to be able to recognize these various types of clauses, but to be alert to some of the words used to introduce them. Study the following list:

1. Coordinating conjunctions: *and, or, nor, for, but, neither . . . nor, either . . . or, both . . . and, not only . . . but also*
2. Adversative coordinating conjunctions: *but, except*
3. Emphatic coordinating conjunctives: *yea, certainly, in fact*
4. Inferential coordinating conjunctives: *therefore, then, wherefore, so*
5. Transitional coordinating conjunctives: *and, moreover, then*
6. Subordinating conjunctions: *when, because, if, since, although, that, where*
7. Subordinating relative pronouns: *who, whose, whom, which, that*

The exegete will observe, however, that where one would logically expect some type of subordination, Hebrew generally coordinates by means of a series of waw-conversives.[13] Only when dealing with problems of this nature should the exegete at this point supplement his examination of the surface structure (grammar and lexical forms) with an examination of the semantic structure (i.e.,

13. See the brief statement in Ronald J. Williams, *Hebrew Syntax: An Outline* (Toronto: University of Toronto, 1967), § § 482, 484. See also A. B. Davidson, *Introductory Hebrew Grammar: Hebrew Syntax*, 3d ed. (Edinburgh: Clark, 1902), § 137; and G. B. Caird, *The Language and Imagery of the Bible* (Philadelphia: Westminster Press, 1980), pp. 117–18.

the meaning of the whole paragraph and section). This, then, will be a partially logical and partially grammatical step.

Clauses can also be classified by grammatical function: (1) noun clauses, (2) relative clauses, (3) adverbial clauses, and (4) miscellaneous clauses.

1. A noun clause is any clause that functions as a noun. In Hebrew on rare occasions these noun clauses are marked by the use of the article, or, when they are equivalent to the accusative case, they may have the Hebrew particle אֵת or אֶת (the direct object sign). Noun clauses may function (a) nominatively ("*That David had escaped* was told to Saul," I Sam. 23:13 [cf. I Sam. 27:4]—note noun clauses often appear after וַיְהִי); (b) accusatively ("The Lord saw *that the wickedness of man on earth was great*," Gen. 6:5); and (c) appositionally ("If it is proven true *that this detestable thing has been done among you*," Deut. 13:14).

2. Relative clauses perform the same function as an adjective by modifying or qualifying a noun.

3. Adverbial clauses function as an adverb and modify or qualify a verb, adjective, adverb, or prepositional phrase. The main types of adverbial clauses are (a) circumstantial ("while . . ."), (b) temporal ("when . . ."), (c) conditional ("if. . ."), (d) purpose ("in order that . . ."), (e) result ("so . . . that . . ."), (f) concessive ("although . . . ," "even though . . ."), (g) causal ("because . . ."), and (h) restrictive ("only . . . ," "if . . . not . . .").

4. Among the miscellaneous clauses are (a) the adversative clause, (b) the equational clause (X is Y), and (c) the existential clause (a quasi-verbal clause). These are not as important as the previous three classifications and are generally limited to Hebrew.

The other component part of the paragraph besides main or independent propositions and clauses is the phrase. A phrase is a group of related words without a subject and a predicate. In function there are three basic types of phrases: (1) prepositional phrase (a group of words lacking a verb and introduced by a preposition), (2) participial phrase (a group of words introduced by a participle acting as an adjective), and (3) infinitive phrase (a group of words introduced by the word *to* followed immediately by a verb). Infinitive phrases may be: (a) adverbial (they may modify verbs or the like—*"she is going to try"*); (b) adjectival (they may modify nouns or the like—"Joseph had so many *mouths to fill"*); or (c) nominal (they may have the function of a noun—"One thing she loved was *to go ride her camel"*).

This slightly technical discussion was most necessary to set the stage. It has dealt with the very fabric of paragraph analysis. Exegetes would be well advised to begin their work on a paragraph by: (1) isolating the theme proposition or sentence; (2) identifying all natural divisions in the paragraph as suggested by Hebrew accent marks, Greek particles, and overall punctuation; (3) underscoring all connectors such as relative pronouns, prepositions, conjunctions, and transitional adverbs; and (4) noting the antecedents for each subordinated or coordinated word, phrase, clause, or sentence so that work on the mechanical diagram or syntactical display can begin immediately. ("Antecedent" is here to be understood as a prior or preceding [usually] element to which the word [phrase, clause, or sentence] in question relates or on which it depends.)

The Syntactical Display

In order for the exegete to study a paragraph in terms of both its internal operation and external interrelations, we are advocating the use of a syntactical display or "block diagram." (In studying this section it would be well for the reader to refer periodically to the illustrations in chapter 8 [pp. 166–81]). Each proposition, clause, and phrase is written out in the *natural order* of the text (using Hebrew, Aramaic, Greek, or English). Each syntactical unit (down to the smallest component part that represents a semantical unit) is isolated on a separate line (this is especially important if it appears in a series or there is another unit that functions in a similar way). The theme proposition is brought out to the left-hand margin (right-hand in the case of Hebrew). Syntactical units which directly modify or qualify the theme proposition are slightly indented. Material which modifies or qualifies the syntactical units subordinate to the theme proposition is indented one step further, and so on. It is plain that all subordinate clauses and phrases will be attached to some other grammatical element in the sentence, thereby modifying or qualifying it. By drawing arrows immediately to the left (or to the right in the case of Hebrew) of all subordinate syntactical units, the exegete can graphically indicate to which elements these units are linked.

"Block diagraming" must be sharply distinguished from "line diagraming." A line diagram is what many of us drew in our junior-high English classes. Each sentence was analyzed by itself and basically formed a one-line diagram. The purpose was to aid the student in identifying the parts of speech and the grammatical function of each word in the sentence. A block diagram is much different. It attempts to analyze all the sentences in a paragraph and to put them into a graphic design so as to show how they function together as a paragraph and how the arrangement of that paragraph compares with the arrangement of related paragraphs.

A block diagram arranges all the material, regardless of its length, so that the interrelationships of whole sentences, clauses, and phrases might be visually apparent at a glance. The advantages of block diagraming over line diagraming are: (1) it forces us to focus on the total flow and thread of meaning throughout the whole paragraph rather than on isolated abstractions of individual words or phrases; and (2) it offers invaluable preparatory assistance for preaching and teaching because we can immediately see what is nuclear in the paragraph (the theme proposition) and what is subordinate.

The Theme Proposition

The nucleus of every paragraph is the theme or topic sentence/proposition. While this sentence usually comes at the head or beginning of each paragraph, it may come in the middle or at the end of the paragraph. But all of this is of no real concern to the exegete; the theme-sentence's position in the paragraph will not affect in the least its meaning or the analysis of the passage. The only effects position will have on the syntactical display of the paragraph are that the various levels of indentation will appear in different order and the arrows indicating how supporting material is to be related to its antecedents and coordinates will be drawn downward when the theme is withheld until later in the paragraph.

Since a paragraph usually is only one part of a group of paragraphs belonging to one section of a book, the topics (theme sentences, propositions) of all of the paragraphs in that section should add up to the total message of that section. Hence the importance of identifying the theme proposition cannot be stressed too much.

Independent Propositions

All of this discussion assumes (1) that there will always be only *one* theme or proposition and (2) that it is always *expressed*. But what if there are several independent or main propositions all of which appear to vie for the designation of *the* theme or *the* topic proposition? This phenomenon may occur in one of two forms. Either there is no *explicitly* stated theme, but only two or more propositions which are closely related; or there are two or more propositions which *together* will form and make up one complete theme proposition.

In the first situation, it will be necessary for the exegete to abstract the implicit theme from the several independent propositions in the paragraph. However, the interpreter must be sure that this cluster of competing main propositions do as a matter of fact all belong to one paragraph and are therefore closely related in topic and theme. Furthermore, they should be of equal rank semantically and function the same way within the paragraph. Only when each of these tests has been passed should the exegete assume that this paragraph is an exception to the normal rule and that there is no explicitly stated theme or topic sentence here. In this event, a theme will need to be formulated so as to accurately reflect what each and all of the vying propositions have asserted. For the mechanical layout or the syntactical display, the competing main propositions should be brought out *almost* to the margin and bracketed together, and the theme implied in all of them should be written in brackets running along the whole paragraph display (see fig. 4.1, layout A).

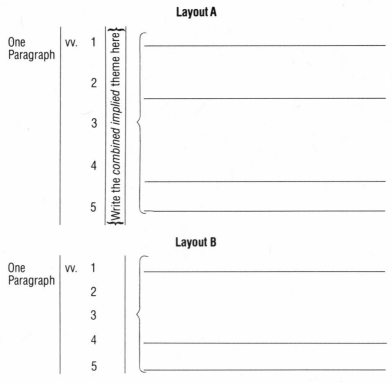

Fig. 4.1 Mechanical layouts for paragraphs lacking a single, explicit theme
proposition

The other situation is not as difficult. It may happen that a
paragraph has a stated theme which is not found complete in any
single proposition, but only when two or more propositions are
taken together. This case may be cared for simply by bringing out
to the margin and bracketing together all the propositions that are
to be included in the theme (see fig. 4.1, layout B). Remember to
preserve the precise *order* and sequence of the sentences and
clauses of the text being analyzed. The main propositions will be
grouped together by the bracket on the margin even though they
may be separated on the layout by some subordinate material.

Regardless of what method is used to find the theme of a paragraph, it must be identified. Ultimately the very substance and

organization of what the exegete will wish to proclaim to his contemporaries will depend on the proper identification of the theme
in every paragraph.

But what of the additional problem of those troublesome independent propositions and clauses which belong to a paragraph
but have no explicit or implicit connection with the theme statement of that paragraph? These independent clauses or sentences
often will have no conjunction or connecting particle attached to
them to indicate how they relate to the rest of the paragraph. (The
technical term for a lack of conjunctions between coordinate elements is *asyndeton* [Greek: "without conjunctions"].) If there is
absolutely nothing in the paragraph to which such a clause or
sentence is subordinate, the exegete must place it parallel with
another clause or sentence (preceding or following) that functions
in the same way and bracket the two together. Once again, the
exegete must, with great reluctance, momentarily leave his sole
reliance on surface-structure signals (since there are none in this
particular case) and use the meaning pattern or semantic structure
to aid his positioning of this independent element as it relates to
the theme sentence of the paragraph. Perhaps this admission that
we must at times use a semantic structure to aid us in interpretation does indicate that surface structure is not intended to give
everything the interpreter needs. It is also legitimate to note that
even though semantic structure often follows surface structure,
there are times when the former may outstrip the latter.[14]

Transitions Between Paragraphs

Once the exegete has mastered analysis of an individual paragraph, the next step is to trace just as diligently the connections
that exist between paragraphs. Fortunately, the same techniques
by which sections and paragraphs were distinguished from one
another will provide the very criteria for establishing the relationship of one paragraph to another.

14. See Beekman and Callow, *Translating*, pp. 268–71.

The best signal is a conjunction, connecting particle, or related expression. A change in the person, number, mood, or tense of the verb will also often indicate which direction the new paragraph will take.

Where no connectors exist and no explicit indicators orient our thinking, the word patterns or ideas may serve as a clue to the relationships between paragraphs. Or perhaps when all the paragraphs in a particular section are laid out in relation to one another, it will be clear how an apparently unrelated paragraph does as a matter of fact continue the development. All of this is to say that it is just as important to observe the connections between paragraphs, especially when they belong to a particular pericope that has been selected for exposition and proclamation, as it is to observe the connections within a paragraph.

We have seen, then, that at the heart of exegesis there should be a detailed syntactical analysis which involves identification of (1) the theme proposition; (2) the relationship (coordinate or subordinate) of all other sentences, clauses, and phrases in the paragraph to that theme proposition; and (3) the connection of the paragraph with other paragraphs. Without such analysis the results of exegesis fall stillborn on the ears of the congregation; and exegesis remains only a segment, and usually a poor one, of isagogics. Parsing of verbs, translating into smooth English, and identifying certain interesting grammatical forms can hardly be a substitute for the riches exegesis might have entailed. Furthermore, the gap between the text and the listener will widen. Thus, parallel to the demands of a legitimate higher criticism with its investigation into literary criticism, form criticism, rhetorical criticism, and redaction criticism, we may now add at the heart of the exegetical process syntactical criticism.

Chapter 5

Verbal Analysis

Words and idioms are the most basic of all the linguistic building-blocks of meaning. Through the accumulation of words and idioms a writer expresses the distinctive thought he has in mind.

Usually the particular meaning a word has in a particular situation is clearly specified by the grammatical constructions in which it occurs. Modern linguists refer to this as the *syntactic* sign of meaning.[1] Thus the same word *stone* may appear in one sentence as a noun, but in another as a verb. In these instances, then, the meaning of the term is indicated by the grammar, that is, by the syntactic construction.

In other situations, the meaning of a word may be marked by the interaction of that word with the meaning of the terms which surround it. This is called the *semotactic* sign of meaning. The key element here is not the grammatical use of the word, but a striking application of that word in a totally new context, with the result that a new meaning is conveyed. Eugene A. Nida and

---

1. E.g., Eugene A. Nida and Charles R. Taber, *The Theory and Practice of Translation*, Helps for Translators, 8 (Leiden: Brill, 1969), pp. 56–98.

Charles R. Taber illustrate semotaxis with the expressions, "a *hand* of bananas, to *chair* the meeting, the vine *runs* over the door."

The wide spectrum of usage that a single word may display in several different contexts can be illustrated by the word *board*.[2] A *board* is a sawed piece of timber. It is also a table on which food is placed (cf. a festive *board*), and the people who eat from it often must pay their *board*. But when people gather around that table for business, they become a *board* of trustees. Use that lumber on the deck of a ship and one will step *on board*; he may even fall *overboard* into the sea.

The same may be said for *fast*. Some run *fast* while confidence men pull *fast* deals. Some men anchor their boats *fast*, while others observe a *fast* on special days.

It is plain to see that words, like people, are known by the company they keep. It is essential that we always be aware of the surrounding words (i.e., the company) as they were intended by the author who wrote them. He is the final court of appeal as to the use of his own words when it comes to determining meaning.

The Author's Meaning

But how do we as exegetes know with any degree of certainty what the author meant by his own use of these words? Here are some general principles that should aid us in lexical enterprise:

1. The meaning of words is determined, in the first place, by custom and general usage current in the times when the author wrote them. No intelligent writer deliberately departs from this *usus loquendi*, that is, the current usage that is prevalent in a particular age, without having a good reason for doing so and without furnishing some explicit textual clue that he has done so.

2. In assigning meaning to a word, the exegete is on the most solid basis when the author himself has defined the term he uses.

2. Milton S. Terry, *Biblical Hermeneutics: A Treatise on the Interpretation of the Old and New Testaments* (New York: Phillips & Hunt, 1890; reprint ed., Grand Rapids: Zondervan, 1964), p. 191.

For example, the writer to the Hebrews defines "perfect" in Hebrews 5:14 as those "who by practice have [their] senses trained in the discrimination of good and of evil."

3. A word may be explained by the immediate attachment of a genitival phrase, an appositional phrase, or some other defining expression. This process is sometimes referred to as *glossing*. It may be illustrated by Ephesians 2:1—to his declaration that "you are dead" Paul immediately adds the explanation, "in trespasses and sins." Often an author may add an editorial comment by way of explanation. For example, in John 2:19 Jesus says, "Destroy this temple and in three days I will raise it up." John explains in verse 21, "He spoke this of the temple of his body." Again, Jesus says in John 7:37–38, "If any one thirsts, let him come to me and drink. The one who believes in me, as the Scripture has said, 'Out of his inner being will flow rivers of living water.' " John knew this would be a troublesome phrase for many who had not personally heard Jesus, so he explains in verse 39, "This he said about the Spirit which those who believed in him were to receive."

4. As we have already seen in our discussion of syntactic signs, the grammatical construction of a word may be another clue to its meaning. For example, "shepherd" may be used as either a noun or a verb. At other times the subject or predicate will serve to limit and define a word which may have different meanings in different contexts. Milton S. Terry shows how the Greek word μωραίνω means "to be tasteless" in Matthew 5:13 because it is used with the subject "salt"; but when it is used of men, as in Romans 1:22, it means "to become foolish" (cf. I Corinthians 1:20: "Did not God make foolish the wisdom of the world?").[3]

5. The meaning of some words may be determined by contextual antitheses and contrasts. Some passages are developed mainly by the method of contrast. In II Corinthians 3:6–14 letterism (γράμμα, not γραφή) is opposed to the Spirit, while the ministry of death is set off against the ministry of the Spirit. And in Romans 8:5–8 Paul contrasts those who live "according to the flesh" and those who live "according to the Spirit."

3. Ibid., p. 186.

6. In Old Testament poetry, often one of the best ways to determine the meaning of a word is by means of Hebrew *parallelism*. Instead of featuring a balance of sound between line A and line B, Hebrew poetry often uses either a synonymous or antithetic parallelism. In *synonymous parallelism* a thought the same as or similar to that of line A is repeated in a slightly different way in line B. In *antithetic parallelism*, an opposite or contrasting thought is presented in the line that completes the poetic couplet. This topic will be presented more definitively in a separate chapter.

7. A careful comparison of *parallel passages* may help an exegete. A writer may return elsewhere in his writings to a discussion of the same word (*verbal parallel passage*) or at least a treatment of the same subject matter or topic (*topical parallel passage*). It may also happen that another writer has discussed the same word or topic. Though a less certain procedure, parallel passages can be compared in this case as well. If the word or subject does prove to be the same or quite similar after a close investigation, then that which is clear in one context may be used to illuminate what is obscure or doubtful in another. (See pp. 125–27 and 134–40 for cautions about using this method.)

Once again, we must deal with the old canard that every word in the Scripture has several levels of meaning which the author was unaware were there. One can cite an impressive list of scholars who would espouse this polyvalence theory for Biblical words. Even the great Brooke Foss Westcott gave credence to this false theory: "I should not of course maintain that the fulness of meaning which can be recognized in the phrases of a book like the Epistle to the Hebrews was consciously apprehended by the author. . . . No one would limit the teaching of a poet's words to that which was definitely present to his mind. Still less can we suppose that he who is inspired to give a message of God to all ages sees himself the completeness of the truth which all life serves to illuminate."[4]

---

4. Brooke Foss Westcott, *The Epistle to the Hebrews: The Greek Text with Notes and Essays*, 2d ed. (London: Macmillan, 1892; reprint ed., Grand Rapids: Eerdmans, 1950), p. vi.

The same opinion continues in our own generation. No Roman Catholic has been more active in working on this problem in exegesis than Raymond E. Brown. His candor is disarming for every conscientious exegete: "Let us apply the term *sensus plenior* [*"fuller sense"*] to that meaning of his [the author's] text which by the normal rules of exegesis would not have been within his clear awareness or intention but which by other criteria we can determine as having been intended by God."[5]

But in whose hands does the final court of appeal rest for deciding what is normative and authoritative for contemporary readers of Scripture? Roman Catholic scholars have the magisterium, tradition, and the Church in general to fall back on if the going gets too rough. What shall Protestants use in place of these?

One Jesuit scholar, Norbert Lohfink, illustrates the agony of this search for authority and normativeness once one declares a text is free and autonomous from its author. At first he conjectured that inspiration must now be restricted to the meanings found in the "final redactor" of the Biblical text. However, he eventually shifted his ground to what the whole Bible teaches— refined, of course, by the sieve of historical and literary criticism! Thus, above, behind, and beyond that which exegesis establishes to be the original sense of a Biblical statement, claimed Lohfink, must be another meaning, namely, that which the whole Bible teaches. It is to be found by a process of exegesis separate from that which we use to find out what an author meant by his words.[6]

But what is it that the whole or unity of Scripture teaches that is not also in the individual books or in the grammar and syntax of individual passages? Lohfink, trapped by his own logic, turns, as some evangelicals also do (for entirely different reasons, at least in the present generation), to a *sensus plenior* or "fuller sense" that goes beyond the consciousness of the original author.

This theory of *sensus plenior* would make the inspired writer a secondary element in the process and even a nuisance at times,

5. Raymond E. Brown, "The *Sensus Plenior* in the Last Ten Years," *Catholic Biblical Quarterly* 25 (1963): 268–69.

6. Norbert Lohfink, *The Christian Meaning of the Old Testament*, trans. R. A. Wilson (Milwaukee: Bruce, 1968), pp. 32–49.

while God, the principal author, is viewed as supplying directly to interpreters many additional meanings that exceed those originally intended by the human authors. According to this view, though the same words are being investigated, normal rules of exegesis fail to yield as high a payload as when the exegete digs into the "fuller sense"!

In a brilliant analysis Bruce Vawter sees this theory as misusing the old scholastic analogy of instrumental causality: ". . . if this fuller or deeper meaning was reserved by God to Himself and did not enter into the writer's purview at all, do we not postulate a Biblical word effected outside the control of the human author's will and judgment . . . and therefore not produced through a truly *human* instrumentality? If, as in the scholastic definitions, Scripture is the *conscriptio* of God and man, does not the acceptance of a *sensus plenior* deprive this alleged scriptural sense of one of its essential elements, to the extent that logically it cannot be called scriptural at all?"[7]

Vawter has slammed the door on *sensus plenior* as a *Scriptural* meaning. Whatever else may be said for this deeper meaning, *it is not a Biblical sense*. The words of Scripture may have been the catalyst which primed the pump and perhaps hastened an individual reception of a heavenly revelation, or something of that sort, but by no known method of exegesis can the words of any one passage be proven to yield this fuller sense. This is admitted by definition. God's meanings supposedly obtained by *sensus plenior* cannot be drawn from Scripture.

Joseph Coppens found a major difficulty with the *sensus plenior* method: if it opens up such new vistas of faith and theological harmony between the Old and New Testaments, why in fact did this "fuller sense" escape the sacred writers? Had they not composed their writings under the divine promptings of the Holy Spirit? Coppens concluded that *sensus plenior* is possible only if the apostles and prophets wrote *better* than they knew, a fact

7. Bruce Vawter, *Biblical Inspiration*, Theological Resources (Philadelphia: Westminster, 1972), p. 115. See the analysis of some related problems in Walter C. Kaiser, Jr., "The Fallacy of Equating Meaning with the Reader's Understanding," *Trinity Journal* 6 (1977): 190–93.

which successive generations have supposedly discovered by an act of faith, by rereading the text, and by systematically studying Biblical images.[8]

But we protest that if the writers "wrote better than they knew," revelation has ceased to be a disclosure or unveiling. And where shall we turn to demonstrate this point? Certainly, I Peter 1:10–12 can never be used to prove that the prophets were totally unaware or even quasi-ignorant of what they wrote. To be sure, they wished revelation had included something about *time*, but they knew what they were saying about that salvation God revealed in the Old Testament. They knew it related to Christ's death and triumph and that it had implications for the believers who were to come in the Church (v. 12).

Nor can our understanding be "better" than an author's understanding unless we mean by "better" that we can complete and enlarge on what was left unfinished concerning the subject and topic with which that Biblical word dealt or that we can clarify certain assumptions or guiding principles which an author used without consciously reflecting on them or explicitly stating them.[9]

A more sophisticated procedure avoids the dilemma just posed. It announces, much as Westcott hinted, that language has a life of its own, independent of its user. In its extreme form, this view announces that a literary work is totally autonomous of its author and must be understood apart from the intentions of the writer or the circumstances of its origin.

In a more modified form David J. A. Clines argues:

> Once it is recognized that the text does not exist as a carrier of information, but has a life of its own, it becomes possible to talk about *the* meaning of a text, as if it had only *one* meaning. . . . [But] meaning is seen to reside not in the text but in what the text

8. Joseph Coppens, "Levels of Meaning in the Bible," in *How Does the Christian Confront the Old Testament?* ed. Pierre Benoit, Roland E. Murphy, and Bastiaan van Iersel, Concilium: Theology in the Age of Renewal: Scripture, 30 (New York: Paulist, 1968), pp. 135–38.

9. See the insightful discussion of these ideas in Otto Friedrich Bollnow, "What Does It Mean to Understand a Writer Better Than He Understood Himself?"

becomes for the reader. . . . Thus the original author's meaning,
which is what is generally meant by *the* meaning of a text, is by
no means the only meaning a text may legitimately have (or rather
create). We cannot even be sure that a literary text (or any work
of art) "originally"—whatever that was—meant one thing and
only one thing to its author; even the author may have had multiple meanings in mind. . . . [Therefore] it is not a matter of being
quite wrong or even quite right: There are only more or less
appropriate interpretations . . . according to how well the world
of the [literary piece] comes to expression in the new situation.[10]

What is all this but a surreptitious way of advocating a return
to some type of fourfold (or more) sense of Scripture as practiced
by some in the patristic and medieval Church? The Antiochian
school with its advocacy of a single meaning to the text (the
author's meaning) is far and away a much better position methodologically, historically, and theologically than is the Alexandrian school of allegorizing.

It does not matter whether one adopts the method of linguistic
analysis—with its stress on the fact that language has a force and
meaning of its own even apart from man as its user—or a White-
headian process-form of understanding language—where language is important more for the number of "lures for feeling"[11]
that it can elicit from a reader than for its presentation of certain
facts in some kind of logical relationship. The bottom line will still
be: Which meaning? Which use of language? *Which* lure and
personally interesting feature of the text *is the valid one* and therefore normative and divinely authoritative for our generation?

These questions spoil everything for some exegetes who have
uncritically drunk deep gulps of modernity. These questions bring
those exegetes back to precisely those problems that the modern

10. David J. A. Clines, *I, He, We, and They: A Literary Approach to Isaiah 53,
Journal for the Study of the Old Testament*, Supplementary Series, 1 (Sheffield: Sheffield
University, 1976), pp. 59–61. See also idem, "Notes for an Old Testament Hermeneutics," *Theology, News and Notes* (March 1975): 8–10.
11. See, e.g., Barry A. Woodbridge, "Process Hermeneutic: An Approach to Biblical Texts," in *Society of Biblical Literature 1977 Seminar Papers*, ed. Paul J. Achtemeier
(Missoula, Mont.: Scholars, 1977), p. 80.

ethos had hoped to escape. It must be admitted by all exegetes that only those propositions identified with the text's meaning as indicated by the author's use of his linguistic symbols can serve as the source for making any decisions about normativeness. Barry A. Woodbridge complains that such an admission is a retrogression which is tantamount to "worshipping the past."[12]

We cannot agree. Had we not used just such a hermeneutic, we would never have heard the complaint against our own position with any degree of accuracy. It never ceases to amaze me how those interpreters who wish to fight the theory that meaning is singlefold and always a return to the author's own meaning demand that all who read their own papers and books do so with the understanding that their meaning is singlefold and must be understood literally. But though we have granted this privilege to them, they then wish us to resume interpreting all other texts as they advocate—with this new polyvalence theory of meanings!

Any successful exegete must face the question of intentionality. We are most confident that the meaning of any given word (and therefore its text and context) will be discretely contained in a single intention of the author. If it is to be found anywhere else and extricated by some means other than the usual methods of exegesis, no one has as yet spelled out how that process works or how we may authenticate the additional meanings at which that process arrives.

But the quest must be pushed even further. What constitutes authorial intentionality and therefore the meaning of the words of a text in some of the more difficult areas?[13] In facing the question of intentionality should we or should we not deal with matters like archaic world-views, culturally conditioned statements, accommodation to quasi-scientific categories, the use of loose expressions, approximation in numbers? Is it possible to distinguish an author's overriding intention, which may communicate divine truth in matters of faith and practice, from other intentions

12. Ibid., pp. 82–83.
13. This discussion is stimulated in part by Gerald T. Sheppard, "Biblical Hermeneutics: The Academic Language of Evangelical Identity," *Union Seminary Quarterly Review* 32 (1977): 85–86.

which that author may have had in mind; for example, an intention merely to report what the fool had said in his heart? We must now treat some of these matters in detail.

Cultural Terms

Two extremes are often found in the discussion of customs, cultures, and Biblical norms. One tends to level out all features in the Bible, including its cultural institutions and terms, and to make them into normative teaching on a par with any other injunction of Scripture. The other extreme tends to jump at any suspected culturally-conditioned description in the Bible as an excuse for reducing the teaching connected with that text to a mere report of a now defunct situation. Both of these approaches usually are examples of what not to do in responsible exegesis of Scripture.

To be sure, there are a whole host of cultural details involving foods, clothing, institutions, society, economics, politics, and customs. Where these features are merely the cultural vehicle for the truth that they contain, the exegete's task is clear. In these situations the exegete must recognize the cultural aspects for what they are without evaporating the enclosed divine revelation one whit.

This is often easier said than accomplished. But this difficulty must not deflect us from our task any more than it deterred Peter's exegesis of Paul, which he admitted was a difficult task (II Peter 3:16, "Some things in [our beloved brother Paul's letters] are hard to understand").

What, then, is culture? H. D. McDonald has reminded us that *cultura* originally meant "the act of tilling the soil to prepare it for growing crops." But it has now taken on a wider significance; it is "the climate of opinion, and network of ideas and values which form the social environment within which each individual lives his life."[14]

14. H. D. McDonald, "Theology and Culture," in *Toward a Theology for the Future*, ed. David F. Wells and Clark H. Pinnock (Carol Stream, Ill.: Creation, 1971), pp. 239, 241. See also Edwin M. Yamauchi, "Christianity and Cultural Differences," *Christianity*

God's revelation in Scripture made a discriminating use of those cultural materials that were available to the writers in their day. Thus they gladly borrowed, reshaped, and reapplied such items as the Canaanite sea monster named Leviathan (Ps. 74:13ff.), the mythological dragon Rahab (Job 26:12–13), the Hittite vassal treaty (as a form for the covenant structure of the Book of Deuteronomy), and the pagan titulary of "sons of God" as a designation for autocratic and unresponsible officials in the state (Gen. 6:1–4).

But it is just as clear that Scripture refused to fall into some cultural containments which might thereby reduce the *content* of the message. One good example of this resistance is the Bible's rejection of the "three-tiered" universe model. To see in certain poetical portions of Scripture the pre-Copernican cosmological model which had a solid dome, flat earth, and an abyss beneath the earth (along with supporting pillars and slits in the dome for rain and stars!) is either an exegetical contrivance or a failure to spot the use of figurative language.[15]

The exegete must then ask when it is appropriate to adopt both the *content* and the *form* of the cultural item. The easiest way to illustrate this problem is to point to passages in Scripture for which some translators have chosen to give a "dynamic equivalent" while others offer a "formal correspondence." The Willowdale Report points, for example, to Romans 1:17,[16] which the Revised Standard Version translates word for word from the Greek: "For in it [the gospel] the righteousness of God is revealed through

---

Today, 23 June 1972, pp. 5–8; John R. W. Stott and Robert T. Coote, eds., *Gospel and Culture: The Papers of a Consultation on the Gospel and Culture*, William Carey Library Series on Applied Cultural Anthropology (Pasadena, Calif.: William Carey, 1979), pp. 5–33; Alan Johnson, "History and Culture in New Testament Interpretation," in *Interpreting the Word of God: Festschrift in Honor of Steven Barabas*, ed. Samuel J. Schultz and Morris A. Inch (Chicago: Moody, 1976), pp. 128–61.

15. See my detailed argument on this point and related features in Walter C. Kaiser, Jr., "The Literary Form of Genesis 1–11," in *New Perspectives on the Old Testament*, ed. J. Barton Payne, Evangelical Theological Society Symposium Series (Waco, Tex.: Word, 1970), pp. 52–54, 62–63 (nn. 16–20); see also John N. Oswalt, "The Myth of the Dragon and Old Testament Faith," *Evangelical Quarterly* 49 (1977): 163–72; Bruce K. Waltke, *Creation and Chaos* (Portland: Western Conservative Baptist Seminary, 1974), pp. 1–17.

16. Stott and Coote, eds., *Gospel and Culture*, p. 8.

faith for faith." Today's English Version, while abandoning a strict formal correspondence, nevertheless does capture with its dynamic equivalent what Paul was saying: "For the gospel reveals how God puts people right with himself: it is through faith from beginning to end."

Yet some Biblical forms ought to be retained because they are intimately bound up with the conceptual truth contained therein, for example, the cross, the Lamb of God, the cup. A more difficult decision must be made regarding the concept of the "blood," which is found in both the Old Testament sacrificial system and our Lord's own sacrifice. The problem here is that the target culture (in our case Western civilization) hears the expression "blood of Christ" in only one way—an incorrect way. Westerners immediately think of a hospital situation and connect the term with a life-imparting transfusion of blood. But the Biblical meaning is just the opposite; it is life being spilt and yielded up in death. Obviously, in this case the conceptual truth is intimately bound up with the cultural form of Old Testament sacrifices. Perhaps it would be worth the effort to explain the cultural form rather than trying to save the truth of the idea by means of a dynamic equivalent which would translate "blood" as "life yielded up to death so that others might live."

Let us try to spell out some exegetical principles for approaching cultural terms in the text:

1. Those items which reflect the specific times, culture, and temporal forms in which the message was given should be identified. But remember that not everything that is cultural is necessarily devoid of timeless principles and theology—even in its cultural *form*, an item may still retain its significance for the present. The author and his context must be the final arbiter as to how each one of these items is to be handled.

2. Where a distinction between the cultural form and its content is to be made,[17] the following guidelines can be used to distinguish timeless truth from that which is temporary and contingent:

17. See Robert C. Sproul, "Controversy at Culture Gap," *Eternity* 27 (May 1976): 13–15, 40.

a. The exegete must determine when the writer is merely *de-scribing* something and setting a background for his abiding principle, and when he is *prescribing* something for his time and afterwards. For example, are the government of the early Church and its officers given as something to be followed to the letter or are there hints that some or all of these notices are merely descriptive?

b. The exegete must determine whether the passage is inculcating a theological principle by means of a handy *illustration* from the culture of that day. In this case the principle remains regardless of whether or not the illustration continues. For example, the principle of humility remains, though the requirement that rich parishioners be seated on the floors of our churches so that the poor might be seated on the pews does not (James 2:1–7).

c. The exegete should ask himself whether the same theological principle may not be recognized just as fully today through an equivalent but not culturally identical medium. For example, as a form of greeting, shaking hands may function in Occidental cultures just as a holy kiss does in Oriental cultures (I Cor. 16:20). And a servantlike attitude may be an equivalent of the custom of footwashing (John 13:12–16).

d. There is something to be learned whenever Scripture itself, in a later historical situation, applies a different form or sanction to the same content. Thus the teaching on incest continues into the New Testament, yet without the form of the sanction provided for in the Old Testament, namely, death. Instead, the New Testament recommends excommunication from the Church until there is public repentance.

3. If a *reason* for a practice or for what might appear to be a culturally-conditioned command is given and that reason is located in God's unchanging nature, then the command or practice is of permanent relevance for all believers in all ages. Genesis 9:6 requires that the state use capital punishment against all who commit first-degree murder "because God made man in his own image." As long as men and women continue to be made in the image of God, this sanction is to be used—not as compensation for the victim's grieving family, not as a warning to other potential

criminals, not as a relief from anxiety for a threatened society, but as a consequence of man's being made in the image of God. In this connection note that Leviticus urges time and again, "Be ye holy," and then adds, "Because I the Lord your God am holy."

4. There are times when the principle of *ceteris paribus* ("other things being equal") may be attached to some of these commands. While those commands based on God's nature will allow no exception, often there are times when circumstances will alter the application of those laws which rest only on the word of God addressed to a particular time or situation. For instance, the command that no one was to eat "the bread of the presence" except the priests (Lev. 24:5–9) was set aside in favor of David's famished men (I Sam. 21:1–6) and used by Jesus as a precedent for His meeting of emergency needs on the Sabbath (Matt. 12:1–5; Mark 2:23–25; Luke 6:1–4). What appeared, at first blush, to allow no exception, actually had the principle of *ceteris paribus* attached to it. But let it be carefully noted that this principle must be used with care and strictly limited.[18]

5. Special emphasis must be placed on the *context* every time the exegete meets what is suspected of being a strictly cultural item. No issue demonstrates the need of this more than those New Testament passages dealing with the sphere of authority assigned to women:

a. The use of explicit doctrinal and theological statements interspersed throughout a passage which treats some local or cultural problem indicates that serious teaching is involved even if the form of the custom is not always to be retained. For example, I Corinthians 11:3 announces that "the head of every man is Christ, the head of every woman is her husband, and the head of Christ is God" in a passage on women that quickly brings all sorts of emotional responses as to its permanent value for the Church today. Nor is that all; verses 7–9, 11–12, and 16 are all heavily didactic and theological in nature. Ac-

18. James Oliver Buswell, *A Systematic Theology of the Christian Religion*, 2 vols. (Grand Rapids: Zondervan, 1962–1963), 1:368–73.

cordingly, whatever is said about this passage must show a
deep respect for the theology inculcated here.

b. If the context rejects a practice or custom mentioned in the
text being examined, we may be sure the practice or custom
was never normative for believers. We have already seen
(pp. 76–77) that in I Corinthians Paul has responded to a series
of questions which the Corinthians had asked of him in a letter.
Occasionally he uses the introductory formula περὶ δὲ ("Now
concerning") (I Cor. 8:1; 12:1; 16:1). But sometimes he quotes
directly from that letter without using the introductory formula. For example, in I Corinthians 6:12 and 10:23 Paul says,
"All things are lawful." But he quickly refutes that position
by adding, "But not all things build up [are helpful]." Likewise
in I Corinthians 14:34–35 Paul again quotes the letter from the
Corinthians. It must have contained a reference to the Rabbinic law which required silence from a woman except at home.
Paul's rejoinder is almost ruthless: "What! Are you men the
only ones [μόνους–masculine; not μόνας–feminine!] the Word
of God has reached? Did the Word of God originate with you?
If anyone thinks he is a prophet, . . . let him acknowledge
[this as well]." When we take all this into consideration together with I Corinthians 11:5, where Paul has just acknowledged that women are permitted to prophesy publicly (as
defined in I Corinthians 14:3—giving encouragement and hope
as well as speaking to men in order to build them up in the
faith), and the context of I Corinthians 14:31, where the "all"
who can learn and be encouraged is the same as the "all" who
can prophesy, it is apparent that the passage is rejecting, not
teaching a cultural practice.[19]

c. A more difficult decision is to be made when the immediate
passage is not qualified by anything except an explanatory
clause(s) or sentence(s) that follows it. I Timothy 2:8–15 is
just such a passage. After depicting men and women in the
same public act of prayer ('Ωσαύτως, v. 9), Paul gives one
command ("Let a woman learn," v. 11) and then one piece of
advice ("I would not permit a woman to teach or to exercise
authority over a man," v. 12). Now all of this appears to hinge

19. See my case in Walter C. Kaiser, Jr., "Paul, Women, and the Church," *Worldwide Challenge* 3 (1976): 9–12.

on the γάϱ ("because") statement that follows this command
and assertion. The exegete must diligently work to determine
what the reasons were, for on their proper identification will
hinge whether the injunctions given in the text are to be regarded as permanent or provisional. Do we have here the argument from the orders of creation; or do we have an argument
from the fact that the men in Timothy's church, like Adam,
had teaching which the women did not have, and thus the
women, like Eve, would be more vulnerable to deception and
trickery in situations that called for an adequate grounding in
the Word? Regardless of one's answer, the point is that interpretation of the context (the γάϱ statement explaining why
women are not permitted to teach) is the most crucial exegetical move in deciding what is of abiding value and what is
merely of a temporary nature.

d. Finally, strict attention must be paid to the Bible's own *definition* of its terms as found in context. Too often there is an
easy substitution of contemporary values for these terms. For
example, some interpreters have wanted to build a Biblical
case for homosexuality and have taken Paul's term *natural*
(φυσικὴν) in Romans 1:26–27 to mean sexual relations which
are "natural" for an individual given his biological makeup,
earlier experiences, and orientation to life. But Paul is using
"natural" in corporate and moral terms; he is not thinking of
distinctive, individual (and degenerate) natures.[20] The source
of such readjustments to the text is the behavioral sciences
and modern ideologies, not the text itself.

The point is this: The historically or culturally conditioned nature of some of the Bible's ethical demands or general teachings
should not embarrass the interpreter. Particularity is often nothing
more than a specific application or illustration within the universal

20. See the fine critique of this error in Mark Kinzer, "Misunderstandings of Scripture's Ethical Teaching: A Case Study: Scanzoni's Views on Homosexuality," *Pastoral
Review* 3 (1979): 93–98. Charles H. Kraft often judges the text in terms of the cultural
context, but this reverses the process of exegesis we are advocating in this book. See
his "Interpreting in Cultural Context," *Journal of the Evangelical Theological Society*
21 (1978): 357–67; and his "Toward a Christian Ethnotheology," in *God, Man and
Church Growth: A Festschrift in Honor of Donald Anderson McGavran*, ed. A. R. Tippett
(Grand Rapids: Eerdmans, 1973), pp. 109–26.

to which it belongs. Thus the exegete may not, and in a fair number of cases *should not*, universalize or "principlize" every injunction or description in Scripture (though, of course, many will need to be handled as abiding truths).

The decision must be based solely on those contextual clues supplied by the author himself.[21] It is simply not true that there are as many approaches to the text of Scripture as there are cultures and societies.[22] Squaring such relativism with the high claims made by the writers of Scripture for their text is impossible. The word of the text may not be removed by modern cavalier techniques.

Tropes and Figurative Terms

Words in all languages function so regularly that we may describe what will generally happen to these words as laws of grammar. However, in order to increase the power and image-making ability of certain words, a writer will at times *consciously* and *purposely* set aside these laws so that new forms or figures of speech arise. Such departures from what would otherwise be a word's literal or natural meaning was called by the Greeks a "trope" (from the Greek word τρόπος, "a turn"). The Romans referred to the same phenomenon as a *figura* ("a shape or figure"); hence "figures" of speech (note also the Latin *fingere*, "to form"). The Greeks reduced these new forms to a science and gave names to over two hundred figures of speech. The Romans carried on this science, but it was almost lost during the Middle Ages.

A figure of speech is a conscious departure from the natural or fixed laws of grammar and syntax. It cannot be a mere mistake

21. Cf. the discussions in Elmer A. Martens, "The Problem of Old Testament Ethics," *Direction* 6 (1977): 23–37; and Philip Nel, "A Proposed Method for Determining the Context of the Wisdom Admonitions," *Journal of Northwest Semitic Languages* 6 (1978): 33–39.

22. As advocated in Charles R. Taber, "Is There More Than One Way to Do Theology? Anthropological Comments on the Doing of Theology," *Gospel in Context* 1 (1978): 4–10. See my partial critique in Walter C. Kaiser, Jr., "Meanings from God's Message: Matters for Interpretation," *Christianity Today*, 5 October 1979, pp. 30–33.

in grammar, or arise from ignorance or by accident. Figures of speech, on the contrary, must be *legitimate departures* from the normal use of words for special purposes. Thus, they are limited in number; they can be described, named, and defined in accordance with known examples.[23]

How shall we decide when something is figurative? The exegete may be guided by these tests:

1. Is there a mismatch between subject and predicate if the sentence is interpreted naturally? For example, in the statement, "God is our Rock," an animate subject (God) is identified with an inanimate predicate noun (Rock).
2. Is a colorful word followed by a word which immediately defines it (and thereby restricts the range of its application); for example, "we were dead—in our *trespasses* and *sin*"?
3. Would the statement be absurd or even contradictory to the rest of revelation or the usual order of creation if one took the statement literally; for example, "the mountains *clapped their hands*"? (This would exclude supernatural and miraculous interventions, of course.)
4. Is there a reason for using a figure of speech at this point in the text? For example, does the text require a heightened feeling, some dramatic emphasis, or some mnemonic device for retaining the message?
5. Are examples of this figure of speech to be found elsewhere?

The problem with language is that the average person has only some twenty thousand to forty thousand words available to identify, describe, and discuss literally hundreds of thousands of identifiable parts, experiences, and happenings in his world. Because of this poverty of linguistic units, we begin to say we feel *blue* and tables have *legs*.

In addition to conveying a meaning, figures of speech create a *picture* for the reader or listener. When Jesus said, "It is easier for a camel to go through the eye of a needle than it is for a rich

---

23. This description is heavily indebted to the definition given in E. W. Bullinger, *Figures of Speech Used in the Bible: Explained and Illustrated* (London: Eyre and Spottiswoode, 1898; reprint ed., Grand Rapids: Baker, 1968), p. xi.

man to enter the kingdom of God," He was deliberately using exaggeration for a certain purpose. But the delightful imagery of attempting to thread a camel through a needle will never be wasted on all who will pause to think about it for a minute.

The best handbook on figures of speech is still available today: E. W. Bullinger, *Figures of Speech Used in the Bible* (Grand Rapids: Baker, 1968 reprint). Bullinger catalogued over two hundred figures of speech by their Greek, Latin, and English names, defined them, and gave some eight thousand illustrations of their employment in the Scripture! This book should be on every exegete's shelf alongside the Greek and Hebrew lexicons and grammars.

A few suggestions for handling these figures of speech are in order at this point:

1. Notice precisely what the point of the trope is. Is it comparison, addition, relation, or contrast?

   a. Figures of Comparison:
     Simile—an *expressed* or *formal* comparison between two things.
       — A is *like/as* B: "He shall be like a tree" (Ps. 1:3).
     Metaphor—an *implied* or *unexpressed* comparison where an idea is carried over from one element to another without directly or expressly saying that A is "like" ("as") B. A is B: "Go tell that *fox*" (Luke 13:32).

   b. Figures of Addition:
     Pleonasm—a redundancy of expression where more words than are necessary are used in order to obtain a certain effect on the mind of the listener or reader.
      "The butler did not remember, but forgot" (Gen. 40:23).
     Paronomasia—the repetition of words that are similar in sound, but not necessarily in sense or meaning.
      "Having all sufficiency in all things" (παντὶ πάντοτε πᾶσαν (II Cor. 9:8).
     Hyperbole—a conscious exaggeration to increase the effect of what is said.
      "I am weary with my sighing; yea, I make my bed swim" (Ps. 6:6).

Hendiadys—the use of two words when only one thing is
  meant.
  "It rained fire and brimstone" (=burning brimstone)
  (Gen. 19:24).
c. Figures of Relation:
  Synecdoche—the exchange of one idea for another associated
    idea; thus a part may be used for the whole or the whole
    for a part.
    "*All* the world went to be taxed" (Luke 2:1).
  Metonymy—the exchange of one noun for a related noun.
    "They have Moses and the prophets" (=the *books* these
    men wrote) (Luke 16:29).
d. Figures of Contrast:
  Irony—the use of words to convey the opposite of their literal
    meaning.
    "Behold, man is become one of us" (Gen. 3:22).
  Litotes—a belittling of one thing to magnify another.
    "I am but dust and ashes" (a remark of Abraham in-
    tended to magnify God's greatness) (Gen. 18:27).
  Euphemism—the exchange of a harsh, disagreeable, or indel-
    icate word or expression for a more pleasant, gentler,
    or modest one.
    "He covers his feet" (one's garments fall around his
    feet when he stoops [as we would say with another eu-
    phemism] to go to the bathroom) (Judg. 3:24;
    I Sam. 24:3).

2. Find passages (by the same author if possible) where the
same figure has been employed. Compare the usage and legitimacy of the figure in these several instances.

3. Consult various guides to figures of speech such as that of
E. W. Bullinger or John Albert Bengel's famous *Gnomon of the
New Testament* (one hundred figures of speech are defined in the
index).

Figures of speech can be a joy to the interpreter. But we must
never label an expression as a figure of speech just to avoid difficulties. One has never settled an issue by proclaiming with a
wave of the hand or shrug of the shoulder, "Oh, that is just fig-

urative. We need not bother with it!" The truth of the matter is that once we have recognized an expression as a figure of speech, we have only started our work. We must go on to name the figure of speech, define it, and state what textual clues force us to claim that the writer was using a figure at this point.

Most important of all, the exegete must now say what the figure represents or is about. If the natural meaning is not intended, then we must determine what meaning is in fact intended. Consider, for example, Genesis 2:7: "The Lord God formed man out of the dust of the ground and breathed into his nostrils the breath of life." To say that this is a figurative expression because God does not have a corporeal form with hands, mouth, and the like is only part of the exegetical process. The next step is to determine what the expression means. Obviously, the text represents an accommodation to our weakness. So that we might understand, God is pictured as if He were a man (*anthropomorphism*). The meaning of the text is that God is indeed most directly and most immediately responsible for both man's shape and his vitality, breath, and life. This, we believe, is how an exegete should approach figures of speech.

Parallel Passages

When the immediate context of associated words and sentences will not aid the interpreter in discovering the meaning of a passage, he may be able to utilize parallel passages which are found elsewhere in Scripture. There are two kinds of parallel passages: verbal parallel passages and topical parallel passages.

A *verbal parallel passage* makes use of the same word in a similar connection or with reference to the same subject. The word *mystery* may be baffling in one passage of Paul, but in one of his nineteen other usages of the word, it may be explained in a much clearer way. There is a danger, however, in supposing that every reference including the word is parallel to all the others. Or in supposing that there is a connection just because the word reoccurs in the same context.

A *topical parallel passage* deals with similar facts, subjects, sentiments, or doctrines, though the words, phrases, and clauses in the passage under investigation may be different. Prime examples are the synoptics in the Old Testament (Samuel, Kings, Chronicles) and the synoptics in the New Testament (Matthew, Mark, Luke). There is also the phenomenon of repeated passages (Ps. 14 and 53; Ps. 18 and II Sam. 22; Ps. 96 and I Chron. 16; Jude and II Peter).

Often the slight variation in wording is not the result of textual corruption, but rather of a deliberate choice of words to aid the audience to understand a special nuance the writer was giving to the subject. In these cases, the exegete may gain just the needed perspective in order to better understand the unclear or ambiguous words or concepts in the parallel context under investigation.

A caution must be raised again. There are some passages where a similarity and likeness exists without any true parallelism. The sentiments of Proverbs 22:2 ("The *rich* and the *poor* meet together; the maker of all is the Lord") and Proverbs 29:13 ("The *poor* and the *man of oppressions* meet together; the enlightener of the eyes of both of them is the Lord") appear to be the same. But it would be wrong to assume that the man of oppressions is the rich man simply because both texts have the "poor" and "meeting together" in common. Nor should the "maker" be identified with the "enlightener of the eyes." Making and enlightening are not the same act even if they are performed by the same Lord. It should also be said that in both cases the "meeting together" is not necessarily in the grave.

A better example of topical parallel passages is Luke 14:26 ("Whoever does not hate his father and his mother . . ."—a sentiment which puzzles us since it appears to contravene the fifth commandment) and Matthew 10:37 ("He who loves father or mother more than me is not worthy to be my disciple"). Another example of a true parallel passage is Matthew 7:13–14 and Luke 13:23–25. Though the contexts in which these passages occur are different, the meanings are identical. In Matthew, Jesus affirms during the Sermon on the Mount: "Strait [notice: not straight] is the gate and narrow is the way that leads to life, and few there be that find it." In Luke, while journeying toward Jerusalem, Jesus is asked the very specific question: "Will few [or many] be saved?" The answer is "few," because "the door [or gate] is narrow."

If the interpreter is careful, parallel passages will supply a small, but helpful, bit of assistance when a word is ambiguous or the context sheds very little light on the subject.

The most difficult words of all to deal with are the *hapax legomena*, "words used [spoken] only once" in the known texts at our disposal. Since dictionaries, lexicons, and related tools are based on collecting instances of usage from a number of contexts, they too, once in a while, let us down because of a lack of sufficient examples.

One illustration of a *hapax legomenon* is a word used by our Lord in the prayer He taught His disciples. "Give us this day our ἐπιούσιον bread." The same petition occurs in Matthew 6:11 and Luke 11:3. Did our Lord mean daily bread, enough for tomorrow (from ἐπὶ + εἶμι, "to go toward, approach")? Or did He mean our essential, necessary bread (from ἐπὶ + εἰμὶ; cf. οὐσία, "existence, subsistence")? The truth is that no one can say for sure. The word has not been found in this form in any other Biblical contexts or related contexts in cognate languages. Nevertheless, we know basically what our Lord meant even if we do not know which of the two renderings He intended.[24]

Key Theological Terms

Many terms were invested with such significance either at the time of their first occurrence or in subsequent appearances that

24. For recent studies on this word, see Werner Foerster, "Epiousios," in *Theological Dictionary of the New Testament*, ed. Gerhard Kittel and Gerhard Friedrich, trans. and ed. Geoffrey W. Bromiley, 10 vols. (Grand Rapids: Eerdmans, 1964–1976), 2:590–99; or Wilhelm Mundle, "Epiousios," in *The New International Dictionary of New Testament Theology*, ed. Colin Brown, 3 vols. (Grand Rapids: Zondervan, 1975–1978), 1:251–52, 253 (bibliography). For an excellent study on how to use dictionaries and what to look for in them, see John Edward Gates, *An Analysis of the Lexicographic Resources Used by American Biblical Scholars Today*, Society of Biblical Literature Dissertation Series, 8 (Missoula, Mont.: Society of Biblical Literature, 1972).

they came to act somewhat as trigger-words (if we may use that expression) to call to the audience's mind most (if not all) of the preceding theology which "informed" the texts in which they occur (see the next chapter for more on "informing theology"). These words are especially important in passages presenting the messianic doctrine and the doctrine of salvation.

In these words, which received an extraordinary amount of attention (perhaps the writer made a decisive comment at the time of their first appearance, or they may have been juxtaposed with a message about deserved judgment), a technical status was born. Not that the words became isolated and detached from their contexts—thereby earning the just rebuke and scorn of James Barr's *Semantics of Biblical Language*.[25] In fact, the reverse was true, for the whole context of what had been said on a previous occasion made the word all the more significant in its new context. The new writer obviously enjoyed recalling all that had been earlier specified as part of that word, and he made this the basis for what he went on to say by the revelation of God.

C. S. Lewis refers to a related process of building onto the meaning of words as "ramification." The analogy to be kept in mind, warns Lewis, is not that of an insect undergoing metamorphosis, but of a tree putting out new branches.[26]

This is the process we believe we observe in theological words. Just to begin the exegete's list of words which signal a large background of antecedent theology, we would point to "seed," "servant," "Holy one" (חָסִיד), "Branch," "land," "rest," "inheritance," "house" (dynasty), "day of the Lord," "fear of the Lord," "believe," "covenantal love," "forgive," "atone," "earnest," "reconciliation," and a host of others.[27] The point is that within the overall canon there exists a theological center; and to the key passages which unfold this center are attached certain

25. James Barr, *The Semantics of Biblical Language* (New York: Oxford, 1961).

26. C. S. Lewis, *Studies in Words* (Cambridge: Cambridge University, 1960), pp. 8–11.

27. For a suggestion or two see David Hill, *Greek Words and Hebrew Meanings: Studies in the Semantics of Soteriological Terms*, Society for New Testament Studies Monograph Series, 5 (London: Cambridge University, 1967); Norman H. Snaith, *The Distinctive Ideas of the Old Testament* (London: Epworth, 1944); and James Kennedy, *Studies in Hebrew Synonyms* (London: Williams and Norgate, 1898).

words which, like barnacles on a ship, refuse to let go. These are the words the exegete must school himself in: first, by studying and exegeting key contexts, and second, by developing some skill in the study and practice of Biblical theology. It is to this type of analysis that we will turn in the next chapter.

Words, then, are the basic blocks for building meaning. We repeat, they must not be torn from their contexts. They will become untrustworthy guides if this happens. But when they are viewed and treated in their distinctive roles as part of the larger context, they serve the exegete well.

Chapter 6

Theological Analysis

Nothing could be more frustrating and discouraging to the interpreter than to have a message fall flat and lifeless on an audience after the interpreter has met all the requirements of investigating the grammar, syntax, literary structure, and history of a given text. After the exegete has invested all those hours conscientiously translating the text, parsing the verbs, investigating the historical backgrounds, and tracing the syntactical relationships, there is a feeling of betrayal when all that labor fails to deliver a credible message that will speak to modern men and women. Clearly, something further is needed. But what is it?

The missing ingredient in most sermon preparation is theological exegesis. The most subtle trap, especially for the new pastor sporting a brand new diploma from a theological institution, is the trap of historicism or sheer "descriptionism." The Achilles' heel for many among the trained clergy is the failure to bring the Biblical text from its B.C. or first-century A.D. context and to relate it directly and legitimately to the present day.

Unfortunately, Biblical learning goes to seed when it rests its case after it has disassembled the passage being examined into its various grammatical, syntactical, historical, and literary units, and then fails to go any further. It cannot be stressed too vigorously that such work, important as it may be, is no more than a preparation for one of the most crucial steps needed to finish the job of studying a text with a view to proclamation. To stop at that point is like carrying the football to within twenty-five yards of the end zone and then asking God's people to carry the ball the rest of the way—perhaps with a wave of the hand and a passing allusion to the wonderful ministry of the Holy Spirit in each believer's life.

Actually, what happens in such a case is frightening to behold. We have laid before God's people a mass of assorted Biblical facts, often interspersed with some contemporary trivia and humorous anecdotes, without assisting them in discerning what in that word remains normative and authoritative to the present moment. How can they without further aid sense what in that text is God's specific and immediate address to them?

Nowhere is this problem more graphically seen than when an Old Testament text has been chosen. Of course, many pastors and Bible teachers solve that problem by avoiding the Old Testament as a matter of practice. But this can hardly be a praiseworthy solution, for how can they acquit themselves before God and say with Paul that they "have not failed to declare the whole counsel of God" (Acts 20:27) when it is obvious that seventy-five percent of that divine counsel has been deliberately bypassed?

Some pastors and exegetes will attempt to avoid the trap of historicism and pure descriptionism by resorting to such reprehensible practices as moralizing, allegorizing, psychologizing, spiritualizing, or subjectively editorializing on a selected Biblical text. Very quickly, many so-called interpreters become very adept at one or all of these practices. There is the further allurement in each of these abominable practices that they are real timesavers for the already overworked and harried pastor, whose time allocations could easily be parceled out in a thousand directions as it is, without the additional imposition of another twenty to thirty hours of study a week for two solid Biblical messages. Thus all sorts of unsolicited testimonies come drifting back to the theological training centers from which some of these "newly-converted" timesaving exegetes previously graduated. The word is simply this: "Forget about using all those historical, literary, and grammatical tools in the preparation of sermons; they are useless!"

What has happened is clear. These exegetes have found that the professional obligations of accurately locating a text within the Biblical writer's space and time situation, of patiently identifying the literary form and grammatical structures, have yielded a purely analytical result. No one can fault the instincts of this group; after all, they have sensed something more is needed. It is just too bad that they took the easiest route available at the time and began to assign in an arbitrary manner various spiritual or practical values regardless of what the original writer of the Biblical passage may have had in mind. Fortunately for them and their people, many of these same values can be found somewhere else in the Biblical text, if only one knew where to turn in the Bible. Instead, people and pastor continue to go blithely on their way, unaware that instead of experiencing God's Word from the passage under investigation, they are bringing in material from some unknown location in the Bible and foisting that material onto the present text.

Meanwhile, the very text which presumably is the focus of attention for congregation and speaker alike, continues to go begging for lack of an interpreter. In the very act which could have unveiled that text for God's people, it is instead being buried more deeply under more tradition, anecdotes, and faddish practical chatter—all in the hopes that divine authority is their source.

By now, it is clear that something is wrong somewhere. Somehow the departments of exegesis (Hebrew and Greek) and practical theology (homiletics) in our theological training centers have failed in some crucial step in the exegetical and homiletical procedure. And we believe that the most frequently misplaced tool on the exegete's shelf is theological exegesis.

For successful exegesis, there must be some procedure for identifying the center or core message of the passage being examined. Only when the core of that text and the assemblage of books which were available in the canon *up to the time of the writing of that text* have been identified will the interpreter be enabled to determine God's normative Word. Again, it must be stressed, however, that in no way may a theological grid be arbitrarily dropped over the text as a substitute for a diligent search for a unifying theological principle through the process of induction. Simply to impose a theological grid on a text must be condemned as the mark of a foolish and lazy exegete. Further, the facile linking of assorted Biblical texts because of what appears on a *prima facie* reading to be similar wording or subject matter (usually called the proof-text method) must also be resisted since it fails to establish that all of the texts being grouped together do indeed share the same theological or factual content.

The Analogy of (Antecedent) Scripture

One solution to the dilemma we have traced above is to employ the principle of the "analogy of faith" (*analogia fidei*). The term apparently was first employed in this connection by the early Church father Origen.[1] He had appropriated it from Romans 12:6 ("according to the analogy of faith")—however, in the context of Paul's usage of the phrase, it referred not to a body of theological truth, but to the exercise of one's spiritual gift in accordance with the appropriation of personal faith.

The Reformers made extensive use of this phrase, which in their time became established with a meaning that related to a very distinct set of circumstances. The Church of Rome had issued the *Glossa ordinaria*, a commentary that enjoined uniformity in all matters relating to faith and practice. But the Reformers objected to this *regula fidei* ("rule of faith") because it was held to be an authority *independent* of Scripture.

The Reformers courageously argued that all faith and practice must be based on Scripture alone (*sola Scriptura*). But the Scripture still had to be interpreted. The Reformers' solution was to

---

1. Origen, *De principiis*, 4.26.

announce that "Scripture interprets Scripture" (*Scriptura Scripturam interpretatur*). The analogy of faith became a corollary of "Scripture interprets Scripture."

However, what the analogy of faith means has not always been clearly defined. John F. Johnson has one way of defining it: "To put it tersely: *analogia* or *regula fidei* is to be understood as 'the clear Scripture' itself; and this refers to articles of faith found in those passages which deal with individual doctrines expressly (*sedes doctrinae*). Individual doctrines are to be drawn from the *sedes doctrinae* and must be judged by them. Any doctrine not drawn from passages which expressly deal with the doctrine under consideration is not to be accepted as Scriptural."[2] For Johnson, the analogy of faith is restricted to what we would describe as an insistence that doctrine be derived initially from large teaching passages where that doctrine is most fully developed (a fine practice, incidentally). Our problem here is whether the analogy of faith is a hermeneutical tool that is an "open [theological] sesame" for every passage of Scripture.

On this particular issue there has been confusion resulting in past and current abuse of the principle. Many have forgotten that *analogia fidei* as used by the Reformers was a *relative* expression especially aimed at the tyrannical demands of tradition. "It was intended solely to deny that tradition was the interpreter of the Bible."[3] Accordingly, it did not mean that all the teachings of Scripture are everywhere announced with equal clarity. Neither was it intended to exclude the use of grammars, commentaries, or a trained ministry. If it had been so intended, it would have made the Reformers' own writing of commentaries and use of various hermeneutical tools extremely hard to explain.

Nor, most important of all, did it mean what Matthias Flacius, the Hebrew professor at Wittenberg and Jena, wrote in his *Key*

2. John F. Johnson, "Analogia Fidei as Hermeneutical Principle," p. 253.
3. Herbert Marsh, *A Course of Lectures, Containing a Description and Systematic Arrangement of the Several Branches of Divinity . . .* , 7 parts (Boston: Cummings and Hilliard, 1815), 3:16.

to the Scriptures (1567): "Everything that is said concerning Scripture, or on the basis of Scripture, must be in agreement with all that the catechism declares or that is taught by the articles of faith."[4] This was a complete reversal of position and a return to a set of traditions which again not only assumed authority *independent* of Scripture, but acted as its interpreter and as arbitrator among competing views concerning it.

In our judgment, when the analogy of faith is used as a part of the exegetical process, it would be better to redefine it, in John Bright's terminology, as a theology that "informs" each Biblical text.[5] In Bright's view, every Biblical text has within it some facet of theology expressed in such a way as to be part and parcel of the fabric of its contents. While that theology cannot be torn from that text, it, nevertheless, often has roots which were laid down *antecedent* to that text.

This last item is the real key here. The only correction that we know for past and present abuses that have taken place in the name of doing theological exegesis is to carefully restrict the process to (1) examination of explicit affirmations found in the text being exegeted and (2) comparisons with similar (sometimes rudimentary) affirmations found in passages that have *preceded* in time the passage under study. Thus the *hermeneutical* or *exegetical* use of the analogy of faith (if we may still use this terminology in exegesis as well as in systematic theology, where it might seem to be more appropriate) must be carefully controlled diachronically (i.e., we must ever be aware of the various time periods in the sequence of the progress of revelation). So serious are we about this point that we would prefer to rename this procedure the "analogy of [antecedent] Scripture" when it is applied to exegesis in order to avoid any possible confusion in concepts. But

4. Cited in Daniel P. Fuller, "Biblical Theology and the Analogy of Faith," in *Unity and Diversity in New Testament Theology: Essays in Honor of George E. Ladd,* ed. Robert A. Guelich (Grand Rapids: Eerdmans, 1978), p. 198. Fuller's discussion of this problem is a brilliant analysis of some troublesome aspects of the Reformer's hermeneutics.
5. John Bright, *The Authority of the Old Testament,* pp. 143, 170. See also Walter C. Kaiser, Jr., *Toward an Old Testament Theology* (Grand Rapids: Zondervan, 1978), pp. 14–19.

in any event the definition is the most important feature here regardless of the particular terminology employed.

Surely most interpreters will see the wisdom and good sense in limiting our theological observations to conclusions drawn from the text being exegeted and from texts which preceded it in time. But it will strike many that this is hardly any help in determining the "antecedent theology" within a given Biblical text. Here again we contend that the theology must be objectively derived from the text; it is not to be subjectively imposed on the text by the interpreter.

There are some clues to the antecedent theology within a text:

1. The use of certain *terms* which have already acquired a special meaning in the history of salvation and have begun to take on a technical status (e.g., "seed," "servant," "rest," "inheritance").
2. A direct reference or an indirect allusion to a previous *event* in the progress of revelation (e.g., the exodus, the epiphany on Sinai) with a view to making a related theological statement.
3. Direct or indirect citation of *quotations* so as to appropriate them for a similar theological point in the new situation (e.g., "Be fruitful and multiply . . ."; "I am the God of your fathers").
4. Reference to the *covenant*(s), its *contents* of accumulating promises, or its formulae (e.g., "I am the Lord your God, who brought you up out of the land of Egypt [Ur of the Chaldees]"; "I will be your God; you shall be my people, and I will dwell in the midst of you").[6]

What we are now arguing for is nothing less than a full involvement of Biblical theology as a part of our exegesis. As we have conceived of that discipline and its special mission in the curriculum of divinity, it must be organized along diachronic lines so as to make its main contribution not to systematic theology (as

6. Kaiser, *Toward an Old Testament Theology,* pp. 32–35.

it sometimes has been said to do in the past), but to the discipline of exegesis.

Consequently, Biblical theology should gather for the exegete all of the pertinent theological materials and organize them in selected historical groupings (e.g., patriarchal, Mosaic, premonarchial, etc.). But this assemblage of doctrine must be more than just a potpourri of materials vaguely related in some way or another to faith or practice in Israel and the Church.

Such an "informing theology" will have significance only if there is a canonical center to this accumulating body of theology. But therein lies another modern problem, for current writers in the field are reluctant to adopt any specific elements as this organizing principle or center of Biblical theology. No one can blame most of these Biblical theologians for their reluctance, for in part they are justifiably afraid of falling into the once all-too-prevalent temptation to impose almost any kind of philosophical or theological grid upon the text. In the past grids that had been devised outside of the text were dropped in place over the text to yield some theological payload from the Bible. But everyone knows this is as wrong as sin itself. At best, it restructures the Bible according to one's favorite schema or pet doctrine; but what authority and guidance are left after the text has been treated so subjectively?

On the other hand, can such excesses be a justifiable excuse for abandoning the search for a theological center of the Biblical materials? We think not; for if there is such a thing as a Biblical theology of either Testament or of both Testaments together, then the ultimate aim should be to locate and identify that inner unity that binds all the various writers, themes, and histories together. Nor will it do to say that ultimately that unity is hidden from us or that God alone is that unity. For the former case mocks the very concept of *revelation*. It contradicts the claim of the text to be an unveiling and disclosure of God to mankind. The latter case merely states who the *subject* of theology is; it fails to give us a predicate of any sort.

Up until recently, the one unifying principle held in highest esteem among Biblical theologians was that *history* is the chief medium of divine revelation and presumably the cohesive factor that holds all of the various "theologies" of the various Biblical writers together. But even this idea has fallen on hard times.[7]

There is, however, a canonical center of the theology of the Old and New Testaments. It is not imposed, but may be *inductively* derived from a careful reading of the writers of Scripture themselves. It is God's word of *blessing* (to use the word especially prominent in the pre-Abrahamic materials) or *promise* (to use the New Testament word which summarizes the contents of the Old Testament) *to be* Israel's God and *to do* something for Israel and *through them* something for *all the nations* on the face of the earth. At first this word comes as a surprise from God. Then, throughout the Bible its substance is repeated in various ways. The formula itself appears time and again; new provisions are added to it and accumulate; history shows how it has been and is being fulfilled. And all of this is focused around that one center![8]

Thus the discipline of Biblical theology must be a twin of exegesis. Exegetical theology will remain incomplete and virtually barren in its results, as far as the Church is concerned, without a proper input of "informing theology." The exegete should keep on his desk a well-marked textbook of Biblical theology along with the lexicons and grammars. It will also be most helpful if that textbook has a Scripture index and a theme index so that the exegete may use this tool quickly without having to leaf through the whole book to find pertinent comments on the subject under investigation.

It is impossible to stress too much the importance of this new role for Biblical theology and the difference that it will make in the exegetical procedure. This should adequately fill the gap left by the commentators from the Reformation and early post-Reformation period who were so strong on theological exegesis. We believe the methodology urged here will more adequately present what those writers themselves had in mind.

7. For a fairly extensive discussion, see ibid., pp. 25–32.
8. See my detailed argument for the "promise" in ibid., pp. 1–69.

Should someone complain that no Christian exegete can or should forget that part of the Bible which was completed after the text under investigation, we respond by saying, "Of course, no one expects the exegete to do that." Subsequent developments in the revelation of theology (subsequent to the passage we have under consideration) may (and should, in fact) be brought into our *conclusion* or *summaries after* we have firmly established on exegetical grounds precisely what the passage means. We do, in fact, have the whole Bible; and we are speaking (usually) to a Christian audience. Therefore, in our summaries we should point out these later developments for the sake of updating and putting everything in its fullest context. However, in no case must that *later* teaching be used exegetically (or in any other way) to unpack the meaning or to enhance the usability of the individual text which is the object of our study.

Theological Wordbooks

Another way to unpack the theological meaning of a text is to resort to a unique type of tool which has arisen in our century: wordbooks. These volumes are not to be confused with lexicons, Bible dictionaries, commentaries, or concordances; they have a distinctive format and purpose. A wordbook seeks to define the leading theological concepts of the Bible by tracing (1) the meaning that these words have in the various contexts where they receive major development, and (2) the history of these same words throughout Biblical literature.[9] Thus, these tools should help the exegete to check that work already done in Biblical the-

9. For a description and review of these books, see James P. Martin, "Theological Wordbooks: Tools for the Preacher," *Interpretation* 18 (1964): 304–28; Xavier Léon-Dufour, "Introduction," in *Dictionary of Biblical Theology,* ed. Xavier Léon-Dufour, trans. P. Joseph Cahill (New York: Desclee, 1967), pp. xv–xxi; Gerhard Friedrich, "Prehistory of the Theological Dictionary of the New Testament," in *Theological Dictionary of the New Testament,* ed. Gerhard Kittel and Gerhard Friedrich, ed. and trans. Geoffrey W. Bromiley, 10 vols. (Grand Rapids: Eerdmans, 1964–1976), 10:613–61; and James Barr, *The Semantics of Biblical Language* (New York: Oxford, 1961).

ology, including conclusions which have been drawn about the terms in the passage under consideration.

The earliest textbook of this type which is still available is Hermann Cremer's famous *Biblico-Theological Lexicon of New Testament Greek*.[10] Cremer sought to find in the extrabiblical usage of theological words the distinctive nuance of meaning in each. By exploring this total range of meaning both inside and outside the Scriptures, he hoped to pinpoint the precise affinities and differences between the Biblical and extrabiblical use of these words. Cremer did not, however, extend his investigation to patristic Greek.[11]

Cremer's pioneering work was enlarged upon by Gerhard Kittel and Gerhard Friedrich's ten-volume *Theological Dictionary of the New Testament*.[12] Included are every theologically important noun, verb, and preposition, and even the names of many Old Testament persons who had theological significance in the history of salvation. The basic plan was to study each word, where possible, from the standpoint of its usage in the Old Testament, the Septuagint, classical sources, Hellenistic sources, Rabbinic Judaism, and finally the New Testament itself.

Kittel felt that his work was clearly different from such Greek lexicons as those of Joseph Henry Thayer, Walter Bauer, and George Abbott-Smith. His work concerned itself with "inner lexicography" so as to show the distinctiveness of each theological concept. Friedrich, who took over the work on Kittel's death, did not agree with Cremer's conclusion that New Testament words exhibit special meanings not found in secular Greek. Any newness in the language is rather to be traced to its new relation to Jesus Christ, concluded Friedrich.

In what sense, if any, does the Biblical usage of words exhibit newness? Cremer had adopted Friedrich Schleiermacher's con-

---

10. Hermann Cremer, *Biblico-Theological Lexicon of New Testament Greek*, 3d ed., trans. William Urwick (Edinburgh: Clark, 1883).

11. This task had to wait until G. W. H. Lampe, *A Patristic Greek Lexicon*, 5 fascicles (Oxford: Clarendon, 1961–1968).

12. For full bibliographical data see n. 9 above.

cept of the "language moulding power of Christianity"[13] and Richard Rothe's conclusion that the Bible uses a language of the Holy Spirit. Adolf Deissmann, however, showed from the papyri that New Testament Greek was actually colloquial, common, or, as it came to be known, Koine Greek.[14]

But this conclusion may have been too strong. Nigel Turner, who completed the third volume of James Hope Moulton's *Grammar of New Testament Greek*, felt differently about the subject of the newness or uniqueness of New Testament words. He declared, "We now have to concede that not only is the subject matter of the Scriptures unique but so also is the language in which they came to be written or translated."[15]

At the same time as Turner was saying this, James Barr was criticizing the basic methodology of Kittel's *Theological Dictionary of the New Testament.*[16] Barr's basic complaint against Kittel is that words tell us very little in and of themselves. It is only when words are joined together in sentences that we begin to get the special nuance of the meaning that a particular word had for an author.

Furthermore, Barr is especially upset (and rightfully so) about what he calls "illegitimate totality transfer":[17] the semantic value of a word in one context is added to the semantic value of that same word in a second and third context, and then the sum of all these values is declared to be the particular value in every individual context. Barr illustrates this fallacy with the word ἐκκλησία

13. Friedrich Schleiermacher, *Hermeneutik und Kritik mit besonderer Beziehung auf das Neue Testament,* ed. Friedrich Lücke, Sämmtliche Werke, Erste Abteilung zur Theologie, 7 (Berlin: Reimer, 1838). Quoted in Martin, "Theological Wordbooks," p. 305.

14. Adolf Deissmann, *Light from the Ancient East: The New Testament Illustrated by Recently Discovered Texts of the Graeco-Roman World,* new rev. ed., trans. Lionel R. M. Strachan (New York: Doran, 1927; reprint ed., Grand Rapids: Baker, 1978). Cf. also James Hope Moulton and George Milligan, *The Vocabulary of the Greek Testament, Illustrated from the Papyri and Other Non-Literary Sources* (London: Hodder and Stoughton, 1930; reprint ed., Grand Rapids: Eerdmans, 1949).

15. Nigel Turner, in James Hope Moulton, W. F. Howard, and Nigel Turner, *A Grammar of New Testament Greek,* 4 vols. (Edinburgh: Clark, 1906–1976), 3:9. Cited in Martin, "Theological Wordbooks," p. 308.

16. James Barr, *The Semantics of Biblical Language* (New York: Oxford, 1961).

17. Ibid., p. 218.

(Church). In different contexts it means (1) the body of Christ, (2) the body as the first installment of the kingdom of God, or (3) the bride of Christ. Now all these meanings, according to Barr, do apply to the word *Church*. But they cannot *all* be regarded as the meaning of Church in each individual passage, say, in Matthew 16:18.

While Barr is correct, of course, in vigorously insisting that meaning is found in clauses and sentences (i.e., words must be considered as parts of a whole clause or sentence), the criticism must not go too far. Words do have a fairly limited range of referents which any given context may modify only within certain rather restricted boundaries.[18]

The lesson to be learned here is that wordbooks (and textbooks of Biblical theology as well) cannot be substitutes for the exegete's own work with the immediate context. If he does not first thoroughly examine the immediate context, it will be all too tempting to adopt every and any theological meaning a given word might have and to read all those meanings into every particular occurrence of that word. Thus wordbooks are tools to be consulted, but they should never be a crutch for the lazy exegete.

What is the procedure, then, for doing one's own personal word studies before consulting some of these wordbooks?

First, one must *select* those words which are significant. A word may be considered significant if it meets one of the following criteria: (1) it plays a key role in the passage being exegeted; (2) it has occurred frequently in previous contexts; or (3) it is important in the history of salvation as revealed up to this point. If the exegete is new at this process, it might be best to emphasize criterion (1). As the exegete gains experience from reading widely and interpreting many books of the Bible, the other two criteria

18. This point is made by Gustaf Stern, *Meaning and Change of Meaning, with Special Reference to the English Language,* Indiana University Studies in the History and Theory of Linguistics (Bloomington: Indiana University, 1931), p. 85; and Stephen Ullmann, *The Principles of Semantics: A Linguistic Approach to Meaning,* 2d ed. (Oxford: Blackwell, 1959), p. 218. I am indebted for these references to Anthony C. Thiselton, "Semantics and New Testament Interpretation," in *New Testament Interpretation: Essays on Principles and Methods,* ed. I. Howard Marshall, pp. 75–104. Thiselton's article is a masterful one.

will be used more frequently. In the meantime, it would be well to ponder one or two textbooks of Biblical theology to develop a feel for theological themes and vocabulary.

The second step is to *define* the word selected in terms of its function in the *immediate context*. Be sure to consider other usages of the same word in the same book, making sure to proceed by moving out into each of the book's other sections as one would through ever enlarging concentric circles. The reason for doing this is that the author's use of the word may undergo development. There may be a progression of nuances of meaning within his own book.

The third step is to examine the usages of the same word in other authors who wrote during the same period of time.

We will now need more tools to aid us in our study. Sometimes it is helpful to study the root(s) from which the word came or even its etymology. This is the fourth step. One must be very careful, however, not to commit the "root fallacy," for the meanings of words often change drastically over the history of their usage. Anthony C. Thiselton illustrates this trap with the English word *nice*, which is derived from the Latin *nescius* (ignorant); the word *hussy,* which originally meant "housewife"; and the word *good-bye,* which is a contraction of "God be with you."[19] The father of modern linguistics, Ferdinand de Saussure (1857–1913) made a ringing protest against this preoccupation with the history of words. He compared linguistics to chess: The issue is not the history of the game, but the state of the board.[20]

One place where etymological considerations may be of some help, however, is in cases of homonymy: two words with the same lexical form (spelling) but with different meanings. But the interpreter must be very hesitant to use such studies in other situations, even though Francis Brown, S. R. Driver, and Charles A.

19. Thiselton, "Semantics," pp. 80–81; idem, "Sense and Nonsense in Interpreting Bible Words," *Eternity* 27 (March 1976): 16–17, 33–35.
20. As cited in Thiselton, "Sense and Nonsense," p. 17. Cf. Stanley D. Toussaint, "A Method of Making a New Testament Word Study," *Bibliotheca Sacra* 120 (1963): 35–41; and Ernest D. Burton, "The Study of New Testament Words," *The Old and New Testament Student* 12 (1891): 136ff.

Briggs appear to encourage this process by arranging their lexicon by what they consider to be the root of every lexical form. The truth of the matter is that quite frequently no one knows what the etymology is and in some instances we may never know. But never mind, nothing essential to the interpretive process has been lost in almost all of these cases.

𝄪 A fifth step may now be taken. Consult an exhaustive concordance for the following data: (1) the total number of times the word appears in the Bible; (2) the period in which there is the highest concentration of usage; (3) any limited context that exhibits an extraordinary number of usages—this might well be the place where the largest teaching block about the word is located; and (4) those contexts that illustrate its usage *prior* to the selected text we are exegeting. The principle here is the same as what we were advocating in our discussion of the "Analogy of [Antecedent] Scripture." What was written after the text in question is of no use or helpful only for the sake of comparison. The object of (4) will be to make sure we have not neglected pieces of pertinent data in our study.

Once again the warning must be issued that in studying a word, the exegete must be concerned with the meaning derived from the context, not with the total range of possible semantic values. Some of the concordances available to the exegete are listed in the bibliography at the end of this chapter.[21]

The sixth step, for the advanced exegete, will involve consulting the various cognate languages to find additional (including contrasting) usages, especially for those words which occur infrequently in the Bible or even only once (*hapax legomena*). For Hebrew one may often consult the grammars and lexicons for Ugaritic, Akkadian cuneiform (both Babylonian and Assyrian), Arabic, Aramaic, Egyptian hieroglyphics, and at times even Coptic.[22]

Mention should be made of Edwin Hatch and Henry A. Red-

---

21. For further discussions on concordances of the Septuagint, Vulgate, and English versions, consult Frederick W. Danker, *Multipurpose Tools for Bible Study*, 2d ed. (St. Louis: Concordia, 1966), pp. 1–17.

22. A preliminary listing of some of these tools may be found in ibid., pp. 106–11.

path's *Concordance to the Septuagint*,[23] for often the trail of the New Testament usage of Greek words begins in the Greek translation of the Old Testament in the third century B.C. Then, too, Koine Greek may share a particular aspect of its range of meanings with the vernacular usages found in the papyri. In this area Adolf Deissmann's *Light from the Ancient East* and James Hope Moulton and George Milligan's *Vocabulary of the Greek Testament* will afford the student of word studies much color and many helpful insights.[24] For example, Paul promised Philemon to repay all that Onesimus had taken from him (v. 18). By citing a papyrus which uses the same phraseology ("charge that to my account"), Deissmann shows that since Paul wrote this statement with his own hand (v. 19), Philemon could have used it much as we use a check today and held Paul financially liable for Onesimus's debt. Though this illustration operates only on the cultural level, there are similar examples on the theological level.

We should now be ready to check our work and compare it with what others have done. For the student's convenience we have listed some of the more prominent wordbooks in the bibliography that follows.

---

23. Edwin Hatch and Henry A. Redpath, *A Concordance to the Septuagint and the Other Greek Versions of the Old Testament*, 2 vols. (Oxford: Clarendon, 1897).

24. Adolf Deissmann, *Light from the Ancient East: The New Testament Illustrated by Recently Discovered Texts of the Graeco-Roman World*, new rev. ed., trans. Lionel R. M. Strachan (New York: Doran, 1927; reprint ed., Grand Rapids: Baker, 1978); James Hope Moulton and George Milligan, *The Vocabulary of the Greek Testament, Illustrated from the Papyri and Other Non-Literary Sources* (London: Hodder and Stoughton, 1930; reprint ed., Grand Rapids: Eerdmans, 1949).

Bibliography

Old Testament Concordances

Lisowsky, Gerhard, and Rost, Leonhard. *Konkordanz zum hebräischen Alten Testament.* Stuttgart: Württembergische Bibelanstalt, 1958.

Mandelkern, Salomon. *Concordance on the Bible.* Edited by Chaim Mordecai Brecher. 2 vols. New York: Shulsinger Brothers, 1955.

Wigram, George V., ed. *The Englishman's Hebrew and Chaldee Concordance of the Old Testament.* 5th ed. London: Bagster, 1890. Reprint. Grand Rapids: Zondervan, 1972.

New Testament Concordances

Moulton, W. F., and Geden, A. S. *A Concordance to the Greek Testament According to the Texts of Westcott and Hort, Tischendorf and the English Revisers.* Revised by H. K. Moulton. 5th ed. Edinburgh: Clark, 1978.

Schmoller, Alfred. *Handkonkordanz zum griechischen Neuen Testament.* 14th ed. Stuttgart: Württembergische Bibelanstalt, 1968.

Wigram, George V., ed. *The Englishman's Greek Concordance of the New Testament.* 9th ed. London: Bagster, 1903. Reprint. Grand Rapids: Zondervan, 1970.

Old Testament Wordbooks

Bauer, Johannes B., ed. *Sacramentum verbi: An Encyclopedia of Biblical Theology.* 3 vols. New York: Herder and Herder, 1970.

Botterweck, G. Johannes, and Ringgren, Helmer, eds. *Theological Dictionary of the Old Testament.* Translated by John T. Willis and David E. Green. 4 vols. to date. Grand Rapids: Eerdmans, 1974–.

Girdlestone, Robert Baker. *Synonyms of the Old Testament: Their Bearing on Christian Doctrine.* 2d ed. London: Nisbet, 1897. Reprint. Grand Rapids: Eerdmans, 1948.

Harris, R. Laird; Archer, Gleason L., Jr.; and Waltke, Bruce K., eds. *A Theological Wordbook of the Old Testament.* 2 vols. Chicago: Moody, 1980.

Wilson, William. *The Bible Student's Guide to the More Correct Understanding of the English Translation of the Old Testament, by Reference to the Original Hebrew.* 2d ed. London: Macmillan, 1870. Reprint. *Old Testament Word Studies.* Grand Rapids: Kregel, 1978.

New Testament Wordbooks

Brown, Colin, ed. *The New International Dictionary of New Testament Theology.* 3 vols. Grand Rapids: Zondervan, 1975–1978.

Kittel, Gerhard, and Friedrich, Gerhard, eds. *Theological Dictionary of the New Testament.* Translated and edited by Geoffrey W. Bromiley. 10 vols. Grand Rapids: Eerdmans, 1964–1976.

Robertson, A. T. *Word Pictures in the New Testament.* 6 vols. New York: Smith, 1930–1933. Reprint. Nashville: Broadman, 1943.

Trench, Richard Chenevix. *Synonyms of the New Testament.* 9th ed. London: Macmillan, 1880. Reprint. Grand Rapids: Eerdmans, 1948.

Vincent, Marvin R. *Word Studies in the New Testament.* 4 vols. New York: Scribner, 1887–1900. Reprint. Grand Rapids: Eerdmans, 1946.

Vine, W. E. *Expository Dictionary of New Testament Words.* Westwood, N.J.: Revell, 1956.

Chapter 7

Homiletical Analysis

Exegesis is never an end in itself. Its purposes are never fully realized until it begins to take into account the problems of transferring what has been learned from the text over to the waiting Church. To put it more bluntly, exegesis must come to terms with the *audience* as well as with what the author meant by the words he used.

Traditionally this is the very place where theological education has failed in its program. None of the theological departments has been specifically charged with assisting the student in the most delicate maneuver of transferring the results of the syntactical-theological analysis of the text into a viable didactic or sermonic format. In fact, everyone has assumed that this is so very obvious to anyone who has spent hours analyzing the Biblical text, that it would be a work of supererogation to even delve into the matter at all!

It is our new contention here that we must now charge this duty to the department of exegesis. The reason we have chosen this department is that the exegetical process and the hermeneutical circle have not been closed or completed until the exegete comes to terms with his own and his intended audience's response to the text.

Recently this point has been felt to be so intrinsic to the whole interpretive process that modern hermeneutical theory has cared less (and sometimes, not at all) about what a text mean*t* when it was written than what it mean*s* to us today. This turn of events was traced in chapter 1. While we were critical, we also said that we have heard—loud and clear—what lies behind this turn of events. What good, indeed, is it to know something happened or was said unless it has some relationship to me the reader or listener? The point is well taken.

From our viewpoint, it is to be regretted that modern men and women have also decided that they can do just as well without a decision on whether the author actually wrote what is found in the text or whether the events described really happened. It is almost as if modern men and women have grown tired of waiting for the exegetes and have summarily changed the ground rules so that finally something relevant and of personal value can come from the texts.

If we are not mistaken, for every move in the exegetical process, as we have attempted to trace it up to this final step, there is a matching function in what we are calling here homiletical analysis. This is not to say that we are now attempting to rival or to supplant the discipline of homiletics; that would be a total misunderstanding of our proposal here. To be absolutely clear about what we are doing in this chapter, we might have entitled it "Preparations for Homiletical Usage." The basic thrust of the chapter will be what we call "principlization," the final task in the exegetical process before a text can be turned over to the special concerns of the department of pastoral theology and homiletics.

In those happy instances where the Biblical materials are cast into a straight didactic form, such as the exegete finds in much of the Book of Romans, there is hardly any need for what we are here calling "principlization." There the problem is relatively simple, in that the only demand on the exegete is that he put the teachings and doctrines of Romans into the form of propositions (i.e., main points in a preaching outline) that will call the hearers to some type of response. When truth is not internalized within the hearers, but is left as just so many notions floating around outside their experience, the exegete is in effect a mere dilettante—a trifler in the art of interpretation.

But most texts are not cast into a straight didactic form. The problems in each of these instances are far more complex.

As we have already seen, it ought to be possible for the interpreter to summarize in a brief sentence the meaning of each paragraph in the portion of Scripture on which he has chosen to preach. (This preaching portion will usually be limited to two or three paragraphs, a total of eight to fifteen verses.) The interpreter must make sure that his focus is identical with the author's truth-intention. And accordingly, it will be proper to designate the brief sentence summarizing the paragraph as the author's theme sentence/proposition.

The theme sentence/proposition should give the essence of what the paragraph is about. The only situation in which this process could become troublesome and complicated is in those rare instances (1) where the theme is *implied* or (2) where independent sentences are connected to the expressed topic sentence of the paragraph (in effect a compound theme). In case (1) it will be necessary to propose a theme; in case (2) it will be necessary to enlarge the theme proposition to include those attached independent clauses which rank on an equal basis with the so-called topic sentence.

But most situations an interpreter will meet have a single and expressed theme. The themes of the two or three paragraphs that have been selected for exposition should be grouped together.

Now we are ready to begin the process of principlizing these themes. To put it most succinctly, in formulating the main points of his message the exegete must restate these paragraph themes without diluting or expanding their content. Furthermore, these restatements must simultaneously embrace the author's *purpose* in writing the whole section and the timeless and abiding truth he intended to convey in each paragraph.

It is of utmost importance that the restated theme not be a purely descriptive narration of the past events. This will immediately prejudice moderns against giving it their attention. Thus, it is imperative that each main point (one per paragraph please, unless the scope of our exegesis and message is only one paragraph) avoid the use of the past tense of the verb (a reporting style) and the use of all proper names (with the understandable exception of God's names).

The exegete's eye will be drawn from the author's overall purpose to his manner of carrying it out in the paragraphs being examined. This in turn will raise the question, what did the first speaker (i.e., the author) of these words expect from his audience when they first heard these words? With this in mind, let us define "principlization." To "principlize" is to state the author's propositions, arguments, narrations, and illustrations in timeless abiding truths with special focus on the application of those truths to the current needs of the Church. Contemporary applications will often be suggested by analogous applications made by the original writer of the Biblical text. The remainder of this chapter will focus on the various steps to be followed in principlizing a passage.

The Subject of the Text

The first step in the process of principlization is to determine the subject of the Biblical passage (and hence of the message to be preached). It should reflect the major concern of the ancient writer. It is best if that concern can be described in a way that shows how that same concern is shared by most, if not all, of humanity.

In order to accurately describe what the subject of a passage is, the exegete must now back up and ask once again what the

Biblical book as a whole is all about. That Biblical book must be classified as to kind and subject matter.

Then the major sections or parts of the Scriptural book should be studied once again to note what, if any, progress or development there is in the argument, narrative, or injunctions as the reader moves along. The whole scope of the work should be understood in relation to the contribution that the individual parts make. By analyzing the relationships that exist at this level, the interpreter may find solutions to some of his problems.

But our concern as interpreters and proclaimers of the Word must be much more restricted if we are to do an intensive and detailed analysis of the text. As we have already suggested, pastors and teachers have almost uniformly experienced that one cannot do a good job of exegeting a passage of more than two or three paragraphs. Usually it is best to treat about six to eight verses when one is working with didactic material. If one is working in historical narrative, of course it will be easier and more practical to focus on a larger body of material (perhaps up to twenty or even thirty verses). Determination of the subject of this group of two or three paragraphs is the most critical move for the proclaimer, for it will in turn determine the subject of the pastor's message.

The exegete must resist the temptation to impose a mold over the text by forcing that text to answer one of his favorite questions or to deal with one of the contemporary issues that our culture wants to have solved. Instead, the careful interpreter will gather the following data to determine the subject that best fits the uniqueness of the passage under investigation: (1) the theme sentence or topic proposition of each of the paragraphs; (2) repeated terms which are defined, or are stressed, or give the text an unusual flavor; and (3) the special part that these paragraphs play in the overall theme or argument of the whole book and the section in which they are found.

Some examples of this process might help. When the exegete undertakes an examination of a text like Isaiah 40:12–31, he or she is immediately struck by the division of the text into three major strophes (poetic paragraphs). Two of these strophes begin with virtually identical questions: "To whom then will you compare God, or what likeness will you make with him?" (Isa. 40:18, 25). It is this repeated question (and hence the theme or topic proposition) that supplies the exegete with the subject of the passage and therefore the topic of the message to contemporary men and women: "The Incomparability of God."

Other passages are a little more subtle in the way they yield up their topic and central subject matter. Take, for example, the historical narrative of Numbers 20:1–13, which deals with an incident that occurred during the forty years of wandering in the wilderness. The issue for the Israelites was a lack of water. But the words that make a major difference and suddenly tip the whole narrative on its head, as it were, are the unexpected blasts from Moses' lips: "Listen now, you rebels; must *we* [!] bring water for you out of this rock?" (Num. 20:10). These words are not repeated, nor are they key theological terms, but they are undoubtedly the pivotal words in this text. They immediately bring to mind the contrast between the words and actions of men and the words and actions of God—for water did pour forth from that rock in spite of what God's leaders had done. Therefore, we believe the subject of this passage is and the topic of the message should be: "Letting God Be God." Moses and Aaron robbed God of His glory by "speaking rashly," as a later Psalm would editorialize on this event (Ps. 106:32–33).

Once in a while the very words of the subject will be expressed in the body of the text itself. One example is Malachi 2:17–3:10. There, almost at the heart of the text and functioning much as a pivot or a fulcrum, is Malachi 3:6—"I the Lord do not change." When this central assertion is juxtaposed with the charges that introduce the passage ("Where is the God of justice [anyhow]?"), the sermon subject naturally suggests itself: "A Call to Trust in Our Unchanging Lord."

The subject of a passage might also be suggested in the opening words or heading of a section. In Malachi 1:6–14, God asks of the Jews through His prophet, "If I am [your] father, where is my honor? And if I am [your] Lord, where is my fear?" (Mal. 1:6). And there is the point of the whole passage: "A Call to Authentic

Sonship." It is all too easy to claim that we are sons and servants of the living God without demonstrating the same! No other subject dominates these nine verses.

When we have extracted the subject from the text instead of imposing a subject on it, we may speak with more confidence that the word we share for moderns has an authority which is not our own, but is borrowed from the text. We would urge exegetes to study (1) the theme sentences, (2) distinctive or unusual features of the passage, (3) pivotal statements that may act as a fulcrum for the passage, and (4) the opening words or headings that set the stage for all that the passage wishes to develop.

The Emphasis of the Text

The next step is to find the *emphasis* of the text under consideration. Within this selected passage there will be important words and key terms. These words and terms may be identified by frequent occurrence in the group of paragraphs being investigated. Or they may occupy a strategic position; for example, they may appear in the theme propositions. Or they may be explicitly defined. One other clue to recognizing these words is that they will usually give us trouble in our exegesis since they add special nuances to the passage.

The original author's leading concepts are sometimes marked by special vocabulary. In those cases where the text and its author have thus pointed to the concepts which they want to stress, it behooves the interpreter to follow this same pattern if he wishes to be a trustworthy exegete. Often, identification of this stress or emphasis will help the exegete to give a unity to his preparation of the passage for teaching or preaching.

Whenever a series of sentences or clauses is linked together by the same introductory word ("because," "since," "therefore," or the like), it may be possible to organize the message around these key words.[1] In this case each major point in the sermon will be a development of the subject from the same perspective and angle. For example, if the word *therefore* is sprinkled throughout the paragraphs under investigation, then we may safely make our major points in the sermon a discussion of the *consequences* of the announced subject. Alternatively, if the word *because* recurs frequently, we may develop our message around a series of *reasons*.

One example that comes to mind is Isaiah 9:1–7. Here the repeated "for" ("because") at the head of verses 4, 5, and 6 introduces the reasons why there is "joy to the world." Another example is Isaiah 58. As it talks about true spirituality in dedicated social action, it balances "if" conditions (אִם) with "then" consequences (אָז).

Sometimes the repeated phenomenon is only a point of grammar or syntax. Thus in I Thessalonians 4:1–8 the stress is on the three infinitival forms in verses 3b, 4a, and 6a. They function almost like purpose clauses to develop the subject of "Knowing the Will of God" (I Thess. 4:3a). Or in I Peter 1:1–12, the Greek form εἰς ("unto, to") is used in verses 3b, 4a, and 5b to indicate all the things into which believers have been "born anew."

Time and again the exegete may be saved from would-be disaster and the perils of subjectivism by relying on the text's own pattern of emphasis as it is often indicated by some stylistic, grammatical, or rhetorical device that supplies the authoritative basis for principlizing that text. Where such emphases in words, terms, stylistics, rhetorical devices, or even repeated grammatical forms are lacking, the interpreter must rely on other factors to guide him in the principlizing or application stage.

The Main Points of the Message

Now we can begin to determine the main points of our lesson or message. In this step, it will be most advantageous if the in-

---

1. For a description and list of possible "key words," see Faris D. Whitesell and Lloyd M. Perry, *Variety in Your Preaching* (Old Tappan, N.J.: Revell, 1954), pp. 75–94 (chap. 5); James Braga, *How to Prepare Bible Messages: A Manual on Homiletics for Bible Students* (Portland: Multnomah, 1969), pp. 101–3.

terpreter has already laid out a syntactical display or block diagram such as was discussed in chapter 4.

The advantages of analyzing each paragraph or strophe in a mechanical display that concentrates on tracing the syntactical connections between sentences, clauses, and phrases are enormous. The most important is that the theme proposition or topic sentence (even if it is only implicit) plainly declares what that particular paragraph or strophe is all about. When the two or three propositions or topic sentences (if our selected text includes that many paragraphs) are studied together, the exegete must ask, "What do these propositions have in common? How can these propositions or topic sentences be stated so as to retain the perspective and stance adopted as a result of the first two steps in the process of principlization—determination and investigation of the subject and key words?"

We are saying only that the exegete, teacher, and preacher must locate the important sentences in each targeted text. Usually there will be only one such sentence for each paragraph. It will be the theme proposition or what we have also designated as the topic sentence of the paragraph.

It will be from these sentences that the interpreter will build the main points of the message or lesson. This will be best accomplished by weighing each topic sentence against the author's major concern in the whole text under scrutiny (see again chapter 3, pp. 69–85; and pp. 152–55). Armed with this perspective, the interpreter should begin to see a way in which these topic sentences can be formulated into major points which will not only preserve the precise meaning of the original text, but will also provide an invitation, challenge, and instruction to moderns.

The main pitfall to avoid in formulating these main points of the message is that of using dated statements. The tendency is to merely transfer from the text all proper names, places, incidents, and descriptions. This of course immediately makes more difficult a modern audience's efforts to hear God's "new" word to their generation from an admittedly old text. Therefore, the teacher or preacher will be well advised to delete all proper names from his main points (except for God's names). Likewise, anything that would tend to focus the listeners' attention more on the "then-ness" of the text than on the "now" of God's new challenge must be studiously avoided. At the same time each proposition must be so worded as to preserve the abiding, permanent, and fixed teaching of the text.

For example, if one were to preach on Numbers 22, his main points might easily be a historicized narration of just passing interest without any contemporary challenge:

    I. Balaam Sought—Numbers 22:1–20
   II. Balaam Fought—Numbers 22:21–27
  III. Balaam Taught—Numbers 22:28–38

This would be a fairly good message if we were preaching to Balaam, but can we expect God's people today to respond to such a message? Instead we would suggest that there is a subject in the passage which is relevant to Balaam and to us in our day—the problem of "Knowing and Doing the Will of God." There are three *ways* (our key word here) in which we can know and do the will of God:

    I. By Keeping the Faith ("once for all delivered to the saints")—Numbers 22:1–7 [the expositor should call attention to the informing theology of Gen. 12:3 and the relationship of Moab and Midian to Abraham]
   II. By Obeying God's Word—Numbers 22:8–22
  III. By Observing the Obstacles—Numbers 22:23–35

The same material has been expounded, but this time the message is relevant to all.

It is also important to make sure that the main points are in a parallel structure—if one is a phrase, then all should be phrases instead of a single word or a sentence. If one is in the imperative form or an interrogative, then it is best that the others also follow suit. Likewise, nouns should correspond with nouns, verbs with verbs, and prepositions with prepositions. Thus, if the first point begins with a preposition, so should each of the other main points.

It might also be noted that until the interpreter has acquired a wide range of experience, it might be best to let the main points follow the same order as the sequence in the paragraphs themselves.

It is not always an easy matter to formulate these main points. Beside the few hints we have already given, there is the need for meditation and prayer. Beyond all the science of exegesis and hermeneutics there is another side which we may call the *art* of preparing a text for proclamation. Those who have few gifts in this creative and reflective area should follow the guidelines we have suggested above as a minimum. This procedure will not lead the interpreter away from what we call the *art* of preparing a text; rather it will put the proclaimer in the best possible position to do further reflection and meditation on the specifics of the text.

The Subpoints of the Message

Next to be considered are the subdivisions of the main points. Here we are involved with the logic and development of a lesson or message. And here is where the syntactical analysis of each paragraph should begin to pay handsome dividends.

The method for extracting the subpoints or subdivisions of the main points ought to be the same in principle as the method used for formulating the main divisions. In fact, the indentations and levels of subordination indicated in the syntactical analysis for each paragraph ought to help us decide which phrases, clauses, or even sentences are to be chosen for highlighting in the subpoints. Only by paying careful attention to the grammar and syntax of the paragraph will our eyes and hearts be directed to follow the thread of the original writer's intentions. And this is what we wish to reproduce in the lives of men and women.

One caution must now be sounded. It is best to limit the number of subdivisions lest the outline tend to make the text seem more complex than it really is. The object ought to be to simplify the structure so as to provide to every listener an insight into the skeleton and linking sinews of the text.

Like the main points, the subpoints must also be in parallel structure. Furthermore, for the sake of simplicity and for the convenience of those who are following the message (ideally, their Bibles should be open to the passage), it again is best to preserve the order of the text. Of course, when there are very good reasons, it is permissible to depart from this order; but this should be the exception. And it must be especially clear at all times just where the expositor is in the paragraph. He should frequently announce the verse(s) in the paragraph he is now examining and the subpoint to which it relates.

The whole objective of what we are here calling "textual expository preaching" is to let the Scriptures have the major, if not the only, role in determining the shape, logic, and development of our message. We want to drive home into the hearts of God's people the Scripture itself as well as the challenge, comfort, and instruction of the message. It is to be hoped that God's men and women will be challenged to reread that very same Biblical text on their own soon after they have heard the message. Even if they cannot recall the outline (they probably will not—sorry!), that Word of Scripture will still speak to them because they have thought through its structure and shape in such a way as to have decisively met God in that text.

We will want to develop our subpoints as the writer did. Thus we will have a list of reasons where he used a series of "because" clauses, or a list of conditions where he had a series of "if" clauses. Regardless of what particular textual device suggests to us the rubric for getting the subpoints in a parallel structure, syntax must lie at the basis of that decision.

Teachers and students of exegesis must pay much more attention to syntax. Only by doing so will they be able to come to terms with what the author meant and only then will they be in a position to come to terms with the audience gathered to hear God's Word. To help in this respect, we strongly urge interpreters to give serious consideration to the method of syntactical display (block diagrams) advocated in this book.

The Theology of the Text

And now, where are we to find the essential substance of a
passage? Or, to put it in another way, what is the permanent,
abiding, and doctrinal part of the passage? Must we import doctrine and theology (from elsewhere in the Bible) to fill out the
word we hope to teach and preach from the selected passage—
especially if it is a narrative text, or an Old Testament passage?

Many have noted that the strength of preachers who follow
rather closely the pattern of preaching found in the Reformers is
that they preach theologically. There is no doubt that when our
teaching and preaching focus on the person and work of God,
there are decided strengths and praiseworthy emphases.

But even these strengths can be subverted when in our methodology we do not heed the Biblical author's own theological
motivations and presumptions—at least to the extent that he has
explicitly referred to an antecedent theology which he believes he
is building onto in this passage. It has been our contention in this
work (see chapter 6) that the *exegete* is responsible for what we
have called the "informing theology" or the "analogy of antecedent Scripture." There are two tools we can employ to identify
this theology: (1) the author's own explicit references, allusions,
and use of terms which in the progress of doctrine had taken on
a technical status by his time; and (2) a good textbook of Biblical
theology that traces the diachronic progress of the doctrine which
is further developed in our preaching passage.

This "emerging theology" must take precedence over the legitimate concerns of a systematic theology. Systematic statements
are useful only when we have completed exegesis of a passage.
Then, in our summaries of each main point, in the sermon outline,
or in the whole passage, we may jump over the centuries and
bring to bear all that God subsequently revealed on the theological
issue being examined. In no case should a later doctrine be used
as an *exegetical* tool to unlock an earlier passage. That would be
an extremely serious methodological mistake, for, in effect, all
revelation would then be leveled out. Virtually every passage deal-

ing with a particular topic would end up saying almost the same thing as the latest revelation of God on that topic.

The proper alternative to this abuse of systematic theology, however, is not to refuse to include any theology; rather, it is to let Biblical theology be the twin tool of syntactical analysis. As "emerging theology" wended its way through the history of redemption, there gradually developed a background against which the deeper or more spiritual emphases of God's most recent revelation were to be understood. Far from imposing any tradition of a later theology (no matter how Biblical and how excellent it is) on an earlier text, this method respects the integrity of the original revelation of God to the writer. Yet it also legitimately enriches that same text by its emphasis on the accumulating, ramifying, and informing theology.

If this was the theology which was central to the interest of the audiences in the writer's day, then could it not also still function for us in the same way? If this informing theology was what made the text timeless and full of abiding values for the people in that day (and we believe that it was), then could not this same diachronic accumulation of theology provide the same heart of the message for all peoples in all times? Yes, for even in the text's historical particularity, it also carried in its very bosom an enduring plan of the everlasting God.

We believe that this informing theology provides the interpreter with the key to all the emphases, applications, appeals, and offers of hope or warnings of judgment which must be made if the text is to mean anything to our day and age. It is for this reason that we have named our method of exegesis after the two most important functions in the exegetical process—the *syntactical-theological* method of exegesis. Without both of these emphases, the message will fall stillborn on baffled ears and hearts.

The Conclusion of the Message

The last step in principlizing a passage is to give the message a strong *conclusion*. The messages of about two hundred years ago that remain in print excel in their ability to draw stirring conclusions. More recently, we have tended to specialize in emphasizing the introduction. In fact, we have usually overindulged ourselves in the art of introducing texts and messages. We have begun with references to the weekly newsmagazines, recent editorials, various opinion polls, and with quotes from prominent authors from the past. Meanwhile, much of our allotted time has been eaten up (sometimes up to one-fifth of it), and we still have not brought God's people near to the text. It is almost as if we were afraid to cut that text loose on God's people.

We need to reevaluate our priorities in this matter of introductions. I would urge God's ministers and teachers of the Word in every type of ministry inside and outside of the Church to severely limit their work on the introduction and to devote that time and those energies of preparation to an expanded and clearly-thought-out conclusion.

Here again we believe the Biblical text itself will suggest what our conclusion might be. At least we ought to begin by asking where the author thought that God was leading the original audience who first heard this message. Usually that is all that we need to observe and the pattern for our own conclusion will be set.

The reader must recognize that there is much more that needs to be done before he can master all the principles and achieve all the goals of good homiletical procedure. We believe that the departments of homiletics in the theological seminary should now take over and carry the student the rest of the way. This book has made an earnest attempt to be the friend of the pastor, teacher, and student along the uncharted and lonely path from exegesis over to the preparation of a sermon. We trust that it has provided an adequate definition and description of the detailed procedure that must be followed in this matter of principlizing a Biblical text for public proclamation of the Word.

Chapter 8

Illustrations of Syntactical and Homiletical Analysis

Now that we have examined in some detail the various aspects of the syntactical-theological method of exegesis, the student should apply to specific texts what has been learned. To assist the student we include here eight sample syntactical displays or block diagrams (four from the Old Testament, four from the New). If necessary, the student should review pages 99–103.

24a Thus says the Lord,

your redeemer,

and your fashioner from the womb:

I am the Lord,

	1	2	
24b	the one making all,		
	the one stretching out the heavens alone,		
	the one spreading out the earth: who was with me?		
25	the one frustrating the signs of liars,	and diviners he makes fools of;	
	the one turning wise men backwards,	and their wisdom he makes folly;	
26a	the one confirming the word of his servant,	and the counsel of his servant he performs;	
			3
26b	the one saying of Jerusalem: she shall be inhabited,	and of the cities of Judah: they shall be built,	and their waste places I will build up;
27	the one saying to the deep: dry up,	and thy rivers I will dry up;	
28	the one saying of Cyrus: my shepherd is he,	and all my pleasure he shall perform,	even to say of Jerusalem: she shall be built,

4
and of the temple: thy foundation shall be laid.

166

Our God's Lordship Is Revealed

כֹּה־אָמַ֣ר יְהוָה֮
גֹּאֲלֶ֒ךָ֒
וְיֹצֶרְךָ֣ מִבָּ֑טֶן

24a

אָנֹכִ֤י יְהוָה֙

I. In His Creation (24b)

2	1
	עֹ֣שֶׂה כֹּ֔ל
	נֹטֶ֤ה שָׁמַ֙יִם֙ לְבַדִּ֔י
	רֹקַ֥ע הָאָ֖רֶץ מֵי־אִתִּֽי ׃
וְקֹסְמִ֣ים יְהוֹלֵ֑ל	מֵפֵר֙ אֹת֣וֹת בַּדִּ֔ים
וְדַעְתָּ֖ם יְשַׂכֵּֽל ׃	מֵשִׁ֧יב חֲכָמִ֛ים אָח֖וֹר
וַעֲצַ֥ת מַלְאָכָ֖יו יַשְׁלִ֑ים	מֵקִים֙ דְּבַ֣ר עַבְדּ֔וֹ

24b A. Of everything

B. Of the heavens

C. Of the earth

II. In His Providence (25–26a)

25 A. By reversing the diviner's forecasts

B. By overthrowing the clever man's advice

26a C. By performing the prophet's predictions

III. In His Predictions (26b–28)

3		
וְחָרְבוֹתֶ֖יהָ אֲקוֹמֵֽם ׃	וּלְעָרֵ֤י יְהוּדָה֙ תִּבָּנֶ֔ינָה	הָאֹמֵ֤ר לִירוּשָׁלַ֙͏ִם֙ תּוּשָׁ֔ב
וְנַהֲרֹתַ֖יִךְ אוֹבִֽישׁ ׃		הָאֹמֵ֣ר לַצּוּלָ֖ה חֳרָ֑בִי
וְלֵאמֹ֥ר לִירוּשָׁלַ֖͏ִם תִּבָּנֶֽה	וְכָל־חֶפְצִ֖י יַשְׁלִ֑ם	הָאֹמֵ֤ר לְכ֙וֹרֶשׁ֙ רֹעִ֔י

26b A. About the restoration of the land

27 B. About the return through the river

28 C. About the Gentile ruler's amazing generosity

4
וְהֵיכָ֥ל תִּוָּסֵֽד ׃

167

5 | Thus says the Lord:

Cursed (is) the man

who trusts in mankind,

( ) makes flesh his arm,

( ) and turns away his heart.

6 | For he will be like a bush in the desert,

and he will not see good when it comes;

but he will inhabit the parched places in the wilderness, a salt plain,

and (it is) not inhabited.

7 | Blessed is the man

who trusts in the Lord

and

(whose) trust is the Lord.

8 | For he shall be as a tree transplanted by the waters,

that extends its roots by the stream,

and will not fear when heat comes,

and its leaves will be green,

and in the year of the drought it will not be anxious,

nor will it cease from yielding fruit.

9 | The heart is deceitful

and it is sick;

who understands it?

10 | I, the Lord, { search the heart and try the reins } to give to every man

according to his ways,

according to the fruits of his deeds.

168

The Lord Who Knows Our Lives and Our Futures

כֹּה׀ אָמַ֣ר יְהוָ֗ה

אָר֤וּר הַגֶּ֙בֶר֙

אֲשֶׁ֣ר יִבְטַ֣ח בָּֽאָדָ֔ם

וְשָׂ֥ם בָּשָׂ֖ר זְרֹע֑וֹ ( )

וּמִן־יְהוָ֖ה יָס֥וּר לִבּֽוֹ׃ ( )

וְהָיָה֙ כְּעַרְעָ֣ר בָּֽעֲרָבָ֔ה

וְלֹ֥א יִרְאֶ֖ה כִּי־יָ֣בוֹא ט֑וֹב

וְשָׁכַ֤ן חֲרֵרִים֙ בַּמִּדְבָּ֔ר אֶ֥רֶץ מְלֵחָ֖ה

וְלֹ֥א תֵשֵֽׁב׃

בָּר֣וּךְ הַגֶּ֔בֶר

אֲשֶׁ֥ר יִבְטַ֖ח בַּֽיהוָ֑ה

וְהָיָ֥ה יְהוָ֖ה מִבְטַחֽוֹ׃

וְהָיָ֣ה כְּעֵ֣ץ׀ שָׁת֣וּל עַל־מַ֗יִם

וְעַל־יוּבַל֙ יְשַׁלַּ֣ח שָֽׁרָשָׁ֔יו

וְלֹ֤א יִרְאֶה֙ כִּי־יָ֣בֹא חֹ֔ם

וְהָיָ֥ה עָלֵ֖הוּ רַֽעֲנָ֑ן

וּבִשְׁנַ֤ת בַּצֹּ֙רֶת֙ לֹ֣א יִדְאָ֔ג

וְלֹ֥א יָמִ֖ישׁ מֵעֲשׂ֥וֹת פֶּֽרִי׃

עָקֹ֥ב הַלֵּ֛ב מִכֹּ֖ל

וְאָנֻ֣שׁ

ה֖וּא מִ֥י יֵדָעֶֽנּוּ׃

אֲנִ֧י יְהוָ֛ה { חֹקֵ֥ר לֵ֖ב   } וְלָתֵ֥ת לְאִישׁ֙

                { בֹּחֵ֣ן כְּלָי֑וֹת } כִּדְרָכָ֔יו

כִּפְרִ֖י מַעֲלָלָֽיו׃

5   I. The Way of the Wicked— The Cursed Man
       A. His description

6   B. His destiny

       II. The Way of the Blessed— The Blessed Man
7   A. His description

8   B. His destiny

       III. The Way of the Lord— The Examining God
9   A. His diagnosis of the heart

10   B. His description
       C. His decisions (on the basis of His diagnosis)
          1. Proportionate
          2. Personalized

1 | Happy is the man

who

does not walk in the counsel of the wicked,

and in the way of sinners he does not stand,

and in the seat of scorners he does not sit down;

2 | but rather, in the Law of Yahweh is his delight,

and in the Law he meditates

day

and night.

3 | That is, he will be like a tree

transplanted by the channels of water,

which yields its fruit in proper time,

and the leaves will not wither;

therefore, in all that he does he will have success.

4 | Not so the wicked,

but rather, they are like chaff

which the wind will drive about.

5 | Therefore

the wicked will not stand in the judgment,

nor sinners in the congregation of the righteous.

6 | For Yahweh knows the way of the righteous,

but the way of the wicked will perish.

170

Our Character and Our Productivity

אַשְׁרֵי הָאִישׁ

אֲשֶׁר |

לֹא הָלַךְ בַּעֲצַת רְשָׁעִים

וּבְדֶרֶךְ חַטָּאִים לֹא עָמָד

וּבְמוֹשַׁב לֵצִים לֹא יָשָׁב :

כִּי אִם בְּתוֹרַת יְהֹוָה חֶפְצוֹ

( ) וּבְתוֹרָתוֹ יֶהְגֶּה

יוֹמָם

וָלָיְלָה :

וְהָיָה כְּעֵץ

שָׁתוּל עַל־פַּלְגֵי מָיִם

אֲשֶׁר פִּרְיוֹ | יִתֵּן בְּעִתּוֹ

וְעָלֵהוּ לֹא־יִבּוֹל

וְכֹל אֲשֶׁר־יַעֲשֶׂה יַצְלִיחַ :

לֹא־כֵן הָרְשָׁעִים

כִּי אִם־כַּמֹּץ

אֲשֶׁר־תִּדְּפֶנּוּ רוּחַ :

עַל־כֵּן |

לֹא־יָקֻמוּ רְשָׁעִים בַּמִּשְׁפָּט

( ) וְחַטָּאִים בַּעֲדַת צַדִּיקִים :

כִּי־יוֹדֵעַ יְהֹוָה דֶּרֶךְ צַדִּיקִים

וְדֶרֶךְ רְשָׁעִים תֹּאבֵד :

1 I. God's Approved Person (1–3)
  A. His consistent conduct

2 B. His constant delight

3 C. His consequent character

4 II. God's Disapproved Person (4–6)
  A. His coarse character

5 B. His end

6 1. The knowledge of the Lord
  2. The judgment of the Lord

171

1 Why do the nations rage,

        and the peoples plot in vain?

2   The kings of the earth take their stand,

        and the rulers gather together

            against the Lord

            and against his Anointed One;

3   Let us break their chains, [they say,]

            and throw off their fetters.

4 The One enthroned in heaven laughs;

the Lord scoffs at them.

5   Then he rebukes them in his anger,

        and terrifies them in his wrath, [saying,]

6   I have installed my King

          upon Zion, the mountain of my holiness.

7 I proclaim the decree of the Lord:

    He said to me,

        You are my Son,

        today I have become your Father.

8   Ask of me,

            and I will make the nations your inheritance,

            and the ends of the earth your possession.

9   You will rule them with an iron scepter;

            like pottery you will dash them to pieces.

10 Therefore, you kings,

        be wise;

        be warned, rulers of the earth.

11   Serve the Lord with fear

        and rejoice with trembling.

12   Kiss the Son

            lest he be angry

            and you be destroyed in your way,

                for his wrath can flare up in a moment.

Blessed are those who take refuge in him.

172

Hebrew	v.	Outline
לָמָּה רָגְשׁוּ גוֹיִם	1	I. Rebellion of the Nations (1–3)
( ) וּלְאֻמִּים יֶהְגּוּ־רִיק׃		A. World insurrection
( ) יִתְיַצְּבוּ׀ מַלְכֵי־אֶרֶץ	2	B. World draft call
( ) וְרוֹזְנִים נוֹסְדוּ־יָחַד		C. World council
עַל־יְהוָה		D. World consensus
וְעַל־מְשִׁיחוֹ׃		E. World proposal
נְנַתְּקָה אֶת־מוֹסְרוֹתֵימוֹ	3	
וְנַשְׁלִיכָה מִמֶּנּוּ עֲבֹתֵימוֹ׃		
יוֹשֵׁב בַּשָּׁמַיִם יִשְׂחָק	4	II. Reaction of God (4–6)
אֲדֹנָי יִלְעַג־לָמוֹ׃		A. God's position
אָז יְדַבֵּר אֵלֵימוֹ בְאַפּוֹ	5	B. God's reaction
( ) וּבַחֲרוֹנוֹ יְבַהֲלֵמוֹ׃		C. God's speech
וַאֲנִי נָסַכְתִּי מַלְכִּי	6	
עַל־צִיּוֹן הַר־קָדְשִׁי׃		
אֲסַפְּרָה אֶל חֹק יְהוָה	7	III. Response of the Messianic King (7–9)
אָמַר אֵלַי		A. Unshakable resolution
בְּנִי אַתָּה		B. Unique relation to the Father
אֲנִי הַיּוֹם יְלִדְתִּיךָ׃		C. Universal dominion
שְׁאַל מִמֶּנִּי	8	D. Unwavering administration
וְאֶתְּנָה גוֹיִם נַחֲלָתֶךָ		
וַאֲחֻזָּתְךָ אַפְסֵי־אָרֶץ׃		
תְּרֹעֵם בְּשֵׁבֶט בַּרְזֶל	9	
כִּכְלִי יוֹצֵר תְּנַפְּצֵם׃		
וְעַתָּה מְלָכִים	10	IV. Recommendation to the Nations (10–12)
הַשְׂכִּילוּ		A. Be smart
הִוָּסְרוּ שֹׁפְטֵי אָרֶץ׃		B. Be instructed
עִבְדוּ אֶת־יְהוָה בְּיִרְאָה	11	C. Serve
וְגִילוּ בִּרְעָדָה׃		D. Rejoice
נַשְּׁקוּ־בַר	12	E. Do homage
פֶּן־יֶאֱנַף׀		
וְתֹאבְדוּ דֶרֶךְ		
כִּי־יִבְעַר כִּמְעַט אַפּוֹ		
אַשְׁרֵי כָּל־חוֹסֵי בוֹ׃		

173

Knowing the Will of God in Dating
(Vv. 1–2 can be used as the conclusion of the passage)
1. Appeal is to brethren
2. Basis is instruction given by Paul through Jesus
3. Obligation is that we *must* please God

I. Abstain from Premarital Sex

II. Know How to Conduct a Christian Courtship

III. Refuse to Cheat Your Future Partner (reasons)

    A. God is a vindicator of wrongs

    B. God has called us to holiness

    C. The indwelling Holy Spirit is defiled by premarital sex

1 Λοιπὸν οὖν, ἀδελφοί,
ἐρωτῶμεν ὑμᾶς
  καὶ
παρακαλοῦμεν ἐν κυρίῳ ᾿Ιησοῦ,
  ἵνα καθὼς παρελάβετε
    παρ᾿ ἡμῶν
    τὸ πῶς δεῖ ὑμᾶς περιπατεῖν
        καὶ
        ἀρέσκειν θεῷ,
        καθὼς καὶ περιπατεῖτε,
            ἵνα περισσεύητε μᾶλλον.
2 οἴδατε γὰρ τίνας παραγγελίας ἐδώκαμεν ὑμῖν
  διὰ τοῦ κυρίου ᾿Ιησοῦ.
3 τοῦτο γάρ ἐστιν { θέλημα τοῦ θεοῦ,
                 ὁ ἁγιασμὸς ὑμῶν,

ἀπέχεσθαι ὑμᾶς ἀπὸ τῆς πορνείας,
4 εἰδέναι ἕκαστον ὑμῶν τὸ ἑαυτοῦ σκεῦος κτᾶσθαι
        ἐν ἁγιασμῷ
        καὶ
        τιμῇ,
5 μὴ ἐν πάθει ἐπιθυμίας
καθάπερ καὶ τὰ ἔθνη
        τὰ μὴ εἰδότα τὸν θεόν,
6 τὸ μὴ ὑπερβαίνειν ⎫
  καὶ   ⎬ /.../ τὸν ἀδελφὸν αὐτοῦ,
  πλεονεκτεῖν ⎭
    ἐν τῷ πράγματι
διότι ἔκδικος κύριος περὶ πάντων τούτων,
    καθὼς καὶ προείπαμεν ὑμῖν
    καὶ
    διεμαρτυράμεθα.
7 οὐ γὰρ ἐκάλεσεν ἡμᾶς ὁ θεὸς
  ἐπὶ ἀκαθαρσίᾳ
  ἀλλ᾿ ἐν ἁγιασμῷ.
8 τοιγαροῦν ὁ ἀθετῶν { οὐκ ἄνθρωπον ἀθετεῖ
              ἀλλὰ τὸν θεὸν
τὸν καὶ διδόντα τὸ πνεῦμα αὐτοῦ τὸ ἅγιον εἰς ὑμᾶς.

174

1 Finally then, brothers,
We ask you
  and
exhort (you) in the Lord Jesus,
    that as you received
            from us (instruction)
        as to how you ought to walk
                and
            to please God,
        as indeed you do walk,

            so that you may excel even more.
2 For you know what instructions we gave you
            through the Lord Jesus.
        3 For this is { the will of God,
                       your sanctification,

that you abstain from fornication,
4 that each of you know how to possess his own vessel

              in sanctification
              and
              honor,
          5 not in passionate lust
                  like the heathen

                  who do not know God,

6 and that no one go beyond ⎤
              and   ⎬ his brother
          defraud ⎦
              in the matter
          because the Lord is the avenger in all these things,
                  as we already told you
                  and
                  solemnly warned you.
          7 For God has not called us
                  to impurity
                  but in sanctification.
          8 Therefore, he who rejects this { does not reject man
                                             but God

              who gives his Holy Spirit to you.

175

The Benefits of So Great a Salvation

I. Our Gifts in the New Birth (3–5)

A. A living hope

B. A sure inheritance

C. A finished salvation

II. Our Joy in the New Birth (6–9)
A. In spite of suffering

B. In a documented faith

C. In the second appearance of Christ

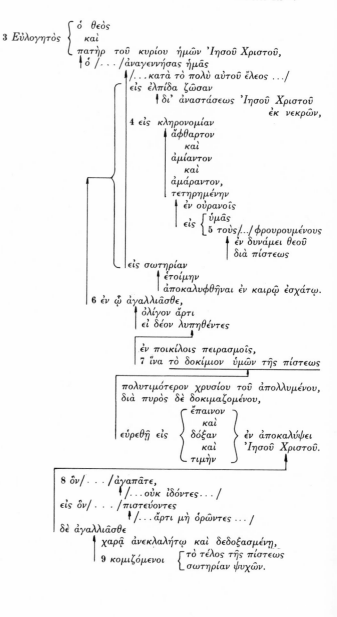

3 Εὐλογητὸς { ὁ θεὸς
καὶ
πατὴρ τοῦ κυρίου ἡμῶν Ἰησοῦ Χριστοῦ,
ὁ /. . ./ἀναγεννήσας ἡμᾶς
/. . .κατὰ τὸ πολὺ αὐτοῦ ἔλεος . . ./
εἰς ἐλπίδα ζῶσαν
δι᾽ ἀναστάσεως Ἰησοῦ Χριστοῦ
ἐκ νεκρῶν,
4 εἰς κληρονομίαν
ἄφθαρτον
καὶ
ἀμίαντον
καὶ
ἀμάραντον,
τετηρημένην
ἐν οὐρανοῖς
εἰς { ὑμᾶς
5 τοὺς/. . ./φρουρουμένους
ἐν δυνάμει θεοῦ
διὰ πίστεως
εἰς σωτηρίαν
ἑτοίμην
ἀποκαλυφθῆναι ἐν καιρῷ ἐσχάτῳ.
6 ἐν ᾧ ἀγαλλιᾶσθε,
ὀλίγον ἄρτι
εἰ δέον λυπηθέντες

ἐν ποικίλοις πειρασμοῖς,
7 ἵνα τὸ δοκίμιον ὑμῶν τῆς πίστεως

πολυτιμότερον χρυσίου τοῦ ἀπολλυμένου,
διὰ πυρὸς δὲ δοκιμαζομένου,
εὑρεθῇ εἰς { ἔπαινον
καὶ
δόξαν
καὶ
τιμὴν } ἐν ἀποκαλύψει
Ἰησοῦ Χριστοῦ.

8 ὃν/. . ./ἀγαπᾶτε,
/. . .οὐκ ἰδόντες. . ./
εἰς ὃν/. . ./πιστεύοντες
/. . .ἄρτι μὴ ὁρῶντες . . ./
δὲ ἀγαλλιᾶσθε
χαρᾷ ἀνεκλαλήτῳ καὶ δεδοξασμένῃ,
9 κομιζόμενοι { τὸ τέλος τῆς πίστεως
σωτηρίαν ψυχῶν.

3 Blessed be ⎰ the God
           ⎱ and
            Father of our Lord Jesus Christ,
       who/ . . . /having given us new birth
                 / . . . according to his great mercy . . . /
                 into a living hope
                      through the resurrection of Jesus Christ from the dead,

4   into an inheritance
                 (that is) incorruptible
                 and
                 undefiled
                 and
                 unfading,
               reserved
                 in heaven
               for ⎰ you
                     ⎱ 5 who are protected
                                 by God's power
                                 by faith
       for a salvation
               ready
              to be revealed in the last time.

6   In this you greatly rejoice,
             though now for a little while
             you may have been distressed

                by various trials,
              7 so that <u>the proof of your faith,</u>

               being more precious than perishable gold,
               even though tested by fire,
                           ⎧ praise ⎫
                           ⎪ and   ⎪
               may be found to result in ⎨ glory ⎬ at the revelation
                           ⎪ and   ⎪ of Jesus Christ;
                           ⎩ honor ⎭

8   whom/ . . . /you love
                   / . . . though not having seen . . . /
   and whom/ . . . /you believe
                     / . . . though you do not see him now . . . /
   and you greatly rejoice
              with an inexpressible and glorious joy,
             9 obtaining ⎰ the goal of your faith,
                          ⎱ the salvation of your souls.

How to Live Wisely

I. Make the Most of Time (16)

II. Understand the Will of the Lord (17)

III. Continue to Be Filled with the Holy Spirit (18–21)
A. By spiritual conversation (19a)

B. By spiritual songs (19b)

C. By continual thanksgiving (20)

D. By submitting to one another (21)

15 /.../ οὖν ἀκριβῶς
Βλέπετε /.../ πῶς περιπατεῖτε,
μὴ ὡς ἄσοφοι
ἀλλ' ὡς σοφοί,
16 ἐξαγοραζόμενοι τὸν καιρόν,
ὅτι αἱ ἡμέραι πονηραί εἰσιν.
17 διὰ τοῦτο
μὴ γίνεσθε ἄφρονες,
ἀλλὰ συνίετε τί τὸ θέλημα τοῦ κυρίου.
18 καὶ μὴ μεθύσκεσθε οἴνῳ,
ἐν ᾧ ἐστιν ἀσωτία,
ἀλλὰ πληροῦσθε ἐν πνεύματι,
19 λαλοῦντες ἑαυτοῖς
ψαλμοῖς
καὶ
ὕμνοις
καὶ
ᾠδαῖς πνευματικαῖς,
ᾄδοντες ⎫
καὶ ⎬ τῇ καρδίᾳ ὑμῶν τῷ κυρίῳ,
ψάλλοντες ⎭
20 εὐχαριστοῦντες
πάντοτε
ὑπὲρ πάντων
ἐν ὀνόματι τοῦ κυρίου ἡμῶν Ἰησοῦ
Χριστοῦ
τῷ θεῷ καὶ πατρί,
21 ὑποτασσόμενοι
ἀλλήλοις
ἐν φόβῳ Χριστοῦ.

15 Careful, then,
Watch how you walk,
　not as unwise men
　but as wise,
　　　16　making the most of every opportunity
　　　　　because the days are evil.
17　Therefore
　　do not be foolish,
　　but understand what the will of the Lord is.
　　18　And do not get drunk on wine,
　　　　　　for that is dissipation,
　　but be filled with the Spirit,
　　　　19　by speaking to one another
　　　　　　　in psalms
　　　　　　　　and
　　　　　　　hymns
　　　　　　　　and
　　　　　　　spiritual songs,
　　　　by singing
　　　　　and　　　} in your heart to the Lord,　·
　　　　making melody
　　　　20　by giving thanks
　　　　　　always
　　　　　　for all things
　　　　　　in the name of our Lord Jesus Christ
　　　　　　to God, even the Father.
　　21　And by submitting
　　　　　　to one another
　　　　　　in the fear of Christ.

I. Our Glorified Body (1)
  A. Is permanent
  B. Is on reserve
  C. Is in heaven
  D. Is made by God

II. Our Present Fears (2–5)
  A. Our "naked" state
    and yearning to be
    clothed
  B. Our "tent" state

C. Our down payment
  (the Spirit) on an
  eternal home

III. Our Present Confidence
  (6–10)

  A. Living by faith in
    God

  B. Living in the sight
    of God

  C. Living in a way
    pleasing to God

---

1 Οἴδαμεν γὰρ ὅτι
  ἐὰν ἡ ἐπίγειος ἡμῶν οἰκία τοῦ σκήνους καταλυθῇ,
  οἰκοδομὴν ἐκ θεοῦ ἔχομεν,
    οἰκίαν ἀχειροποίητον
    αἰώνιον ἐν τοῖς οὐρανοῖς.

2 καὶ γὰρ ἐν τούτῳ στενάζομεν,
    ... ἐπιποθοῦντες,
      ... ἐπενδύσασθαι   τὸ οἰκητήριον ἡμῶν
      3 εἴ γε καὶ   τὸ ἐξ οὐρανοῦ
      ἐνδυσάμενοι
        οὐ γυμνοὶ εὑρεθησόμεθα.

4 καὶ γὰρ οἱ ὄντες ἐν τῷ σκήνει στενάζομεν
      βαρούμενοι,
      ἐφ' ᾧ οὐ θέλομεν ἐκδύσασθαι
      ἀλλ'   ἐπενδύσασθαι,

ἵνα καταποθῇ τὸ θνητὸν ὑπὸ τῆς ζωῆς.
5 ὁ δὲ κατεργασάμενος ἡμᾶς
  εἰς αὐτὸ τοῦτο θεός,
    ὁ δοὺς ἡμῖν
    τὸν ἀρραβῶνα τοῦ πνεύματος.

6 Θαρροῦντες οὖν πάντοτε
  καὶ
  εἰδότες ὅτι
    ἐνδημοῦντες ἐν τῷ σώματι
    ἐκδημοῦμεν ἀπὸ τοῦ κυρίου.
      7 διὰ πίστεως γὰρ περιπατοῦμεν,
      οὐ διὰ εἴδους.
8 θαρροῦμεν δὲ
  καὶ
  εὐδοκοῦμεν μᾶλλον
    ἐκδημῆσαι ἐκ τοῦ σώματος
    καὶ
    ἐνδημῆσαι πρὸς τὸν κύριον.
9 διὸ καὶ φιλοτιμούμεθα,
      εἴτε
      ἐνδημοῦντες
      εἴτε   εὐάρεστοι αὐτῷ εἶναι.
      ἐκδημοῦντες,

10 τοὺς γὰρ πάντας ἡμᾶς φανερωθῆναι δεῖ
    ἔμπροσθεν τοῦ βήματος
      τοῦ Χριστοῦ,
    ἵνα κομίσηται ἕκαστος
      τὰ διὰ τοῦ σώματος
      πρὸς ἃ ἔπραξεν,
        εἴτε
        ἀγαθὸν
        εἴτε
        φαῦλον.

180

1 For we know that
    if the earthly tent which is our house is destroyed,
    we have a building from God,
         a house not made by hands,
         eternal in the heavens.
  2 For indeed in this we groan
           . . . longing
             . . . to be clothed   with our dwelling
                3 because   from heaven,
           being clothed
             we shall not be found naked.
  4 For indeed while we are in this tent, we groan
           being burdened,
              because we do not wish to be unclothed
              but   clothed,

         in order that what is mortal may be swallowed up by life.
        5 Now he who has made us
          for this very purpose is God,
             who gave us
               the Spirit as a pledge.
  6 Therefore, being always confident
            and
          knowing that
            while we are at home in the body
            we are away from the Lord—
                   7 For we walk by faith,
                   not by sight
  8 We are confident, I say,
        and
        prefer rather
          to be away from the body
            and
        at home with the Lord.
  9 Therefore also we have as our ambition,
              whether
          at home
            or   to be pleasing to him.
          absent
         10 For we must all appear
             before the judgment seat
               of Christ,
          so that each may be recompensed
             for the things done in the body
            according to what he has done
                  whether
            good
            or
          bad.

Part

Special Issues

Chapter **9**

The Use of Prophecy in Expository Preaching

One of the signs of a good minister, in the minds of many parishioners today, is that the proclaimer speaks a prophetic word to our generation. To speak prophetically, according to one contemporary usage, is to address the current ills and injustices of society from a courageous, if not also from a somewhat unpopular point of view when judged by those content with the status quo. Therefore, since the Old Testament prophets were known for some similar types of outspoken challenges in their day, they have emerged in modern times as the exemplars of all who would buck the system and speak forthrightly against the prevailing current of thought in society.

Frankly, there is more than a modicum of truth in this picture. The prophets were indeed revolutionaries of a sort,[1] yet they would hardly fit easily into all the modern equivalents of the roles that have been cast for them. For example, to name one huge disparity between those Biblical prophets and their aspiring mod-

1. See Edmond Jacob, "The Biblical Prophets: Revolutionaries or Conservatives?" trans. James H. Farley, Interpretation in Contemporary Theology, 5, *Interpretation* 19 (1965): 47–55.

ern counterparts, the Old Testament prophets did not make their primary appeal to the structures or institutions of their society, but to the individuals who made up those communities and institutions. What is more, the lever they proposed to cause a revolutionary turnabout was the Word of God itself rather than direct sociological tinkering or political agitation. Thus, the Old Testament prophets were revolutionaries who did indeed hate with a passion every form of oppression, injustice, and unrighteousness, but they viewed these ills as being mere symptoms of deeper spiritual problems which cried out for each individual to respond to the declared Word of God.

That the prophets addressed themselves primarily to individuals in their attempt to effect massive changes in society (whether those individuals were judges, other government officials, merchants, or clergy) gives us a clue as to how we might proclaim their message anew in our day. But simply to redirect their message to contemporary men and women is not sufficient in and of itself. It will not help the interpreter/proclaimer merely to state that there is some type of connection between the ancient and modern audience. If exegetical theology is worth anything, it must aid the student and pastor/teacher in bridging the gap between the original situation and the present-day audience.

Inadequate Approaches to Prophetic Texts

Perhaps the best way to proceed is to consider some inadequate ways of approaching the prophetic text. And, in order to stress the point that much of what are today classified as historical books in the Biblical canon (Joshua, Judges, Samuel, and Kings) can more rightfully be classified as prophetic books, we have chosen to deal with a passage from one of them. Indeed, that is the precise category in which they are placed in the Hebrew order of the canon: they comprise the Earlier Prophets while Isaiah, Jeremiah, Ezekiel, and the twelve minor prophets make up the Latter Prophets.

One of the best prophetic texts for illustrating both the difficulties of and the potential for preaching from the prophets deals with the life and ministry of Elijah (I Kings 17 to II Kings 2). And one of the most stimulating books I have read on the problems encountered when preaching on Elijah is a volume by G. Gerald Harrop. By comparing several typical messages on I Kings 21, Harrop has dramatically pointed out that most interpreters tend to approach that text with expectations already well in hand.[2] Worst of all, most interpreters have let their previous prejudices, education, and convictions shape the answers which they earnestly believe they have derived from the text by a methodologically commendable type of textual exposition.

Harrop's chapter on "how to get lost in Naboth's vineyard, and how to begin to find your way through"[3] led me to posit four separate types of *inadequate* exegetical-homiletical approaches to the prophetic texts. The labels and ideas are my own; Professor Harrop must not be thought to be in agreement with my assessments here even though his chapter was tremendously stimulating and of great heuristic value.

Prophetic Typological Preaching

The first inadequate model is "prophetic typological preaching." While there is a legitimate typology in Scripture where the exegete can point to textual clues that some person, event, or institution in the Old Testament illustrated in shadow form the full reality that was to come, that is not what is meant here. Perhaps it would be better to label this deficient approach "contemporary-typology preaching," for the modern situation controls both the shape and almost all of the content of the sermon. In the case of I Kings 21 with its tragic story of Jezebel's ruthless murder of Naboth and Ahab's subsequent appropriation of his vineyard, practitioners of typology preaching begin almost im-

2. G. Gerald Harrop, *Elijah Speaks Today: The Long Road into Naboth's Vineyard* (Nashville: Abingdon, 1975), p. 73.
3. Ibid., pp. 59–86 (chap. 4).

mediately decrying the Ahabs of our day: the exploiters of minority groups, of employees who are overworked and underpaid, and of pensioners who are trapped by the inflationary spirals of our time. Ahabs like these exploit and sap the earth and its inhabitants (the Naboths) until both have very little, if anything, left. The Ahabs do this only to give the stolen booty to the Jezebels of our day who are already living in ivory palaces.[4]

On the whole, this message certainly needs to be proclaimed if that is what the context is asserting. But is this the authoritative point of the writer of I Kings 21? What particular phrases, clauses, or sentences (taken in their own context) would indicate that this is the central message here? Furthermore, how has the paragraph sequence shaped this message? The passage seems to supply little more than two convenient labels for the villains of our time, namely, Ahab and Jezebel. But this is a reverse typology in which present situations reflect the past—an inversion of things, to say the least.

The proof that something is awry here is that the overwhelming bulk of this message focuses on a description of the current ills of society. But where is the divine proclamation in all of this? Where is the gospel note? Does this not replace the redemptive history of God as found in the Old and New Testaments with our own quest for socioeconomic wholeness?[5] To be sure, the call for action is often legitimate and proper; but it must be grounded in something more than merely applying old Biblical names to modern injustices.

Prophetic Action Preaching

A second model for preaching from the prophetic books focuses on what scholars refer to as prophetic actions. In shaping the message this method tends to use more of the text than merely

4. Ibid., pp. 64–65.
5. See the stirring indictment of this reversal of the order of proclaiming and doing (as found in the 1960s) in James Daane, *Preaching with Confidence: A Theological Essay on the Power of the Pulpit,* 2d ed. (Grand Rapids: Eerdmans, 1980), pp. 4–6.

a name or two which have come to stand for ideas or systems in both the past and contemporary culture. In this approach, the preacher notes that Ahab ruthlessly seized Naboth's vineyard and thus the interests of the state triumphed over the interests of the individual. To be sure, Ahab had earlier promised Naboth that he would give him "another and better vineyard" or "fair compensation," but the theme is unmistakable. It is the little man being swamped by the socialism and welfarism of modern democratic societies.[6]

Meanwhile, the text of Scripture still waits for an exposition. Again, the "message" briefly sketched here is hardly a word from God. What in it can be *proclaimed* and announced with the authority of God? As an editorial in a newspaper or an essay in a newsmagazine, this message would be very provocative and stimulating. But it cannot function as a proclamation of God's Word if the text does not explicitly set forth this principle.

In fact, there are aspects of this message that are indeed pertinent to and even border on what is discussed in I Kings 21. The informing theology that lies behind I Kings 21 is the doctrine of the sanctity of property as set forth in the Ten Commandments along with the teaching that, for Israel in particular, real estate and people were to be inseparable. Property could not be bought and sold; it had to remain in the family to whom God gave it since God is the ultimate owner of all the earth and its fulness (Lev. 25:23; Ps. 24:1). But "prophetic action preaching" has veered off course by linking *Ahab's* aggrandizement with *institutional* systems like socialism, welfarism, the New Deal, Fabianism, and big government in general. Elijah charged the man Ahab, not the philosophy, the system, or the program under which he was working. Furthermore, Elijah wanted Ahab to change and to repent; he would not have been satisfied with merely a reversal in the state's policy.

Once again, the exegesis has not gone far enough into the text. The preacher had too much mental baggage which he spread as a grid on top of the text to force it to carry his message. The best

6. Harrop, *Elijah Speaks Today,* pp. 67–68.

we can say for his use of I Kings 21 is that it provided an interesting illustration for his message. But he did not find in the passage at hand a Biblical context which specifically treats the principles he was expounding—and this a preacher must do if he wishes to borrow God's authority for what he is saying. The action of I Kings 21 occurs in a context that sets forth the divine perspective. True, since we are involved in Biblical narrative as well as prophetic materials, the principles will not necessarily be stated in explicit terms. Often they will need to be deduced from the *arrangement* of *all* the details of the prophetic narrative and from the *selection* of the facts included. But the action cannot be abstracted from the context of the surrounding prophetic narratives or from a consideration of all the details included in the story.

Prophetic Motto Preaching

A third form of prophetic preaching we would call "prophetic motto preaching." In a most delightful way, Harrop pictures how a conservative preacher might handle I Kings 21:7: "I [Jezebel] will give you the vineyard of Naboth the Jezreelite."[7] This is the only verse from this context which the preacher uses. It serves him as a motto and a springboard for a dozen or more texts from the Old and New Testaments aimed at women's liberation. If only Ahab had heeded the implicit warning in Genesis 3:17 ("Because you listened to the voice of your wife . . . I will curse the ground because of you"), all would have been well. But no, he and our society have refused to embrace God's order of things as spelled out in Ephesians 5:23. The comparison of several protagonists of the women's liberation movement with Jezebel would appear, to this preacher, to be a proper way to apply I Kings 21:7 and to give it poignant relevancy.

But did the writer of I Kings 21 intend this text to be an evaluation of the legitimate spheres of authority for women? And even if we should decide that I Kings 21:7 is the focal point and the central reference of the passage, we still must demonstrate how

7. Ibid., pp. 71–73.

the whole pericope of I Kings 21 is related to this alleged pivotal statement.

But we remain unconvinced. Why would the author put his key statement for interpreting the whole passage into the mouth of one of the villains of this story—especially since shortly thereafter a word from God is uttered by the prophet Elijah (I Kings 21:17–26)? We cannot help but feel that the wish was again parent to the thought: the message came first and then a motto was selected from the Scriptures. But this can never qualify either as legitimate exegesis or as a textual exposition of Scripture.

Motto preaching may please the masses in that it is filled with a lot of epigrammatic or proverbial slogans and interesting anecdotes, but it will always be a powerless word lacking the authority and validation of Scripture. It cannot compare with the full and honest proclamation of God's Word, for that kind of proclamation is attended by the confirming and convincing work of the Holy Spirit to the truthfulness of the Scriptures.

Prophetic Parable Preaching

The fourth model for preaching from the prophets is the method we would call "prophetic parable preaching." Instead of selecting a name, or a particularly interesting action, or a sentence from the text, this approach employs the whole text in that it devotes the first part of the message to telling the story of Naboth and his vineyard as it moves through its various episodes to the climactical tragedy of Naboth's death and Ahab's appropriation of his private property.

Midway through this type of message, a sudden shift immediately transports the listener to a present-day situation. Once again a story form is utilized. One episode after another is related until a similar concluding note of pathos and tragedy is struck. In brief, there is a "dynamic analogy"[8] in which there is an expressed comparison between the tensions in ancient Israel and the stresses in the present community. Note that this is an extended and ex-

8. The term is from James A. Sanders, *Torah and Canon* (Philadelphia: Fortress, 1972), p. xvi.

pressed comparison. By the development of a story one situation is shown to be like another situation.

Harrop constructs a contemporary parable based on I Kings 21.[9] It happened that the building program of an expanding university finally came into conflict with a widow's home and property. The administration and crooked town officials tried one scheme after another to dislodge this stubborn but gallant soul. "Is there no note of grace? Is evil and wrong forever to be enthroned?" asks the practitioner of this model. No, there are saving features. One college official spoke up in defense of this poor woman and came to her aid. Thus, Auschwitz, Jezreel, and oppression of the widow cannot be the last word. The last word may be found in "the inalienable rights of the least of these little ones who believe in the Lord in whose name we are gathered. Amen."[10]

Is that all? Are we to expect nothing else from I Kings 21? What validates the analogy we have drawn from this passage? Have we arrived at the conclusion and principles at which the writer who gave us this passage wanted us to arrive?

We do not think that this approach fulfills the demands of rigorous textual exposition any more than the three preceding methods did. The narrative is shorn from the prophetic word of judgment and promise that accompanies it in I Kings 21:17–29. True, on critical analysis some will feel that these judgments are not part and parcel of the original text and therefore are of no importance to an authentic hearing of this text. But that approach is likewise vulnerable in that it violates the canon of textual evidence, and the canon of taking the text on its own terms until there is sufficient contrary evidence (whether it come from legitimate literary, form-critical, or redaction-critical methods). However, most will agree that confidence in the integrity of the narrative in its present shape is more than justified by the evidence. Therefore, we must insist that no proclamation will suffice until it embraces the passage in its wholeness and until it brings the listener

9. Harrop, *Elijah Speaks Today,* pp. 145–48; see also pp. 87–129.
10. Ibid., p. 148.

to hear the prophetic words of judgment and hope with which the passage concludes. But here is where most pastors and teachers falter. These words seem so foreign to and distant from our day and needs. So that we may do effective textual exposition of such passages, we will now discuss basic principles for interpreting the prophets.

The Central Message of the Prophets

There is no royal road to legitimate exegesis or authentic textual exposition of any Biblical passage, much less that of the prophets. But homiletics, if it means anything at all, is the art and science of "saying the same" thing that the text of Scripture says (*homo*, "the same," and *lego*, "to speak or say"). And in the case of I Kings 21 we do find an example of one of the great principles for interpreting the prophets to modern audiences. Two alternatives are presented: blessing and judgment. Which of the two will come to pass depends on whether the hearers of that prophetic word in all ages repent in response to it.

This is true for both the individual and the believing community at large. Both are summoned to "repent," or, more simply put in its Hebrew idiom, to "turn" or "return" to the Lord. So prevalent was this message of the prophets that the prophet Zechariah was able to sum up in one sentence all the prophets who had preceded him: ". . . the earlier prophets proclaimed: Thus says the Lord of Hosts, Turn from your evil ways and doings" (Zech. 1:4).

Every message of judgment and hope had attached to it either an implied or expressed "unless" or "if you do [or do not] turn to me." This conditional aspect of prophecy is put into a formal principle in Jeremiah 18:7–10: "Whenever I announce that a nation or kingdom will be uprooted, torn down and destroyed, if that nation which I spoke against will repent of its evil, then I will relent and not bring on it the evil I had intended to bring. And whenever I announce that a nation or kingdom will be built up and established, if it does evil in my sight and does not obey me, then I will relent and not do good to it as I had intended to do."

Perhaps the best illustration of this conditional aspect which is found in almost all prophetic writings[11] is in the Book of Jonah. In fact, suspicion that God would indeed relent from His announced threat that He would destroy Nineveh in forty days should the Ninevites suddenly listen and turn from their evil ways led Jonah to abandon his prophetic calling and take a ship to Tarshish (4:2). When Jonah finally went to Nineveh to preach this word after being "down in the mouth" for a while, he had his worst fears confirmed. God relented after all and did not destroy Nineveh because men responded to Jonah's preaching.

What is true for nations is also true for individuals. This is demonstrated in the concluding section of I Kings 21. "When Ahab heard these words, he ripped open his clothes, put on sackcloth, fasted . . . and went about meekly [before the Lord]" (I Kings 21:27). Thereupon, God instructed Elijah to declare to this threatened sinner that the awful judgments which had been announced in I Kings 21:21–22 (without any notice of conditionality—in this case it was implicitly understood as it was in the Book of Jonah) would not be carried out on Ahab, but on his son.

Thus, even a temporary repentance (in I Kings 22 Ahab consults false prophets just before his death in a battle that a prophet of Yahweh had told him to abandon) brought God's word of hope and blessing to pass. And there are the intended theology and teaching of this passage. Amidst the gross evils of society, government, and institutions of our day, a healing process starts when individuals "turn" to God and "repent" of their sin.

This truth is put in a formal proposition in II Chronicles 7:14: "If my people, who are called by my name, will humble themselves and pray and seek my face and turn from their wicked way, then I will hear from heaven and forgive their sin and heal their land." Some feel that this is a promise totally reserved for Israel as a nation. But the text has included its own principlizing feature

11. Of course the Abrahamic–Davidic promise, the new covenant, and the promise of the new heavens and the new earth are totally unconditional. See Walter C. Kaiser, Jr., *Toward an Old Testament Theology* (Grand Rapids: Zondervan, 1978), pp. 231–34; see also pp. 93–94, 111, 130, 156–57.

for all times and ages—"my people, *who are called by my name*," that is, those "over whom I have called my name" and, therefore, whom I own. This will include all believing Gentiles as well as believing Jews. Notice also the promise to *heal the land* of God's people. A connection between people and the soil can be traced back to creation itself. The fortunes of men and the soil on which they lived were closely linked in that God made man from the dust of the ground. Furthermore, when mankind's representatives (Adam and Eve) fell, the dirt also was cursed and will remain so until the whole creation is redeemed when the Lord returns again with glory (Rom. 8:20–22).

The same theme is sounded by one prophet's message after another. Time after time the prophets decried the abuse and evil they witnessed in the state, the halls of justice, and society at large (whether in Israel or the Gentile nations surrounding them) and appealed to men and women to repent of these sins which were symptomatic of the fact that the hearts of the community were not right with God. And when men and women failed to respond to the word of God, out of His love God sent them one tragic event compounded on top of another to drive them back to Himself. Still, in many cases the people did not repent. Note that the refrain, "and yet you did not return unto me," is repeated five times in Amos 4:6–12.

The programmatic statements found in Leviticus 26 and Deuteronomy 28 are useful for interpreting all the prophets. Both of these chapters clearly lay down the alternative prospects: increased degrees of blessing or judgment.

Similar statements can be found at the end of the Old Testament as well. Haggai 1 called the generation of 520 B.C., as well as our own, to reflect on the significance of shortages in harvests and food supplies, spiraling costs, and inflation. It was (is) high time to repent.

Preaching from the prophets can have a great contemporary appeal if we emphasize repentance as the condition for experiencing the favor of God. Only if this call to repent is heeded will there be answers to many, if not all, of the ills of abused and downtrodden minorities, to injustices and unrighteous acts. And only then will men of high and low position experience the grace of God to which all are called.

By this time it will be obvious to the reader that the best way to arrive at and explain to contemporary audiences the central message in a prophetic passage is to use the method we have been advocating in this book. In other words, the best model for preaching from the prophets is that approach which proceeds by carefully observing the syntactical-theological constructions within the paragraphs or strophes of the various sections of the prophetic books.

Chapter 10

The Use of Narrative in Expository Preaching*

Nothing can be more discouraging and disheartening for contemporary believers gathered to hear the Word of God than to listen to a simple recounting or bare description of an Old Testament or Gospel narrative. This kind of preaching is nothing more than narrating a "B.C. story" or "first-century A.D. homily." This kind of preaching merely strings verses or events together. It does not attempt to come to terms with the truth taught by the writer in that narrative. It is, then, a poor excuse for expository preaching.

What is needed in preaching on such narrative portions is some method of pointing out the abiding meanings and continuing significance for all believers of all times. This method we have already designated the syntactical-theological method of exegesis, which employs the special technique of principlization. While the term *grammatico-historical exegesis* has had the honored place in exegetical procedure since 1788 when Karl A. G. Keil first coined it, we have felt that the results of that method could be

*Reprinted with changes from "The Use of Biblical Narrative in Expository Preaching," *Asbury Seminarian* 34 (1979): 14–26. Originally part of the Ryan Lectures given at Asbury Theological Seminary in September 1978, this material is used by permission.

sharpened even more by (1) stressing the *syntactical* relationships within the unit under discussion and (2) tracing the antecedent theology. Once these two features have been identified, the matter of principlizing then becomes most important in treating historical and narrative texts.

Principlizing a Biblical passage is, as we have argued in chapter 7, that procedure which seeks to discover the enduring ethical, spiritual, doctrinal, and moral truths or principles which the writer himself set forth by the way in which he selected his details and arranged the contextual setting of his narrative. Principlization seeks to bridge the "then" of the text's narrative with the "now" needs of our day; yet it refuses to settle for cheap and quick solutions which confuse our own personal point of view (good or bad) with that of the inspired writer.

The Abuse of Narrative

Examples of confused and subjectivistic exegesis are all too plentiful. Consider the message from II Kings 4:1–7, which tells of the seminarian's widow who realized that she was now unable to meet her numerous debts—perhaps tuition bills! You will remember that the prophet Elisha instructed her first to gather all the empty vessels she could borrow from her neighbors. Then she was to shut the door of her house and begin to fill them all from what was left in the jar of oil she owned. The text records that the oil did not stop—it did not stop until the last vessel was filled. Now a message I once heard on this passage stressed the point that to the degree that we are in a condition of being empty of self, the Holy Spirit is accordingly enabled to fill us with Himself. Further, since oil is *always* [!] a symbol of the Holy Spirit, it should be noticed that the flow of the Holy Spirit was not stopped until the last empty vessel was filled.

As I left that service, I overheard a few people who might be described as "certain . . . fellows of the baser sort" (cf. Acts 17:5, KJV) complain, "Humph, the speaker never finished his text, for the woman was told in verse 7 to go out and sell the Holy Spirit and pay her debts." Though the attitude of these complainers left something to be desired, their point was well made. Indeed, it is the author's prerogative to tell us what he wants to say before we attach a significance of our own to his text. Such a subjective use of narrative must fall into the category of spiritualizing rather than exegeting a text.

Another improper use of Old Testament narrative material can be seen in Origen's work on Exodus 1:22–2:10. With bold strokes he proclaimed that Pharaoh, the king of Egypt, represented the devil while the male and female children of the Hebrews represented the rational and animal faculties of mankind. Pharaoh wished to destroy all the males, that is, the seeds of rationality and spiritual science through which the soul tends to and seeks heavenly things. However, he wished to preserve all the females alive, that is, all those animal propensities of man, through which he becomes carnal and devilish. Thus, wherever men live in luxury, banquetings, pleasures, and sensual gratifications, one can be assured that there the king of Egypt has slain all the males and preserved all the females alive.

This silliness can be carried one step further. Pharaoh's daughter might represent the Church which was gathered from among the Gentiles. Although she had an impious and iniquitous father, the psalmist said of her, "Harken, O daughter, and consider, incline thine ear; forget also thine own people, and thy father's house; so shall the king greatly desire thy beauty" (Ps. 45:10–11). Her coming to the waters to bathe was tantamount to coming to the baptismal font that she might be washed from the sins which she had contracted in her father's house. But this has gone far enough. Wouldn't Moses have been thrilled if he had known how much was going on when he wrote the narrative?

Many may argue, "But this type of approach affords us such a real blessing! Isn't it important to get something out of a text? What is more, shouldn't the Church and our spiritual lives be at the center of our preaching and teaching?"

Of course I agree, but the point of our message must be derived directly from the text being examined. How is it, then, that many are blessed by an allegorical message reminiscent of Origen? The answer is that they are being taught a truth of God which occurs somewhere in the Scripture, but their finger is on the wrong text. Therefore, I would have to conclude with this assessment of the situation: "good" for the blessing, but "poor" for the text selected.

Then there is the extreme of that dry, detached, and boring recital which makes the greatest ado about the most insignificant nothingness. A hilarious tongue-in-cheek sample of this type of scholarship has come to my attention. It is an exegesis of "Jack and Jill" allegedly published in the *Altschriften für Allgemeinschaftliche Bibelforschungen:*

> Verse 1: "Jack and Jill went up the hill, to fetch a pail of water."
>
> The word "and" presents some difficulties which are not apparent to the casual reader. There is considerable doubt in the minds of most scholars as to whether Jack was actually accompanied by Jill in the sense that the phrase is intended to record an historical event.
>
> In the setting out upon this expedition, which was apparently undertaken for a specific purpose, or, at least, with some definite object in mind, it seems likely that Jack was stimulated to undertake this mission by a basic need for water. Since most functions in the home involving water, such as cooking, washing clothes, scrubbing floors, etc., are normally undertaken by the distaff side, it is widely held that the force of "and" in this context probably means that Jack set out with a strong picture image of Jill in his mind, and several existentialist scholars also insist that her parting words were undoubtedly ringing in his ears.
>
> Grosskopf, in his monumental essay entitled *Jackmitjilldamrotarung,* takes a contrary view. He dates this passage considerably earlier than is generally believed (somewhere between 404 B.C. and the 19th Amendment). On this basis he maintains that the hewing of wood and the drawing of water were exclusively carried on by women at this period, and that the words "Jack and" are a gloss by some later copyist, and did not appear in the original manuscript.
>
> "Went up the hill" is obviously allegorical. The ancients, although probably ignorant of Otis' First Law of Elevation ("what goes up must come down"), were well aware that the transfer of water by artificial means normally involves transportation from

an inferior to a superior position (cf. "The Old Oaken Bucket," "Down by the Old Mill Stream," etc.). Professor Gard de l'Eau, the distinguished hydrographer and mystic, suggests that this anabasis symbolizes man's struggle to rise nearer to ultimate unity with the cosmic. The water, he continues, has precisely the same symbolism as the crossing of the Red Sea, the Jordan, Lindbergh's trip across the Atlantic, and the landing on Omaha Beach in World War II, with which everyone is familiar.[1]

That is enough of this method. If it were not so sad, we could laugh until we cried over such examples of handling Scripture in the name of serious scholarship. It is all too common, even in evangelical circles.

Now there must be an alternative to allegorical spiritualizing and the so-called scholarly, dry-bones-history-and-grammar approach. In contemporary preaching and teaching, no portion of Scripture is more vulnerable to both forms of abuse than is the Old Testament. With no less than 77 percent of God's total revelation at stake,[2] the Old Testament continues to receive very little attention (and what little there is, is very poor) even from its friends, who rightfully protest when any attempt is made to denigrate that Testament. Why do so many pastors admit to having a mental block, feelings of inadequacy, or plain guilt when it comes to preaching the Old Testament?

Very little profit will come from attempting to fix the blame on one factor or another. We all have our own impressions and guesses: shortage of preparation time; topical, theological, and even so-called expository sermons which are jacks of all the texts on the subject and master of none; an exaggerated view of the discontinuity between the Testaments; or just plain old-fashioned laziness. Meanwhile, the crisis in evangelical practice grows to dangerous proportions—dangerous because the generation of interpreters that follows ours will level out their doctrine of Scrip-

1. A student shared with me an abstract of this literary spoof some years ago, but he neglected to note the source from which it had been taken. I have not been successful in obtaining documentation for it.

2. The figure is from Carl Graesser, Jr., "Preaching from the Old Testament," p. 525.

ture to match our exegetical practice, and dangerous also because an enormous famine of the Word of God continues to exist in most evangelical churches. We have talked *about* the Word of God without loosing that Word itself so that the power of God can be demonstrated to all.

All sorts of "shortcuts" and "innovative ideas" are being introduced as substitutes for proclamation of the Word of God. These substitutes include relational theology, transactional therapy, fellowship groups, "what-do-you-think" (pooled ignorance) Bible study groups, topical seminars, and just plain Christian entertainment in music, films, and variety programs. Some of these (in their most wholesome form) may have a function in the body of Christ, but never as substitutes for the declaration of the Word of God! The formula of the Reformation epitomized in I Thessalonians 1:5 still holds: The Word of God plus the convicting work of the Holy Spirit equals dynamite, the power of God and full conviction of men and women.

The Problem of the "Then" and the "Now"

The jump from the "then" of the original text to the "now" of the modern audience has received so little attention in our evangelical training centers and pulpit practice that our best efforts are being crippled. Even what little use is made of the Old Testament narrative in our preaching is questionable in its effectiveness or authority status as a word from the Lord since we cannot or do not leave enough time for the "priesthood of believers" in the pews to decide Biblically whether the assertions made on a given topic are indeed precisely those affirmed by the writer of Scripture.

Our generation is being called upon to test in practice whether the Reformers' principle of *sola Scriptura* is sufficient for a vital, living encounter with our God. Is the Holy Scripture—all of it— the *exclusive* guarantee of the validity and divine authority of the Gospel, of the fulness of the whole counsel of God, of the relevancy of the churches' ministries to men's needs? Or, reminiscent of the past history of the Church, is there a new "tradition" vying for recognition equal to that of Scripture? Is not this new tradition the basis, as C. Trimp concluded in a recent article, for the new growing consensus between the two nonevangelical branches of Christendom?[3] As this consensus would have it, in the sermonic "re-presentation" (the preached word itself) the truth is once again actualized, but apart from its "then" meaning in the text. But if that is true, is it not the same as the claim made by the Roman Church that Christ is actually sacrificed again each Sunday during the celebration of the Lord's Supper?

At what a high price is the problem of the "then" of the Old Testament text solved by the "now" of this *sacramental* view of preaching! Certainly, such modern liberal and neo-orthodox methods successfully avoid the deadening effects of a dry, antique, purely descriptive recital of facts. But such methods have thereby also forfeited the right to claim any *divine authority* for their message since the tradition or preached word is of man's own making and not another revelation equal to Scripture. If it is *man* who has made his message "relevant" apart from what God meant, *man* must also vouch for its authenticity as a divine perspective—all of which is an impossible feat unless those who are delivering the message happen to be the very ones who were prepared by God to stand in the councils of eternity to receive such authentication.

If the dry, detached, so-called scholarly method is Ebionite in that it wrestles only with the historical or earthly aspects of the message, then "re-presentation" or the sacramental view is basically Docetic in that it rejects all historical connections and it isolates the Word from its contextual events into some kind of new "Word-event" of preaching.[4] In that case, every preacher is inspired for thirty minutes each Sunday!

3. C. Trimp, "The Relevance of Preaching (in the Light of the Reformation's 'Sola Scriptura' Principle)," esp. pp. 6–9.

4. The Ebionite heresy accepted the human phenomena about Jesus but rejected any and all supernatural claims. Daniel Lys applies the term *Ebionite* to a "lazy explanation of the text" that stops after it has explained its background, rationale, and purpose. *The Meaning of the Old Testament: An Essay on Hermeneutics,* pp. 38, 150. *Docetism* stressed Christ's divinity but wrongly argued that Jesus did not come in the flesh, that He only *appeared* to be a man. See ibid., pp. 42, 151.

But we must still ask: how *can* the historical distance between the original audience of the Word and later generations be bridged? How *can* the sermon be protected from our superficial analyses of what we consider to be the "human situation" or from our "favorite ideas"? Are there some "bloodless abstractions" to be found in some type of "canon within the canon"? Or are there "sets of rules" for isolating the timeless, rational, moral, and theological truths from the rest of the text?

At this point evangelicals are tempted to appeal to a heretical "double-author theory" as a basis for seeing a dual or even multiple meaning in the text. Support for this is alleged from the so-called double meaning of prophecy and a "dual logic theory" which finds the way in which Old Testament personalities (the prophets and the unbelievers they addressed) understood certain messages to be distinctly separate from the meaning God intended for the Church.

Such bifurcation has been tried historically at Alexandria, Egypt, in the second to fourth centuries A.D. and currently in the neo-orthodox existential separation between what the text *meant* and what it *means* to me.[5] Each has had disastrous effects. Instead of glorifying God and exulting the *sola Scriptura* principle, as one might assume, this bifurcation deprecates the original work of the Holy Spirit and tends to stumble at the same point that offended the Greeks: the scandal of the historical note in Scripture and its particularity which linked its message to specific men in specific times and specific situations.

What, then, is the key? If the older historico-grammatical exegesis as practiced by our Biblical departments has left incomplete the job of preparing a text for preaching (especially Old Testament and first-century A.D. narrative texts) and many of the current "gap fillers" fall into Ebionite, Docetic, or bifurcational errors—what is left?

---

5. For the most famous expression of the distinction between what the text meant and what it means to us, see Krister Stendahl, "Biblical Theology, Contemporary," in *The Interpreter's Dictionary of the Bible: An Illustrated Encyclopedia,* ed. George Arthur Buttrick and Keith Crim, 5 vols. (Nashville: Abingdon, 1962–1976), 1:418–32.

Good preaching has a twofold job: it must teach the *content* of truth as set forth in each passage and it must also suggest a *reproducible method* of Bible study. That is why, unlike allegorizing or spiritualizing, the method of principlizing seeks to derive its teachings from a careful understanding of the text. Rather than importing an external meaning into the Bible (this includes prematurely using the analogy of subsequent doctrines and assigning these new meanings to the details of the earlier narrative, meanings which were not in the mind of the original author), we must receive only those meanings authoritatively stated by the authors themselves.[6]

The Author's Arrangement and Selection of Material

The unique aspect of the narrative portions of Scripture is that the writer usually allows the words and actions of the people in his narrative to convey the main thrust of his message. Thus, instead of addressing us through direct statements, such as are found in doctrinal or teaching portions of Scripture, the writer tends to remain instead somewhat in the background as far as direct teaching or evaluative statements are concerned. Consequently, it becomes critically important to recognize the larger context in which the narrative fits and to ask why the writer used the specific selection of events in the precise sequence in which he placed them. The twin clues to meaning now will be *arrangement* of episodes and *selection* of detail from a welter of possible speeches, persons, or episodes. Furthermore, the divine reaction to and estimate of these people and events must often be determined from the way the author allows one person or a group of people to respond at the *climax* of the selected sequence of events; that is, if he has not interrupted the narration to give his own (in this instance, God's) estimate of what has taken place.

6. On the distinction between the analogy of faith and the analogy of antecedent Scripture, see Walter C. Kaiser, Jr., *Toward an Old Testament Theology* (Grand Rapids: Zondervan, 1978), pp. 18–19; idem, "The Present State of Old Testament Studies," *Journal of the Evangelical Theological Society* 18 (1975): 73–74 and notes 11 and 12.

One clear example of the importance of studying the *arrangement* and *selection* of detail can be seen in the Book of Nehemiah.[7] Nehemiah recorded what God had done for Israel at a
crucial moment in their history after the exile.

Now one method of preaching on Nehemiah would be merely
to tell the story and to feel that all responsibility for edification
and teaching ends when all the historical events, characters, and
speeches have been dutifully trotted out. But this can hardly en-
compass the total purpose why God had this history recorded for
posterity.[8] This is an Ebionite approach to Bible study and
preaching.

But will a Docetic approach to Nehemiah be any better? It
attempts to increase the spiritual value of this book by what
amounts to an allegorization of the text. For example, one might
approach the description of the rebuilding of the ten gates in Nehemiah 3:1–32 in this fashion: (1) the Sheep Gate is a reminder
of the cross and the Lamb of God; (2) the Fish Gate symbolizes
our Lord's promise to make us "fishers of men"; (3) the Old Gate
reminds us that subjection to the will of God involves using the
ancient and tried paths (Jer. 6:16); (4) the Valley Gate is a reminder to be humble (Ps. 84:6—the allusion is to the Valley of
Baca, which means "weeping"); (5) the Dung Gate brings to mind
our need for cleansing from defilement (I John 1:7–9); and so on.
But where is one's authority for all this? If it is argued, and it will
be, that there is no need for fuss because all these truths are
taught elsewhere in the Bible, then let us go to those passages to
teach those truths. Again, we may be teaching good theology, but
obviously it is from the wrong text and therefore devoid of any
power or authority from God.

Then how shall we preach from Nehemiah? As an example of
principlizing a Biblical narrative text, a series of messages on the

7. For a recent and suggestive study on Nehemiah, see Cyril J. Barber, *Nehemiah
and the Dynamics of Effective Leadership* (Neptune, N.J.: Loizeaux, 1976).

8. On the problem of past particularity and present significance, see the early contribution of Patrick Fairbairn, "The Historical Element in God's Revelation," in *Classical Evangelical Essays in Old Testament Interpretation,* ed. Walter C. Kaiser, Jr. (Grand
Rapids: Baker, 1972), pp. 72–79.

following topics would cover the teachings which the writer under the Spirit of God wanted to inculcate in all believers:

I. The Primacy of Prayer in Any Undertaking in Life (Neh. 1).
II. The Significance of Setting Goals (Neh. 2).
III. The Principles of Successful Leadership (Neh. 3).
IV. The Way to Meet Opposition to God's Work (Neh. 4–6).
V. The Way to Encourage Spiritual Renewal (Neh. 8).
VI. The Importance of Learning from History (Neh. 9).
VII. The Necessity of Preserving the Gains Made in the Work of God (Neh. 10–13).

Especially instructive is Nehemiah 6. It provides a great study on how godly men handle personal attacks while attempting a ministry for God. Nehemiah 4 had depicted how open violence was an obstruction to the work of God. Nehemiah 5 focused on the need to deal with internal problems if the work of God was not to be damaged. The attack on God's work in Nehemiah 6 was from an even more subtle angle. This time the enemy resorted to attempting to ruin God's leader through devious tricks.

The four paragraphs of Nehemiah 6 help form the basis for the four major points of our message. Note especially the repetition of similar phrases such as "let us meet together" (Neh. 6:2, 7, 10) and "to make me afraid" (Neh. 6:9, 13, 14, 19). The means by which the enemies of God's work secretly attempted to counter God's servant were: (1) deceptive calls for a conference at which they really intended to harm him (6:1–4); (2) smear tactics (6:5–9); (3) attempts to force Nehemiah into religious compromise (6:10–14); and (4) the pressure of naive friends (6:15–19).

Within each of these four paragraphs the writer recorded a key statement which suggests one of God's abiding helps for Nehemiah and for all subsequent leaders who find themselves hard pressed:

I. "I am doing a great work and I cannot come" (6:3).
II. "Nothing you are saying is true. . . . But now, O God, strengthen thou my hands" (6:8–9).

III. "Then I knew that God had not sent him" (6:12).
IV. "They perceived this work had been accomplished by the help of our God" (6:16).

We are now ready to construct our sermon. God's leaders, we shall proclaim, may use the following God-given helps when they are harassed by intrigue, innuendo, and intimidation.

I. A God-given Sense of Direction (6:1–4).
II. A God-given Spirit of Determination (6:5–9).
III. A God-given Heart of Discernment (6:10–14).
IV. A God-given Demonstration of Approval (6:15–19).

The climactic assertion of verse 16 is clear as to the theology of the passage: the enemy knew that Nehemiah was doing the work of God, for they perceived that what had been accomplished in the rebuilding of the wall had been accomplished only with the help of God. Why, then, should Nehemiah ever fear them? This verse is the "hinge" of the passage and what we would call the "central point of reference" which gives us perspective on the writer's *selection* of incidents. That the incidents in this chapter were selected from among many is made clear in 6:4–5 (there were four other such invitations), 6:14 (other false prophets came with similar so-called revelations), and 6:17 (there were many such letters). Moreover, the *arrangement* of these details not only reflects the chronological order of events, but also the increasing need for spiritual discernment as the enemy even dared to use prophets and friends to defeat the work of God. When chapter 6 is viewed alongside similar materials in chapters 4 and 5, it is clear that the sequence of attacks in chapter 6 is not recorded haphazardly. The climactic assertion of verse 16 offers us the clues we need in determining the authoritative message and use of this passage. The interpreter is now in a better position to suggest possible applications of this message in different areas of our modern world where some of these same tensions arise.

The Theology of the Passage

But there is more: there is also the question of the theology of the passage. What doctrinal aspect of the chapter should the preacher stress to the congregation if the result is to be personal response and growth?

The answer is: the preacher must stress that theology which the writer of Nehemiah 6 explicitly or implicitly had in mind. This theology may be found in quotations from Biblical authors whose writings were available to the writer and audience at that time. It might also be ascertained from the author's special use of words and concepts which had by that time taken on technical status, or from historical events which were an inseparable part of the continuum of God's dealings with Israel and through her with all the nations of the earth. In Nehemiah 6 the theology appears first in a negative form: the slur made by Geshem and Sanballat that Nehemiah had messianic pretensions of becoming a king in Judah (vv. 6–7). But it is also set forth positively in the very work of rebuilding the walls, which was no isolated act of diligence or heroism, but the work of God (v. 16) for Israel and, as such, another piece of God's great plan for history, eternity, Israel and the nations. There is an accumulation here of *antecedent* doctrine (that is, doctrine which had been set forth in books which preceded Nehemiah) about the land and Israel's role as a servant and light to the nations—yes, even to Geshem, Sanballat, and Tobiah themselves. It is the interpreter's duty to examine thoroughly the relationship between this antecedent doctrine and the author's truth-intention.

We propose that preaching on narrative passages will again become effective if: (1) it is *contextually* limited or narrowed in its focus, and careful attention is paid to the sequence of the passage within the book or sections of the book; (2) it is strictly developed according to the *syntactical relationships* observed within the statements of the limited passage being examined; (3) it discloses the part that the *theology which historically preceded* had in "informing" this text within the historical-redemptive plan of God; and (4) it is composed of *timeless principles* drawn solely from the Biblical author's single truth-intention. All four steps must be in evidence; otherwise, either the "then" will overcome the "now," or the "now" will obliterate the significance of the "then" of the text.

Accordingly, the exegete must first come to terms with the Biblical author. Since we know not a syllable from God except through the pens of those who stood in His divine council, we first must go to the human author's words. To find God's meanings and emphases, we must discover what the author's were[9]—first in the book as a whole and then in the particular section and passage we wish to use for our messages.

9. This point has been argued elsewhere: Walter C. Kaiser, Jr., "The Single Intent of Scripture"; and idem, "Legitimate Hermeneutics," in *Inerrancy,* ed. Norman L. Geisler (Grand Rapids: Zondervan, 1980), pp. 117–47.

Chapter **11**

The Use of Poetry in Expository Preaching

The modern era of the study of Biblical poetry commenced in A.D. 1753 with Robert Lowth's magisterial work.[1] Yet the analysis of Biblical poetry still languishes. Part of the problem, concludes Stephen A. Geller, is our failure to distinguish between different aspects of parallelism such as the two *types* of parallelism, namely, semantic parallelism of *meaning* and grammatical parallelism of *form*.[2] Being aware of this distinction is of critical importance because most scholars regard semantic parallelism as the chief feature of Biblical poetry.

Another problem has been the almost fruitless search for some workable formula for meter similar to that of classical literatures. But, alas, no one can convince anyone else as to what that formula should be. Furthermore, even if we could work out a formula, it would no doubt be of marginal significance. Hence we

---

1. Robert Lowth, *Lectures on the Sacred Poetry of the Hebrews.* This is a translation of *De sacra poesi hebraeorum praelectiones academicae* (Oxford: Clarendon, 1753).

2. Stephen A. Geller, *Parallelism in Early Biblical Poetry,* pp. 375–76. Geller goes on to attempt to assign *degrees* of parallelism in a somewhat artificial hierarchical classification of semantic grades. He also mentions *rhetorical* relationships.

will not even trouble the exegete with the impressive speculations which have been made on the subject.

The greatest roadblock to poetical analyses is the vague category which Bishop Lowth called "synthetic parallelism." Unlike the firmly secure categories of "synonymous parallelism" and "antithetic parallelism," synthetic parallelism has always been a problem since Lowth introduced this nomenclature. Exegetes experience such frustration in this one category, which covers more couplets than do the other two categories together, that they begin to distrust the whole approach. This difficulty can be overcome. But before we get into that, let us set out an orderly method of treating poetical texts.

The Distinctive Features of Hebrew Poetry

Despite the wealth of classical poetic form in Greek and Latin sources, most translators and exegetes of the Hebrew Bible continued to be oblivious to the poetic form in the Old Testament. A few medieval commentators such as Ibn Ezra and David Kimchi recognized that a few passages are in a parallel form. But this observation was not applied very widely at all. For this advance, we had to wait until 1753, when Lowth noted that parallelism is the chief characteristic of Biblical Hebrew poetic style.

The definition Lowth supplied has never been superseded: "The correspondence of one verse or line with another, I call parallelism. When a proposition is delivered, and a second is subjoined to it, or drawn under it, equivalent, or contrasted with it in sense, or similar to it in the form of grammatical construction, these I call parallel lines; and the words or phrases, answering one to another in the corresponding lines, parallel terms."[3] From Lowth's day to this, it has never been seriously questioned that parallelism, as he defined it, is the dominant stylistic feature of poetry in the Old Testament.[4]

---

3. Robert Lowth, *Isaiah: A New Translation, with a Preliminary Dissertation and Notes, Critical, Philological, and Explanatory*, 10th ed. (Boston: Peirce, 1834), p. ix.
4. For a review of some of the more important contributions to the study of Hebrew poetry since Lowth, see the survey in T. H. Robinson, "Hebrew Poetic Form: The English Tradition."

The only major development in this field since the 1930s has come with the recent decipherment of the texts from Ugarit. These poetic texts, which date from the fourteenth and thirteenth centuries B.C., were written in a language and a style much like the poetry of Biblical Hebrew. Features of the type of parallelism that they exhibit are virtually identical with many of the features of Old Testament poetry.

The find at Ugarit also had the effect of helping us to isolate and identify another distinctive feature of Hebrew poetry. We discovered that both literatures have several hundred "pairs" of words that appear in a fixed parallel relationship to each other. These conventionally linked pairs of words are balanced off against each other in such a way that the "A" word appears in the "A" line and the parallel "B" word appears in the "B" line. The recognition of "parallel pairs" immeasurably aids our ability to interpret Hebrew poetry.[5] The latest analysis of Ugaritic and Hebrew texts indicates there are some seven hundred pairs of these words. While the order in which these words appear is not always fixed in a rigid sequence, that literally hundreds of words do occur in parallel pairs is now very clear.[6]

Besides the presence of parallelism and parallel pairs of words, Hebrew poetry may also be identified by the absence, or very sparse use, of several grammatical features. Generally speaking, Hebrew poetry avoids: (1) the use of the definite article; (2) the sign of the accusative case (Hebrew אֵת or אֶת—the *nota accusativi*); (3) the conjunction ו (ordinarily translated as "and"); (4) the so-called relative pronoun (Hebrew אֲשֶׁר, "which, who, that") and (5) the consecutive or conversive forms of the verb (such as

5. For a further discussion of parallel pairs, see the brief reference to them in H. L. Ginsburg, "The Rebellion and Death of Ba'lu," *Orientalia* 5 (1936): 171–72; and the magisterial chapter by Mitchell Dahood, "Ugaritic-Hebrew Parallel Pairs," in *Ras Shamra Parallels: The Texts from Ugarit and the Hebrew Bible*, 2 vols. to date, ed. Loren R. Fisher, Analecta orientalia: commentationes scientificae de rebus Orientis antiqui, 49 (Rome: Pontifical Biblical Institute, 1972–), 1:73–382.

6. Besides the 624 parallel pairs listed by Mitchell Dahood in "Ugaritic-Hebrew Parallel Pairs," see his 66 additions in *Ras Shamra Parallels*, ed. Fisher, 2:3–39; and idem, *Psalms*, 3 vols., The Anchor Bible, ed. William Foxwell Albright and David Noel Freedman (Garden City, N.Y.: Doubleday, 1966–1970), 3:445–56. That gives a total of 690 parallel pairs in Ugaritic and Hebrew.

the waw-conversive with the imperfect which gives the narrative past tense; e.g., Hebrew וַיֹּאמֶר, "And he said"). This is not to say that these forms will *never* be found in poetry, but they will appear only rarely, whereas they can be found almost anywhere in a Hebrew prose text. Thus Hebrew poetry does have some very distinctive marks. The exegete may not label a text as poetical merely for reasons of convenience, aesthetics, or apologetics.

The first step that the exegete must make when he suspects a passage may be poetical is to determine if it is indeed poetry. The Revised Standard Version of 1952 was the first English translation to cast all the poetic passages in the Old Testament in the distinctive stichometric format. Prior to that time, only the poetic books of the Old Testament had been given this distinctive form. Now nearly all of the editions and translations of the Hebrew text attempt to indicate in some manner the presence of a poetical format. This does not mean that these decisions must be accepted as final and canonized by the exegete. The tests suggested above should still be run.

The Strophe in Hebrew Poetry

The question of whether it is possible to group lines of Hebrew poetry into stanzas or strophes was stimulated by the work of Friedrich B. Köster in 1831.[7] While some scholars remained skeptical, it is plain from the existence of acrostic poems such as Psalm 119 that such an arrangement is not only possible, but actually required. Hence, what the paragraph is to the exegete of prose, the strophe is to the exegete of poetry.

One of the most prominent devices used for marking off strophes is the presence of refrains. Just as Ugaritic poetry has exhibited the strophic structure by the use of refrains, so have some eigh-

---

7. Friedrich B. Köster, "Die Strophe, oder der Parallelismus der Verse der hebräischen Poesie," *Theologische Studien und Kritiken* 4 (1831): 40–114. See more recently Kemper Fullerton, "The Strophe in Hebrew Poetry and Psalm 29," *Journal of Biblical Literature* 48 (1929): 274–90; and Charles Franklin Kraft, "Some Further Observations Concerning the Strophic Structure of Hebrew Poetry."

teen Psalms (Pss. 39, 42–43, 44, 46, 49, 56, 57, 59, 62, 67, 78, 80, 99, 107, 114, 136, 144, 145). And there are examples from the prophets, such as Isaiah 5, 9–10, and Amos 1, 2, 4. Thus in Psalm 46 verses 7 and 11 have this refrain:

> The Lord of hosts is with us,
> The God of Jacob is our refuge.

An even more elaborate example is the thrice-repeated refrain in Psalm 42:5, 11; 43:5:

> Why are you cast down, O my soul,
> and why are you troubled within me?
> Hope in God; for I shall again praise him,
> my Help and my God.

Isaiah 9:8–10:4 is divided off into strophes by four appearances of the refrain (9:12, 17, 21; 10:4):

> For all this his anger is not turned away
> And his hand is stretched out still.

In addition to the recurring refrain, the Hebrew word סֶלָה is frequently used to mark the end of a strophe. *Selah* occurs seventy-one times in thirty-nine Psalms as well as in Habakkuk 3:3, 9, 13. The problem with suggesting this unusual word as a strophe divider is that we are still uncertain as to what the word means. Furthermore, the word *Selah* occurs in some of the titles of the Psalms, which many have understood to be musical instructions. However, if the meaning of *Selah* is "to raise," as some have conjectured, then the idea that it is a musical notation and a general strophe marker may not be incorrect, since a "lifting up" of voices or a crescendo of instruments might well come at the end of some line of thought in the poetry, namely, at the end of a strophe. It would be unfair, therefore, to rule it out completely as a strophe divider, for the appearance of this term, at what would otherwise be awkward places, must function in some of these cases to mark the end of a strophe. Nevertheless, *Selah* must be used with very great caution as an indication of a strophe division.

A third, but much surer aid is the alphabetic acrostic scheme as found in Psalms 9–10, 25, 34, 37, 111, 112, 119, 145, and Lamentations 1–4. In this arrangement the first word of the initial stanza commences with the first letter of the Hebrew alphabet, the first word of the second stanza with the second letter of the alphabet, and so on. In a few cases every line in the same strophe begins with the same letter. That these poetic lines were intentionally grouped into one strophe cannot be denied.

Charles Franklin Kraft has a number of additional criteria for determining strophes: (1) notable changes in rhythm or length of lines (shortening or lengthening the final line of a strophe); (2) repeated catchwords (such as the reiterated call "Yahweh" and the use of introductory or closing formulae such as "Thus says the Lord" or "Says the Lord"); and (3) chiasmus or "introverted parallelism" (e.g., a four-line strophe is so arranged that the first and fourth line correspond to each other as do the second and third—an ABBA pattern).[8]

Two other devices which will help to identify a few examples of strophic structure are anacrusis and "distant parallelism." Anacrusis is a technical poetical device in which a single word (it may be an interrogative or an exclamation such as "How" in Lam. 1:1) stands outside of the basic pattern of balance and parallelism in the couplets or strophe. The presence of these words has an effect on all that follows them. Frequently this feature appears in strophes containing especially expressive materials.[9] Mitchell Dahood labeled as "distant parallelism" a rhetorical device in which parallel paired words are separated from each other. He illustrated this phenomenon with the parallel pair of מָחַץ ("to smite") and צָמַת ("to annihilate") in Psalm 18. "I smote them" occurs in verse 39 (Heb.) while "I annihilated them" comes in verse 41 (Heb.) with four lines intervening. The ancient listener

8. Kraft, "Some Further Observations," pp. 65–66. The use of chiasmus for detecting strophic structure was demonstrated in Nils Wilhelm Lund, "The Presence of Chiasmus in the Old Testament," esp. pp. 104–9. Kraft warns, however, that D. H. Müller, Hans Möller, and Albert Condamin carried the idea to extremes.

9. R. K. Harrison, "Hebrew Poetry," in *The Zondervan Pictorial Encyclopedia of the Bible*, ed. Merrill C. Tenney, 5 vols. (Grand Rapids: Zondervan, 1975), 3:82.

or reader, in Dahood's view, would have recognized the parallel brace and instinctively linked the two. It would seem that distant parallelism holds some promise as an eighth way in which we might detect the presence of a strophe.[10]

The point in all this, of course, is that the identification of the strophe is not an optional matter for the exegete. As the paragraph stated one central idea and then developed or organized itself around that one theme proposition, so we would contend that the strophe exhibits a central rallying point around which it organizes its content.

Because parallelism occurs basically in two or occasionally in three lines, the most frequent strophic structure will be the simple couplet or triad. Kraft estimates that for 70 to 75 percent of the poetry in the Psalms the strophic unit is one simple couplet.[11] Less frequently it is the triad (three lines) and in extremely rare cases it involves four lines (or a quatrain) or perhaps six lines (e.g., Ps. 19:7–9).

There is one further question as to whether some poems which are composed of couplets (e.g., Pss. 18, 28, 39, and 40; perhaps Pss. 2, 16, 17, 23, and 26) might not occasionally combine two couplets into a quatrain to form *stanzas*. The answer to this probe is not yet clear, but existence of the stanza as such seems secure. Whether couplets may intermingle with triads or occasionally even an isolated line (which must *not* be therefore treated as spurious, i.e., as a later redaction) to make up stanzas must be tested in each individual passage while we await definitive answers based on cognate studies and more exact analyses of all Hebrew poetic texts.

The Couplet in Hebrew Poetry

The variety of strophic pattern by this time should be clear. Psalm 2 has a clear structure of four triads,[12] while Psalm 20 has

---

10. Dahood, "Ugaritic-Hebrew Parallel Pairs," pp. 80–81.
11. Kraft, "Some Further Observations," p. 71.
12. Ibid., p. 85.

two stanzas (each of which is composed of a quatrain or two couplets) and an additional line. Kraft sees Proverbs 8 as a long poem of four stanzas:

Stanza I (vv. 1–9): Three triads.

Stanza II (vv. 10–21): Six couplets, including one quatrain (vv. 14–17), forming an "envelope parallelism"—the quatrain occurs in the middle of the stanza with two couplets before it and two couplets after it.

Stanza III (vv. 22–31): Two triads (vv. 24–26, 27–29) within an envelope of two couplets (vv. 22–23) and (vv. 30–31).

Stanza IV (vv. 32–36): Two final couplets of exhortation.[13]

Now that we are certain that Canaanite and Hebrew poetry were arranged into strophes and in some rarer cases into stanzas, we must ask how we are to analyze the substance of each strophe and stanza. We cannot depend here on the theme proposition or topic sentence as we did in paragraph analysis—at least not in such prosaic forms.

Instead, the exegete must now deal with the couplet. The couplet is indispensable in analyzing the strophe. The couplet is made up of an A and B line. These lines may be in parallel form or they may have no parallel units whatsoever. The tendency, however, in a large number of cases is for these two lines to exhibit the phenomenon of *parallelismus membrorum;* that is, a balancing of units of thought, meaning, and form in the two (three in the case of a triad, four in the case of a quatrain) parallel lines, but not a balancing of sounds as in European poetry.

Recently, Geller has insisted that we clearly distinguish three *aspects* of Hebrew parallelism:[14]

13. Ibid., p. 86. Note Kraft's clear and convincing analysis of 185 lines of Ugaritic text from "The Baal and Anat Cycle" (Cyrus Gordon's text 51:IV–VI:59). Ibid., pp. 74–84. "Three couplets," writes Kraft, "are followed by four triads, possibly another couplet, and then two triads; then in the heat of controversy only brief couplets, isolated lines, or even single stichoi occur; then once more a triad and a unique couplet-enclosed triad are followed by a couplet, two quatrains, and a concluding couplet" (pp. 83–84).

14. Geller, *Parallelism,* pp. 15–16, 31–34, 375–77.

1. Grammatical parallelism exists where words in lines A and B are fully parallel grammatically, that is, in form, but not in meaning. For example, lines A and B may both take the form of subject–verb–direct object, but none of these words are parallel in meaning.

2. Semantic parallelism, on the other hand, is a parallelism in meaning or thought, not just in form.

3. Rhetorical parallelism designates features which are intended to produce a certain literary effect.[15] In our usage here, the term *rhetorical parallelism* refers to such features as the ballast variant, emblematic symbolism, climactic parallelism, chiasm, merism, and paronomasia.

Semantic Parallelism

For the purposes of exegesis, grammatical parallelism is of very little help. Geller would take Lowth's somewhat dubious category called synthetic parallelism (George Buchanan Gray's formal parallelism) and speak instead of grammatical parallelism.[16] But we are very interested as exegetes in the meaning package, semantic parallelism. It has two basic *types*.

The first type is *synonymous parallelism*. Here the second line repeats the idea of the opening line without significant addition or subtraction. When every *grammatical* element in line A has a parallel synonym in line B, we also have grammatical parallelism, or what some have called *complete* matching of grammatical units. Some examples of complete synonymous parallelism are:[17]

a	b	b	c
Israel	does-not		know

a'	b'	c'
My-people	do-not	consider	(Isa. 1:3)

15. Ibid., p. 32.
16. Ibid., pp. 375–85.
17. To approximate better the Hebrew text and the thought units, I have used the hyphenated form to show which words belong together. Usually the translation is my own rendering of the text.

```
        a           b           c
A-wicked-doer  gives-heed  to-false-lips
    a'          b'           c'
And-a-liar   gives-ear   to-a-naughty-tongue   (Prov. 17:4)
```

Oftentimes the parallelism is synonymous, yet one key element (perhaps the subject, the verb, or the object of a transitive verb) will be deleted. In this case there is an incomplete (i.e., grammatically incomplete) synonymous parallelism.

```
        a         b              c
The-earth  is-the-Lord's  and-everything-in-it
    a'      [b']              c'
The-world   [    ]  and-everyone-who-lives-in-it   (Ps. 24:1)
```

But there is a rhetorical device for just such circumstances. This is what Cyrus H. Gordon called a "ballast variant."[18] In those couplets or triads where there was no matching unit for one grammatical element (as seen in Ps. 24:1—"is the Lord's"), both Ugaritic and Hebrew often compensated for the omission by lengthening that line. This may be illustrated as follows:

```
           a          b        c
A. When-came-out  Israel   from-Egypt

   [a']            b'              c'            d'
B. [    ]  The-house-of-Jacob  from-a-people  of-strange-
        (Ps. 114:1; cf. Jer. 17:10b)           language
```

Notice that the "a" unit is left unanswered in the B line, but bulk is added almost as if it were compensating "ballast" for the earlier omission in the line. Thus we would label with Gordon the phrase "of-strange-language" the ballast variant. Another illustration of this same rhetorical device may be seen in Psalm 103:7.

---

18. Cyrus H. Gordon, *Ugaritic Textbook: Grammar, Texts in Transliteration, Cuneiform Selections, Glossary, Indices,* Analecta orientalia: commentationes scientificae de rebus Orientis antiqui, 35 (Rome: Pontifical Biblical Institute, 1965), p. 135.

```
        a              b          c
He-made-known   his-ways    to-Moses

   [a']          b'          c'          d' (ballast variant)
   [    ]    his-deeds    to-the-sons   of-Israel
```

The second type of semantic parallelism is *antithetic parallelism*. In this type, the second line contrasts with or negates the thought or meaning of the first line. The best place to search for examples of antithetic parallelism is in the Wisdom or Gnomic Literature of the Old Testament, especially in Proverbs 10–22. Here are some examples of *complete* antithetical parallelism:

```
        a              b           c
A-soft-answer     turns-away    wrath

        a'             b'          c'
But-grievous-words  stir-up     anger   (Prov. 15:1; cf. 15:2, 20)
```

```
        a             b           c
Righteousness      exalts      a-nation

     a'              b'             c'
But-sin      is-a-reproach   to-any-people   (Prov. 14:34)
```

Sometimes the antithetical thought is not found internally within the couplet, but *externally* between two couplets. A good example can be found in the prophet Isaiah:

```
        a          b          c
The-ox       knows     its-owner

     a'           [b']         c'          d' (ballast variant)
and-the-ass    [    ]    its-master's    crib
```

```
        a          b          c
But-Israel    does-not    know

     a'          b'           c'
My-people    do-not    consider    (Isa. 1:3)
```

The adversative "but" in the middle of the verse helps us to realize that there is a clear external antithesis here between the two couplets—one with a ballast variant.

Rhetorical Parallelism

Besides the balance of form, thought, and meaning, Hebrew poetry uses a number of rhetorical devices to increase both the beauty and the simplicity of the meaning. Already we have observed the operation of the *ballast variant* at work in both types of parallelism, though it would appear that it is more at home in synonymous parallelism.

One interesting feature that marks Ugaritic (Canaanite) and Hebrew poetry off from other Semitic and classical forms of poetry is the feature of deleting the verb.[19] Thus in Ugaritic we have:

```
      a            b          c
You-will-take  your-eternal  kingdom

[a']          b'            c'
[    ]    your-everlasting  dominion   (Text 68:10 or
                                        III: AB, A:10)


      a        b        c        d
For-a-son  is-born   to-me   like-my-brothers

   a'      [b']     [c']         d'
a-scion  [    ]   [    ]   like-my-kinfolks  (II D; 2:14–15)
```

Likewise in Hebrew we have:

```
    a        b         c
Saul      has-slain   his-thousands

   a'      [b']           c'
and-David [    ]    his-ten-thousands  (I Sam. 18:7b)
```

19. Ibid., § 13:105. See also Edward L. Greenstein, "Two Variations of Grammatical Parallelism in Canaanite Poetry and Their Psycholinguistic Background," pp. 89–96.

```
      a         b         c
The mountains  skipped  like-rams

  a'   [b']    c'
hills  [    ]  like-lambs  (Ps. 114:4)

(anacrusis)  a          b          c
Indeed, I-have-slain  a-warrior  for-my-wound

  [a']      b'        c'
  [    ]  and-a-lad  for-my-injury

(anacrusis)  a        b          c
Indeed, Cain  shall-be-avenged  sevenfold

    a'       [b']        c'
and-Lamech  [    ]  seventy-times-seven  (Gen. 4:23–24)
```

Thus, in Canaanite and Hebrew, when the grammatical subject and object correspond or are identical in both lines of the couplet, the verb may be deleted in the *second* line, but never in the first line. With a view to compensating for this gap the ballast variant was added to retain the same general bulk or shape of the couplet; in fact, the deletion of the verb may even have been deliberate in some cases in order to allow for a fuller explanation of the subject or object.

In some couplets one line takes the form of a literal or factual statement, and the other line, in the form of a simile or metaphor, is a figurative illustration. This is called *emblematic symbolism*. Note that the simile or metaphor is italicized in the following examples:

> *As a jewel of gold* in a swine's snout,
> So is a beautiful woman without discretion (Prov. 11:22).

> *As a deer* longs for the flowing streams,
> So longs my soul after you, O God (Ps. 42:1).

> *As cold waters* to a thirsty soul,
> So is good news from a far country (Prov. 25:25).

Table 11.1
Examples of Climactic Parallelism
in Ugaritic and Hebrew Poetry

---

irš • ḥym • laqht • ġzr
irš • ḥym • watnk
   bl mt • wašlḥt
	Request life, O Aqhat lad;
	Request life and I'll give thee
	Immortality, and I'll endow thee.
	    (II Aqht 6:26–28)

bkm • tmdln • 'r bkm • tṣmd • pḥl bkm • tšu • abh	Weeping she saddles an ass, Weeping she hitches a donkey, Weeping she lifts her father. (I Aqht 57–59)

knp • nšrm • b'l • ytbr
b'l ytbr • diy • hmt
tqln • tḥt • p'ny
(wyql • tḥt • p'ny) etc.
	May Baal break the wings of the eagles;
	                         Hrgb
	                         Ṣml
	May Baal break their pinions
	So that they fall at his feet.
	    (I Aqht 107, 114, 118, 122, 128, 132,
	                          136, 142, 148)

bl • ṭl • bl • rbb bl • šr' • thmtm bl • ṭbn • ql • b 'l	Without dew, without rain, Without surging of the two deeps, Without the goodness of the voice of Baal. (I Aqht 44–46)

כִּי הִנֵּה אֹיְבֶיךָ ׀ יְהֹוָה	For, lo, thine enemies, O Lord,
כִּי־הִנֵּה אֹיְבֶיךָ יֹאבֵדוּ	For, lo, thine enemies shall perish;
יִתְפָּרְדוּ כָּל־פֹּעֲלֵי אָוֶן׃	All the workers of iniquity shall be scattered. (Ps. 92:9 [Heb., 10]; cf. Ugaritic text 68:9)
נָשְׂאוּ נְהָרוֹת ׀ יְהֹוָה	The floods have lifted up, O Lord,
נָשְׂאוּ נְהָרוֹת קוֹלָם	The floods have lifted up their voice;
יִשְׂאוּ נְהָרוֹת דָּכְיָם׃	The floods lift up their waves. (Ps. 93:3)
שִׁירוּ לַיהֹוָה שִׁיר חָדָשׁ	Sing unto the Lord a new song:
שִׁירוּ לַיהֹוָה כָּל־הָאָרֶץ׃	Sing unto the Lord, all the earth.
שִׁירוּ לַיהֹוָה בָּרְכוּ שְׁמוֹ	Sing unto the Lord, bless his name.... (Ps. 96:1–2)

כִּי בָא°	...for he cometh,
כִּי בָא לִשְׁפֹּט הָאָרֶץ	For he cometh to judge the earth:
יִשְׁפֹּט־תֵּבֵל בְּצֶדֶק	He shall judge the world with righteousness,
וְעַמִּים בֶּאֱמוּנָתוֹ: [ ]	[ ] and the people with truth.

(Ps. 96:13)

Another rhetorical device, *climactic or staircase parallelism*, involves the repetition and development of a group of two or three words in successive lines—often a triad or quatrain. Taking note of such recapitulation helps the exegete to understand better both the emphasis and the aesthetic beauty of this poetry.[20] This repetition from line to line is frequently seen in Canaanite and Hebrew poetry. Some illustrations of this device appear in table 11.1.

Another feature of Biblical poetry is *chiasm*, the inversion of parallel terms in successive lines or even the arrangement of a quatrain so that lines 1 and 4 correspond to each other as do 2 and 3 (or 1 to 3 and 2 to 4). This device is named after the Greek letter *chi* which resembles our English letter *x*. Examples of various types of chiasm—simple chiasm, line chiasm, and a quatrain with two couplets—are shown in table 11.2. In the last example notice that Rahab cannot be identified with the sea (יָם), but is something *in* the sea, perhaps a large marine animal like a crocodile. Likewise, the fleeing serpent is not the sky itself, but a *feature in the sky,* perhaps an eclipse.

Merismus, or, as we say in English, *merism,* is a figure of speech much like synecdoche (where a part is used to indicate the whole or the whole is used to indicate only a part). It consists of listing the individual parts of a whole, or more frequently only some of them—usually the first and the last or the more prominent of a series—and thereby indicating that the whole group is to be understood.

The best example of a merism is in Malachi 1:11, which speaks

---

20. For further discussion see Greenstein, "Two Variations," pp. 96–105; Samuel E. Loewenstamm, "The Expanded Colon in Ugaritic and Biblical Verse."

Table 11.2
Examples of Chiasm in Hebrew Poetry

Simple Chiasm (abba or abccba)

	a	b	c
A.	Ephraim	shall-not-be-jealous	of Judah

	c '	b '	a '
B.	and Judah	shall-not-harass	Ephraim (Isa. 11:13b)

Line Chiasm (abba)

A. My-son if-your-heart *is-wise*

B. *My-heart* too will-be-glad

C. *My-reins* will-rejoice

D. When-your-lips speak *right-things*   (Prov. 23:15–16)

Quatrain with two couplets (abab)

A. By-his-power *the-sea* is-quiet

B. And-by-his-understanding he-smites *Rahab*

C. By-his-breath *the-sky* is-cleared

D. His-hand pierces *the-fleeing-serpent*   (Job 26:12–13)

---

of the triumph of the kingdom of God "from the rising to the
setting of the sun," that is, over the *whole earth.* A similar point
can be made by speaking of the extent of a king's reign as being
from shore to shore.

Merisms include substantives denoting time, place, persons,
things, and even certain actions. Thus universals can be subsumed
under particulars rather than put into abstract terms. This figure
of speech or rhetorical device occurs in both poetry and prose.[21]

Part of the subtlety and beauty of Hebrew poetry can be found
in the Hebrew poets' love for *paronomasia,* or playing on words.
The Oriental peoples delighted in a good pun.

---

21. For an extended discussion of Biblical examples, see A. M. Honeyman, "*Mer-ismus* in Biblical Hebrew."

Many is the time that a prophet made his point by placing similar-sounding words side by side. In Isaiah 5:7, the prophet declared: God looked for "justice" (מִשְׁפָּט) and "righteousness" (צְדָקָה), but He got only an "outcry" (צְעָקָה) instead.

When Jeremiah was called, God showed him an "almond branch" (שָׁקֵד) and connected this with the fact that He was "watching over" (שֹׁקֵד) His people to bring swift judgment if they did not soon repent. A rough English equivalent (in both sound and culture in that almond branches in Judea are like our pussy willows; viz., the harbingers of spring) would be: God showed Jeremiah a "pussy-willow branch" and said, "This is what I *will-a-do* to my people if they do not soon repent" (with apologies to Jer. 1:11–12).

Thus the exegete has six rhetorical devices to help him glean the special nuance of the divine message. But in all this labor the thought must be to focus in on the central contribution of each strophe so as to garner from it a main point in the message. In developing the subpoints the exegete must analyze the route chosen by the Biblical poet. If, for example, the poet contrasts his statements by using antithetical parallelism, that fact must be reflected in the exegesis.

If it seems that within the stanza or larger strophes it is impossible to detect which of the lines states the theme, the rhetorical devices may be of help. For example, in Psalm 2 there are four triads making up four strophes. It is clear that each of the first two ends with a speech—verse 3 is a speech by the rebels and verse 6 a speech from God. The main theme of the first two strophes, then, comes to focus in verses 3 and 6 respectively. Accordingly, verses 1–2 and 4–5 will be subpoints which develop those main themes.

Likewise in the case of nonparallel units, the exegete must once again lean heavily on rhetorical devices. Of course, if all surface-structure features (under this term we include grammatical parallelism and syntax) supply little or no help, then we must go to semantic structure (i.e., meaning, logic), but we should be warned that the subjective is a far less reliable guide to sound exegesis.

Preaching on Biblical Poetry

The best-known poetry in the Bible is the psalms of David. The Book of Psalms, however, includes many other poets, and this work in turn belongs to a larger group of writings sometimes called the Wisdom Books, namely, Job, Proverbs, Ecclesiastes, and Song of Solomon.

Yet the Wisdom Books hardly begin to exhaust the massive amount of material in the Bible that is written in the poetical form. There are examples of poetry in the historical books: "Lamech's Boastful Song" (Gen. 4:23–24), "Jacob's Blessing of His Sons" (Gen. 49), the "Song of Moses" (Exod. 15), the "Song of Deborah" (Judg. 5), David's "Lament over Saul and Jonathan" (II Sam. 1:19–27). But still more significant are large sections of fourteen of the sixteen writing prophets in the Old Testament. In fact, only seven books in the Old Testament are without any poetry: Leviticus, Ruth, Ezra, Nehemiah, Esther, Haggai, and Malachi. Thus approximately one-third of the Old Testament is written in poetic form.

Nor is the New Testament without examples of poetry. While the New Testament contains no single book that could be identified as poetical, nevertheless, poetry still plays a significant role.

According to Frank E. Gaebelein, five kinds of poetical passages may be identified in the New Testament: (1) quotations from ancient poets (Epimenides of Crete said, "For in thee we live and move and have our being," Acts 17:28; Aratus of Cilicia and Cleanthes the Stoic both said, "For we are his offspring," Acts 17:28; Epimenides was again quoted, "The Cretans are always liars, evil beasts, lazy, gluttons," Titus 1:12; and Menander, the Athenian comic poet, said: "Evil communications corrupt good manners," I Cor. 15:33); (2) quotations from unidentified poetry that may have been first-century Christian hymns (Eph. 5:14 [cf. v. 19]; Phil. 2:5–11; I Tim. 3:16; and II Tim. 2:11–13); (3) passages which are in the mold of Old Testament poetry (the "Magnificat," Luke 1:46–55; the "Benedictus," Luke 1:68–79; the "Gloria in Excelsis," Luke 2:14; and the "Nunc Dimittis,"

Luke 2:29–32); (4) passages which lack rhyme or meter but are in a grand and exalted style filled with intense expression (the Beatitudes or, for that matter, the whole of the Sermon on the Mount; Jesus' lament over Jerusalem in Luke 13:34–35; and parts of the Upper Room Discourse, e.g., John 14:1–7); and (5) apocalyptic imagery such as the Olivet Discourse or the songs and hymns in Revelation (e.g., Rev. 4:8, 11; 5:9–10, 12–13; 7:15–17; 11:17–18; 15:3–4; 18:2, 8, 14–24; 19:6–8).[22]

In most cases, New Testament portions exhibiting poetry are limited in their scope. They are not lengthy enough to be the sole focus of the sermon. There are exceptions to this observation, of course—the Olivet Discourse and the Sermon on the Mount.

But in general, the bulk of New Testament poetry is hymns and songs. Where the style is similar to that of Hebrew poetry, our approach would be similar to our approach to any Old Testament poetical passage. But where the poetry is a combination of non-prosaic form and, say, wisdom materials (as in the Sermon on the Mount) or apocalyptic symbolism (as in the Olivet Discourse), the exegete will want to pay more attention to the special nuances and demands of the particular literary genre involved (wisdom literature, apocalyptic).

One more special comment must be made. In wisdom materials the exegete will usually encounter much smaller units of material—even smaller than the combination of couplets or triads found in many of the Psalms. While individual couplets in Proverbs may combine to make up one strophe, often each couplet forms a unique and separate unit.

This is particularly true of Proverbs 10–22 where there are a great many examples of antithetic parallelism often without any easily discernible relationship *between* the couplets. Where this anomaly appears, contextual analysis will be of little or no help. The exegete should be warned in these cases (other examples are the Sermon on the Mount and James) to proceed carefully by

22. Frank E. Gaebelein, "Poetry, New Testament," in *Zondervan Pictorial Encyclopedia,* ed. Tenney, 4:813–14.

giving full weight not only to the poetic form, but also to the full range of figurative expressions and exaggerated and hyperbolic ways of stating priorities, similarities, contrasts, or consequences, and of characterizing persons by their actions or situations.

The point is that a proverb is so compressed that it may be misunderstood if it is not put back into the total context of teaching from which it was abstracted and raised to prominence for the purposes of emphasis. Thus the following steps will be helpful in approaching wisdom poetry:

1. Determine the character of the proverbial material first of all. Is it a parable (Eccles. 9:13–18), an allegory (Prov. 5:15–18), a simile (Prov. 25:13, 19, 20, 25), or a conundrum requiring a lengthy pause for reflection before the comparison or metaphor is caught (Prov. 26:8)?
2. Where the context is helpful, use it. A good example is Proverbs 16, which is a series of proverbs on "man proposes, but God disposes."
3. Where no connections can be discerned from the context, then use the more obvious line of the Hebrew parallelism to unlock the more difficult and enigmatic line.
4. In applying the principles of wisdom material, note that they are not meant to cover every situation. For example, Proverbs 16:7 says that "when Jehovah delights in the ways of a man, He makes even his enemies to be at peace with him." That is the basic principle, but of course there are some exceptions. It is the nature of proverbial speech to assume that *ceteris paribus* ("all other things being equal"), this then is true.

There is no doubt that the poetical forms in Scripture will always pose more problems for the exegete than most prose sections ever will. But offsetting this added burden there are also an additional beauty and an emotional flavor that usually cannot be contained in prose forms. In principle the basic procedure for exegeting poetry will be the same as that for exegeting prose.

1. Identify the full scope of the poem.
2. Divide the poem up into stanzas or strophes.

3. Locate the theme line or basic affirmation in the parallel structure.
4. Show how that theme proposition is developed or explained.
5. Restate this theme in a principle which is unrestricted by time, persons, cultures, or places. It should also be given in a form that invites some type of response from the hearer to the living Lord who first gave that word.

Part **IV**

Conclusion

Chapter 12

The Exegete/Pastor and the Power of God

With so many instructions, steps, and cautions to be kept in mind when employing the syntactical-theological method, exegetes are likely to throw their hands up in despair and exclaim in exasperation, "Who is sufficient for these things?" In truth, the task is enough to overwhelm almost anyone, and especially those who must gain whatever they derive from Scripture by a slow painful experience of translating, meditating, and comparing results with a number of previous commentators on the passage. That is why we must in all good conscience point to the presence and work of the Holy Spirit as the source of any confidence that we might have in our message even after we have acted most responsibly in the study and preparation of the text for proclamation.

The Exegete and the Holy Spirit

One of the most depressing spectacles in the Church today is her lack of power. Too frequently the Church has little or no impact at all on the society and nation in which she ministers. Therefore, the masses outside the Church, not to mention the additional scandal of those within the Church, are indifferent to her.

At the heart of this problem is an impotent pulpit. And that impotency will not be dealt with definitively until the exegete is armed with an authoritative message based on the single meaning of the text as informed by its antecedent theology, and until there is also a decision to take the time to wait on God until the messenger is "clothed with power from on high" (Luke 24:49). Only then will the Church begin to prove once again that "the gospel . . . is the power of God" (Rom. 1:16).

The best teaching passage on this theme of the source of the preacher-teacher's power in proclaiming the Word of God is I Corinthians 1:17—2:5. The concept of "power" or "the power of God" (δύναμις θεοῦ) occurs five times (I Cor. 1:17, 18, 23–24; 2:4, 5).

The burden of Paul's message is already apparent in the verse with which this great passage begins: "Christ . . . sent me . . . to preach the good news, not with eloquent wisdom, lest the cross of Christ should be emptied of its *power*" (v. 17, italics mine). And as if to bracket off this message, Paul concludes this section with the divine solution to powerless preaching (I Cor. 2:4–5): "My speech and my message were not in persuasive words of wisdom, but in demonstration of the *Spirit* and *power,* so that your faith might not be [anchored] in the wisdom of men, but in the *power of God*" (italics mine).

The "demonstration of the [Holy] Spirit" (ἀπόδειξις) is what is needed to make our poor and inadequate words the power of God. Yes, even when we have faithfully discharged our full range of duties as exegetes and when we have also pressed on to apply that exegesis by principlizing the text paragraph by paragraph into timeless propositions which call for an immediate response from our listeners, we still need the Holy Spirit to carry that word home to the mind and hearts of our hearers if that word is ever going to change men's lives.

Thus purity in our use of the source of our message and accuracy in the method of reproducing that message are not enough; the delivery of the message must likewise be attended by the evident presence and powerful working of the Holy Spirit if the Church is ever going to make an impact on an indifferent world. Rather than this being an impediment to our style or personality, Paul affirmed that "we have this treasure [of the message] in earthen vessels [our bodies] in order to show that the surpassing greatness of the power belongs not to us, but to God" (II Cor. 4:7).

Charles Haddon Spurgeon in his addresses delivered to the students at the Pastors' College sternly warned all proclaimers of the Word of God:

> To us, as ministers, the Holy Spirit is absolutely essential. Without him our office is a mere name. We claim no priesthood over and above that which belongs to every child of God; but we are the successors of those who, in olden times, were moved of God to declare his word, to testify against transgression, and to plead his cause. Unless we have the spirit of the prophets resting upon us, the mantle which we wear is nothing but a rough garment to deceive. We ought to be driven forth with abhorrence from the society of honest men for daring to speak in the name of the Lord if the Spirit of God rests not upon us.[1]

The Power of the Spirit

How then, Spurgeon inquired, shall we obtain this aid of the Holy Spirit? Must we abandon all rational forms of study and come to our pulpits with a blank mind?

To answer his own question, Spurgeon told this story: "After a visitation discourse by the Bishop of Lichfield upon the necessity of earnestly studying the Word, a certain vicar told his lordship that he could not believe his doctrine, 'for,' said he, 'often when I am in the vestry I do not know what I am going to talk about; but I go into the pulpit and preach, and think nothing of it.' His lordship replied, 'And you are quite right in thinking nothing of it, for your churchwardens have told me that they share your opinion.' "[2]

---

1. Charles Haddon Spurgeon, *Second Series of Lectures to My Students: Being Addresses Delivered to the Students of the Pastors' College, Metropolitan Tabernacle* (London: Passmore and Alabaster, 1877), p. 3.

2. Ibid., p. 4.

Spurgeon continued by commenting, "If we are not instructed, how can we instruct? If we have not thought, how shall we lead others to think? It is . . . when we are alone with the Book before us, that we need the help of the Holy Spirit."[3] The Holy Spirit, then, is the *Spirit of knowledge*. That is the same truth to which John pointed in I John 2:27: "His anointing teaches you about all things."

But the Holy Spirit is also called the *Spirit of wisdom*. Knowledge must be accompanied by wisdom, the art of properly using what is known. Involved in this art is the ability to apply the text and to place any given truth in its proper perspective without giving undue prominence to it.

Spurgeon illustrated the harm that such an improper balance of doctrines could produce. He cautioned: "A man's nose is a prominent feature in his face, but it is possible to make it so large that eyes and mouth, and everything else are thrown into insignificance, and the drawing is a caricature and not a portrait: so certain important doctrines of the gospel can be so proclaimed in excess as to throw the rest of truth into the shade, and the preaching is no longer the gospel in its natural beauty, but a caricature of the truth, of which caricature, however, let me say, some people seem to be mightily fond."[4]

The most difficult task of all will be to preach the "whole counsel of God." Some truths are easier to receive than others, and it will not take most pastors very long to discover what audiences enjoy and what they passionately dislike from the teaching of Scripture. But the wisdom which the Holy Spirit imparts to all preachers who ask for it will make them wise in giving a balanced total diet.

The Spirit will also supply the wisdom that is needed to discover the way we should present various truths. "You can cast a man down with the very truth which was intended to build him up. You can sicken a man with the honey with which you meant to sweeten his mouth. The great mercy of God has been preached

3. Ibid.
4. Ibid., p. 6.

unguardedly, and has led hundreds into licentiousness; and, on the other hand, the terrors of the Lord have been occasionally fulminated with such violence that they have driven men into despair, and so into a settled defiance of the Most High."[5]

Yet there is a third work of the Holy Spirit that is needed if we are to preach with power. It is to have our lips touched with a live coal from the altar of God, as Isaiah experienced when he was commissioned by God (Isa. 6). Not only do we need to experience the cleansing of God's forgiveness if we are to handle the holy things of God, we also need the Spirit's gift of the *freedom of utterance.*

Paul urged the Ephesians to pray for all the saints, but especially for him "that utterance might be given [him] in opening [his] mouth to speak with boldness the mystery of the gospel" (Eph. 6:18–19). Such power as this does not come from mere skills of elocution or oratory. We must have the Holy Spirit incite us to declare with boldness the truth we have discovered in the Word of God. From the beginning of the sermon to its end, the all-engrossing force of the text and the God who speaks through that text must dominate our whole being. With the burning power of that truth on our heart and lips, every thought, emotion, and act of the will must be so captured by that truth that it springs forth with excitement, joy, sincerity, and reality as an evident token that God's Spirit is in that word. Away with all the mediocre, lifeless, boring, and lackluster orations offered as pitiful substitutes for the powerful Word of the living Lord. If that Word from God does not thrill the proclaimer and fill the servant who delivers it with an intense desire to glorify God and do His will, how shall we ever expect it to have any greater effect on our hearers?

Again Spurgeon's words are right on target. "We need the Spirit of God, then, all through the sermon to keep our hearts and minds in a proper condition, for if we have not the right spirit we shall lose the tone which persuades and prevails, and our people will discover that Samson's strength has departed from

5. Ibid., p. 7.

him. Some speak scoldingly, and so betray their bad temper; others preach themselves, and so reveal their pride. Some discourse as though it were a condescension on their part to occupy the pulpit, while others preach as though they apologised for their existence. To avoid errors of manners and tone, we must be led of the Holy Spirit, who alone teacheth us to profit."[6]

The Holy Spirit's fourth and final aid to powerful preaching of the Word is a *spirit of supplication and holiness*. It is the Spirit of God who teaches us to pray for ourselves and for all who will hear that Word of God. Therefore, earnest and magisterial preaching requires abundant and Spirit-led prayer. Spurgeon urged: "The habit of prayer is good, but the spirit of prayer is better. Regular retirement [to pray] is to be maintained, but continued communion with God is to be our aim. As a rule, we ministers ought never to be many minutes without actually lifting up our hearts in prayer. Some of us could honestly say that we are seldom a quarter of an hour without speaking to God, and that not as a duty but as an instinct, a habit of the new nature for which we claim no more credit than a babe does for crying after its mother."[7]

And as for our prayers in public, we cannot pray acceptably without the Spirit of God and the daily experience of privately communing with God. Dead praying, warned Spurgeon, will be recognized by our people faster than we think it will, for it is as offensive to them as it is to God.

Likewise a spirit of holiness is important, for we are to be examples both in the pulpit and out of it. Therefore we must pray for God's Spirit to keep ourselves and our family unspotted by the world. It is not a matter of trifles to attend to our families, to our deportment in social circles, and, yes, even to the garments that we wear. We must give no offense so that the ministry be not blamed.

The Absence of the Spirit's Power

Spurgeon completed his famous lecture on "The Holy Spirit in Connection with Our Ministry," which has occupied our atten-

6. Ibid., p. 11.
7. Ibid., p. 13.

tion for some time already in this chapter, by noting that some
ministers may lose the aid of the Holy Spirit. Do not misunder-
stand; neither Spurgeon nor I mean to imply that some ministers
thereby may lose their eternal life with God. Rather, some may
no longer be able to function as powerful ministers of God's Word
because they succumb to those evils which grieve the Spirit's free
work in our lives. Even more tragic, some have failed to recognize
that God's Spirit has been lifted from them. They continue attempting to minister. Like Samson or King Saul, they do not
realize that the Spirit of the Lord has left them (Judg. 16:20;
I Sam. 16:14; 18:12).

Spurgeon's list of evils which grieve the Spirit's free work include a lack of sensitiveness (to His most delicate promptings),
a lack of truthfulness (in that we preach doctrines not because we
believe them, but because we know our audiences love to hear
them), pride (a love of being recognized), an attitude of laziness
(lack of discipline results in neglect of study and private prayer),
and a heart that is deficient and obviously lacking in something.

This last category is most difficult to pin down. The person
with a deficient heart is not dishonest, immoral, bad-tempered,
nor self-indulgent, but something is lacking. In Spurgeon's words:
"[Something] is wanting in the whole man, and its absence spoils
everything. He wants [lacks] the one thing needful. He is not
spiritual, he has no savour of Christ, his heart never burns within
him, his soul is not alive, he wants [lacks] grace."[8]

What will happen to such hapless persons who, after repeated
warnings, suddenly have the Spirit of God taken from them as it
was taken from Saul? It is not for us to say. We know from
Scripture only that there is such a gallery of men and women
whose ministries were terminated when they were deserted by
the Holy Spirit.

For Spurgeon, the saddest and most painful of all of these
Biblical examples was Moses, whose whole life's work was marred
by one moment of speaking unadvisedly toward the close of his
long career (Num. 20:10; Ps. 106:32–33). This was not as gross

---

8. Ibid., p. 19.

a sin as David's nor as startling as Peter's failure of nerve, but it was the sin of God's spokesman, one favored of God beyond all others to lead His people and to represent "that prophet" who was to come.

It behooves us as exegetes and spokesmen for the living God to implore God's Spirit for His protection from ourselves and from our all too common tendency to yield ourselves to sin, and for demonstration of the power of God in our every declaration of His Word.

The Exegete and the Word of God

In the midst of all the feverish activity to restore the Church once again to her former position of influence and respect, all sorts of programs and slogans have appeared. But regardless of what new directives and emphases are periodically offered, that which is needed above everything else to make the Church more viable, authentic, and effective, is a new declaration of the Scriptures with a new purpose, passion, and power. This we believe is most important if the work of God is to be accomplished in the program of the local church.

Once again, we point to I Corinthians 1:17—2:5, which is one of the more definitive statements on the fact that the Word of God is both the wisdom and power of God if we will but use it. Paul deliberately decided to let the *manner* of his preaching be governed by its *matter* and content so that his audiences might know that whatever excellence or power was observed in his presentations, it rested in the direct work of God. Paul feared attracting people to Christ solely on intellectual and aesthetic grounds. This he found repulsive and altogether artificial and anemic.

This does not mean that the Scriptures may be used in a magical way—as if the mere importation of their words into our addresses to the local body makes everything we say sacrosanct. On the contrary, in II Corinthians 2:17 Paul had strong words of rebuke for such "peddling," "hawking," or "huckstering" of the Word of God. Such cheapening of the Word cannot stand up to the test of the heat of the sun. (The Greek word for "sincerity" in

II Cor. 2:17 is made up of the two words εἴλη, "heat of the sun," and κρίνειν, "to judge, or to test.") Therefore, mixing the Word with such foreign elements as civil religion, current philosophies, schools of psychology, political affiliations, and personal predilections is to take the powerful Word of God and to make it ineffective, weak, and despised in the eyes of our contemporaries.

In an ordination charge delivered by James Stalker in 1879, he urged the new pastor:

> This is your work; the Book is put into your hands to-day, that you may unfold its contents to your people, conveying them into their minds by all possible avenues and applying them to all parts of their daily life. . . . this Book will become dearer to you every day; it will enrich every part of your nature. . . . But be true to it! The Bible will be what I have said to you only if you go deep into it. If you keep to the surface, you will weary of it. There are some ministers who begin their ministry with a certain quantity of religious doctrine in their mind, and what they do all their life afterwards is to pick out texts and make them into vessels to hold so much of it. The vessels are of different shapes and sizes, but they are all filled with the same thing; and oh! it is poor stuff, however orthodox and evangelical it may seem.[9]

In order to reverse this dangerous state of affairs, Stalker urged the preachers of his day, just as we would urge those of our day, to thoroughly prepare their Biblical texts for proclamation.

> But preparation of this sort for the pulpit is not easy. It requires time, self-conquest and hard work. Perhaps the greatest ministerial temptation is idleness in study—not in going about and doing something, but in finding and rightly using precious hours in one's library, avoiding reverie and light or desultory reading, and sticking hard and fast to the Sabbath work. I, for one, must ' confess that I have had, and still have, a terrific battle to fight for this. No men have their time so much at their own disposal as

9. James Stalker, *The Preacher and His Models: The Yale Lectures on Preaching, 1891* (New York: Armstrong, 1891; reprint ed., Grand Rapids: Baker, 1967), pp. 273–74.

we. . . . If you lecture, as I trust you will—for it brings one, far more than sermonising, into contact with Scripture—you will know your subject at once, and be able to begin to read on it. The text of the other discourse should be got by the middle of the week at latest, and the more elaborate of the two finished on Friday. This makes a hard week; but it has its reward. There are few moods more splendid than a preacher's when, after a hard week's work, during which his mind has been incessantly active on the truth of God and his spirit exalted by communion with the Divine Spirit, he appears before his congregation on Sabbath, knowing he has an honestly gotten message to lavish on them; just as there can be no coward and craven more abject than a minister with any conscience who appears in the pulpit after an idle, dishonest week, to cheat his congregation with a diet of fragments seasoned with counterfeit fervour.[10]

How can the power of God be present in that kind of weak and lazy preaching? Paul would have none of it and neither should we. It is our pleasant duty to unleash the Word of God in all its authority and power for those who wait to be fed with bread from heaven. While some may argue and debate over whether there is any resident power in such a confident study and use of Scripture, the man of God need only experience the difference in mood and results between a paltry sharing of a few sentiments loosely tied into Scripture and the excited explanation of what God is teaching us in a selected Biblical text. There is a world of difference between the two.

The Exegete and the Audience

When all has been said and done, the question that we have been attempting to answer in this work will continue to be the most difficult aspect of exegetical theology; that is, how can the ancient Scriptures continue to be the living voice of God for the present time? Exegesis has not begun to do its work until it comes to grips with this problem. The Bible must not only be understood

10. Ibid., pp. 276–77.

historically, culturally, grammatically, syntactically, and critically; it must be appreciated for its vertical axis as well as its horizontal orientation. In a sense, the time wrapper must not be shed and peeled off; rather, it must be related to its theological core. To stop short of doing theological exegesis in preparing the texts for homiletical analysis is to fail to complete the task which the Church has a right to expect of us.

There is the "ever-abiding meaning," "the *Ipse dicit*,"[11] that must be ascertained. In the parenetic parts of Scripture, Jac. J. Müller comments, it is easier to observe the *eternal* truth which time does not affect, the meaning for all readers regardless of their age. The historical passages of Scripture do not as easily yield those abiding principles.

Nevertheless, the search for the *übergeschichtliche* (superhistorical) moment is necessary if we are to discover the profound sense and lasting major value of the text. This must not lead us to an easy allegorical method of exegesis anymore than we should adopt some type of *sensus plenior*. The fifth-century church's theory of a fourfold sense to Scripture was expressed in the maxim:

> Litera gesta docet,
> Quid credas allegoria,
> Moralis quid agas,
> Quo tendas anagogia!

> The literal teaches what happened,
> The allegorical what you must believe,
> The ethical what you must do,
> The anagogic whither you are tending.[12]

Possibly the most that can be said for this theory of a fourfold sense is that the early Church was grappling with exactly the same problem that we are raising here. If only their view had been that occasionally one or another of these four *elements* can be found in one text or another, perhaps a more positive foun-

11. Jac. J. Müller, "Exegesis and Kerugma," p. 233.
12. Ibid., p. 234.

dation for present-day exegesis could have been provided. But the whole scheme tended to develop into a search for all sorts of hidden *meanings* which simultaneously existed in the text.

Therefore we must once again assert that meaning is always a single meaning as judged by the author's truth-intentions; significance is multiple and plural as it involves various relationships between that single meaning and various persons, situations, and events.

Yet rejection of a plural meaning to Scripture is not to say that we need not be active in identifying the lasting theological value of the text. Almost all of modern hermeneutics centers around one question: what does the text mean to me? Our quarrel with most of these contemporary procedures is that they have wearied and despaired of determining if there is any valid grounding of the existential *significance* of a text in its single authorial meaning.

Thus, we conclude that we do need an exegesis that is just as patient in its listening for the contemporary voice of the living God as it is in making contextual, grammatical, historical, cultural, and syntactical analyses. It is this voice that distinguishes the Bible from other books.

What good will it do the Church proudly to announce that she possesses the law, the prophets, the writings, and the gospel if there is no response to the Word? Such a situation would be about as ludicrous as that which Jeremiah describes in his famous Temple Gate Message (Jer. 7–10). There he caustically notes that the irrational creatures of God know and *respond* to the ordinances of God much better than do God's rational creatures, for with the approach of the changing season, the birds leave for warmer climes (Jer. 8:7), whereas God's rational creatures refuse to take any action in spite of impending and certain disaster.

Even more tragic, *possession* of the Word of God is no guarantee that men and women will *respond* to it. Israel had three types of leaders, each with a unique type of revelation from God— the priests with the law, the prophets with the word of the Lord, and the wise men with wisdom; yet they did little, if anything, to heal the wound of God's people. Most amazingly, that law, word, and wisdom failed to evoke any response from these leaders themselves, much less the people. They did not even blush when they heard the word (Jer. 8:8–12). It had become a strictly external word and an intellectual exercise.

May God deliver us, the new generation of interpreters, and His Church, from such parochical use of the Scriptures. We cannot be acquitted as scholarly exegetes until we have led the Church to understand how to respond to the very words that we have analyzed most critically and carefully.

Bibliography

Exegetical Methodology

Achtemeier, Elizabeth. "The Artful Dialogue: Some Thoughts on the Relation of Biblical Studies and Homiletics." *Interpretation* 35 (1981): 18–31.

_____. *The Old Testament and the Proclamation of the Gospel.* Philadelphia: Westminster, 1973.

_____. "The Relevance of the Old Testament for Christian Preaching." In *A Light unto My Path: Old Testament Studies in Honor of Jacob M. Myers,* edited by Howard N. Bream, Ralph Heim, and Carey A. Moore, pp. 3–24. Philadelphia: Temple University, 1974.

Bjornard, Reidar B. "Christian Preaching from the Old Testament." *Review and Expositor* 56 (1959): 8–19. Includes bibliography.

Blackman, E. C. "The Task of Exegesis." In *The Background of the New Testament and Its Eschatology: In Honor of Charles Harold Dodd,* edited by W. D. Davies and David Daube, pp. 3–26. Cambridge: Cambridge University, 1964.

Braga, James. *How to Prepare Bible Messages: A Manual on Homiletics for Bible Students.* Portland: Multnomah, 1969.

Bright, John. *The Authority of the Old Testament.* Nashville: Abingdon, 1967. Reprint. Grand Rapids: Baker, 1975. Pp. 161–212, "The Old Testament in the Christian Pulpit: General Hermeneutical Considerations."

Bruce, F. F. "The Earliest Old Testament Interpretations." In *The Witness of Tradition: Papers Read at the Joint British-Dutch Old Testament Conference Held at Woudschoten, 1970,* pp. 37–52. Oudtestamentische Studiën, edited by A. S. Van Der Woude, 17. Leiden: Brill, 1972. Analyzes Old Testament interpretation in the Prophets and in Psalm titles.

249

Bultmann, Rudolf. *Essays: Philosophical and Theological.* Translated by James C. G. Greig. London: SCM, 1955. Pp. 234–61, "The Problem of Hermeneutics."

————. *Existence and Faith: Shorter Writings of Rudolf Bultmann.* Edited and translated by Schubert M. Ogden. New York: Meridian, 1960. Pp. 289–96, "Is Exegesis Without Presuppositions Possible?"

Buttrick, David G. "Interpretation and Preaching." *Interpretation* 35 (1981): 46–58.

Caemmerer, Richard R., Sr. "Why Preach from Biblical Texts? Reflections on Tradition and Practice." *Interpretation* 35 (1981): 5–17.

Chafer, Rollin Thomas. "A Syllabus of Studies in Hermeneutics." *Bibliotheca Sacra* 91 (1934): 457–62; 93 (1936): 110–18, 201–3, 331–35; 94 (1937): 72–94, 207–17, 470–78; 95 (1938): 91–101.

Craddock, Fred B. "Occasion–Text–Sermon." *Interpretation* 35 (1981): 59–71.

Cunliffe-Jones, H. "The Problems of Biblical Exposition." *Expository Times* 65 (1953–54): 4–7.

Daane, James. *Preaching with Confidence: A Theological Essay on the Power of the Pulpit.* Grand Rapids: Eerdmans, 1980.

Dreher, Bruno. "Exegesis and Proclamation." Translated by John Griffiths. In *Theology, Exegesis, and Proclamation,* edited by Roland E. Murphy, pp. 56–66. New York: Herder and Herder, 1971.

Ensign, Grayson H. "The Correct Method of Biblical Hermeneutics: Its Basic Factors Identified and Described." *Seminary Review* 24 (1978): 73–99.

Forstman, H. Jackson. "What Does It Mean 'to Preach from the Bible'?" *Encounter* 21 (1960): 218–31.

Furnish, Victor Paul. "Some Practical Guidelines for New Testament Exegesis." *Perkins School of Theology Journal* 26 (1973): 1–16.

Gowan, Donald E. *Reclaiming the Old Testament for the Christian Pulpit.* Atlanta: John Knox, 1980.

Graesser, Carl, Jr. "Preaching from the Old Testament." *Concordia Theological Monthly* 38 (1967): 525–34.

Greidanus, Sidney. *Sola Scriptura: Problems and Principles in Preaching Historical Texts.* Toronto: Wedge, 1970.

Haller, Eduard. "On the Interpretive Task." Translated by Ruth Grob. *Interpretation* 21 (1967): 158–66.

Hanson, R. P. C. "Biblical Exegesis in the Early Church." In *Cambridge History of the Bible,* edited by Peter R. Ackroyd and C. F. Evans. 3 vols. Cambridge: Cambridge University, 1970. I:412–54.

Hope, Robert. "Preach the Old Testament." *Theological Students Fellowship Bulletin* (1970): 1–2.

Jasper, F. N. "Preaching in the Old Testament." *Expository Times* 80 (1968–69): 356–61.

Johnson, John F. "*Analogia Fidei* as Hermeneutical Principle." *Springfielder* 36 (1972–73): 249–59.

Jones, Peter Rhea. "Biblical Hermeneutics." *Review and Expositor* 72 (1975): 139–47.

Kaiser, Otto, and Kümmel, Werner Georg. *Exegetical Method: A Student's Handbook.* Translated by E. V. N. Goetchius. New York: Seabury, 1967.

Käsemann, Ernst. "Protestant Exegesis on the Way to the World Church: Looking Back." *Australian Biblical Review* 26 (1978): 2–13.

Kessler, Martin. "New Directions in Biblical Exegesis." *Scottish Journal of Theology* 24 (1971): 317–25.

Klooster, Fred H. "Toward a Reformed Hermeneutic." *Theological Bulletin* 2 (1974): 1–16.

Klug, Eugene F. *"The End of the Historical-Critical Method:* A Review Article." *Springfielder* 38 (1974–75): 289–302.

Knight, George A. F. "New Perspectives in Old Testament Interpretation." *Bible Translator* 19 (1968): 50–58.

Kraus, Hans-Joachim. "Calvin's Exegetical Principles." Translated by Keith Crim. *Interpretation* 31 (1977): 8–18.

Landes, George M. "Biblical Exegesis in Crisis: What Is the Exegetical Task in a Theological Context?" *Union Seminary Quarterly Review* 26 (1970–71): 273–98.

Loretz, Oswald. "The Church and Biblical Exegesis." Translated by John Griffiths. In *Theology, Exegesis, and Proclamation*, edited by Roland E. Murphy, pp. 67–79. New York: Herder and Herder, 1971.

Lys, Daniel. *The Meaning of the Old Testament: An Essay on Hermeneutics.* Nashville: Abingdon, 1967. Pp. 146–72, "The Appropriation of the Old Testament."

McCurley, Foster R., Jr. *Proclaiming the Promise: Christian Preaching from the Old Testament.* Philadelphia: Fortress, 1974.

McKenzie, John L. "Problems of Hermeneutics in Roman Catholic Exegesis." *Journal of Biblical Literature* 77 (1958): 197–204.

Malherbe, Abraham J. "An Introduction: The Task and Method of Exegesis." *Restoration Quarterly* 5 (1961): 169–78.

Mare, W. Harold. "Guiding Principles for Historical Grammatical Exegesis." *Grace Journal* 14 (Fall 1973): 14–25.

Marrow, Stanley B. *Basic Tools for Biblical Exegesis.* Rome: Biblical Institute, 1976.

Marshall, I. Howard, ed. *New Testament Interpretation: Essays on Principles and Methods.* Grand Rapids: Eerdmans, 1977.

Mayer, Herbert T. "The Old Testament in the Pulpit." *Concordia Theological Monthly* 35 (1964): 603–8.

Meuer, Siegfried. "What Is Biblical Preaching? Exegesis and Meditation for the Sermon." *Encounter* 24 (1963): 182–89.

Mezger, Manfred. "Preparation for Preaching: The Route from Exegesis to Proclamation." Translated by Robert A. Kraft. *Journal for Theology and the Church* 2 (1965): 159–79.

Milavec, Aaron. "Modern Exegesis, Doctrinal Innovations, and the Dynamics of Discipleship." *Anglican Theological Review* 60 (1978): 55–74.

Montague, George T. "Hermeneutics and the Teaching of Scripture." *Catholic Biblical Quarterly* 41 (1979): 1–17.

Müller, Jac. J. "Exegesis and Kerugma." In *Biblical Essays: Proceedings of the Ninth Meeting of "Die ou-testamentiese Werkgemeenskap in Suid-Afrika"* . . . *and* . . . *of the Second Meeting of "Die nuwe-testamentiese Werkgemeenskap van Suid-Afrika"* . . . , pp. 230–38. Stellenbosch: Pro Rege-Pers, 1966.

Murphy, Roland E., ed. *Theology, Exegesis, and Proclamation.* Concilium: Religion in the Seventies; vol. 70: Scripture. New York: Herder and Herder, 1971.

Piper, Otto A. "Modern Problems of New Testament Exegesis." *Princeton Seminary Bulletin* 36 (August 1942): 3–14.

Preus, Robert D. "How Is the Lutheran Church to Interpret and Use the Old and New Testaments?" *Lutheran Synod Quarterly* 14 (1973): 23ff.

Rad, Gerhard von. *Biblical Interpretations in Preaching.* Translated by John E. Steely. Nashville: Abingdon, 1977. Pp. 11–18, "About Exegesis and Preaching."

Robert, André, and Feuillet, André, eds. *Interpreting the Scriptures.* Translated by Patrick W. Skehan et al. New York: Desclee, 1969.

Robinson, Haddon W. *Biblical Preaching: The Development and Delivery of Expository Messages.* Grand Rapids: Baker, 1980.

————. "What Is Expository Preaching?" *Bibliotheca Sacra* 131 (1974): 55–60.

Rosensweig. Bernard. "The Hermeneutic Principles and Their Application." *Tradition* 13 (1972): 49–76.

Sanders, J. N. "The Problem of Exegesis." *Theology* 42 (1941): 324–32.

Snodgrass, Klyne R. "Exegesis and Preaching: The Principles and Practice of Exegesis." *Covenant Quarterly* 34 (August 1976): 3–29. Includes a brief annotated bibliography for New Testament exegesis.

Stevenson, Dwight E. *Preaching on the Books of the Old Testament.* New York: Harper, 1961. Pp. 1–8, "The Old Testament and the Word of God."

Stuart, Douglas. *Old Testament Exegesis: A Primer for Students and Pastors.* Philadelphia: Westminster, 1980.

Surburg, Raymond F. "The Moral and Spiritual Qualifications of the Biblical Interpreter." *Concordia Theological Monthly* 22 (1951): 472–99.

————. "The Presuppositions of the Historical-Grammatical Method as Employed by Historic Lutheranism." *Springfielder* 38 (1974–75): 278–88.

Thiselton, Anthony C. "The Use of Philosophical Categories in New Testament Hermeneutics." *Churchman* 87 (1973): 87–100.

Thompson, William D. *Preaching Biblically: Exegesis and Interpretation.* Nashville: Abingdon, 1981.

————. "Text and Sermon: A Homiletician's Viewpoint." *Interpretation* 35 (1981): 32–45.

Toombs, Lawrence E. *The Old Testament in Christian Preaching.* Philadelphia: Westminister, 1961. Pp. 13–36, "The Old Testament and Christian Preaching."

————. "The Problematic of Preaching from the Old Testament." *Interpretation* 23 (1969): 302–14.

Trimp, C. "The Relevance of Preaching (in the Light of the Reformation's 'Sola Scriptura' Principle)." Translated by Stephen Voorwinde. *Westminster Theological Journal* 36 (1973–74): 1–30.

Weingreen, J. "The Rabbinic Approach to the Study of the Old Testament." *Bulletin of the John Rylands Library of Manchester* 34 (1951–52): 166–90.

Williams, Jay G. "Exegesis-Eisegesis: Is There a Difference?" *Theology Today* 30 (1973–74): 218–27.

Author-Oriented Hermeneutics— Advocates and Critics

Bollnow, Otto Friedrich. "What Does It Mean to Understand a Writer Better Than He Understood Himself?" *Philosophy Today* 23 (September 1979): 16–28.

Cain, William E. "Authority, 'Cognitive Atheism,' and the Aims of Interpretation: The Literary Theory of E. D. Hirsch." *College English* 39 (1977–78): 333–45.

Caird, G. B. *The Language and Imagery of the Bible*. Philadelphia: Westminster, 1980.

Fuller, Daniel P. "The Scope of Hermeneutics." *Notes on Translation* 51 (1975): 2–15.

Guthrie, Malcolm. "The Bible and Current Theories About Language." *Journal of the Transactions of the Victoria Institute* 86 (1954): 50–60.

Henry, Carl F. H. "The Interpretation of the Scriptures: Are We Doomed to Hermeneutical Nihilism?" *Review and Expositor* 71 (1974): 197–215. Is followed by a response from Morris Ashcraft (pp. 217–23), to which Henry then replies (pp. 225–27).

Hirsch, E. D., Jr. *Validity in Interpretation*. New Haven, Conn.: Yale University, 1967.

Johnson, Everard C. "From an Author-Oriented to a Text-Oriented Hermeneutic: Implications of Paul Ricoeur's Hermeneutical Theory for the Interpretation of the New Testament." Dissertation, Louvain University, 1977.

Kaiser, Walter C., Jr. "Meanings from God's Message: Matters for Interpretation." *Christianity Today*, 5 October 1979, pp. 30–33.

_____. "The Single Intent of Scripture." In *Evangelical Roots: A Tribute to Wilbur Smith*, edited by Kenneth S. Kantzer, pp. 123–41. Nashville: Nelson, 1978.

Nemetz, Anthony. "Literalness and the *Sensus Litteralis*." *Speculum* 34 (1959): 76–89.

Palmer, Richard E. *Hermeneutics: Interpretation Theory in Schleiermacher, Dilthey, Heidegger and Gadamer*. Evanston, Ill.: Northwestern University, 1969. Pp. 60–65.

Wilson, Barrie A. "Hirsch's Hermeneutics: A Critical Examination." *Philosophy Today* 22 (April 1978): 20–33.

Yoder, Perry B. *Toward Understanding the Bible: Hermeneutics for Lay People*. Newton, Kans.: Faith and Life, 1978.

Exegesis of Poetry

Alden, Robert L. "Chiastic Psalms: A Study in the Mechanics of Semitic Poetry." *Journal of the Evangelical Theological Society* 17 (1974): 11–28; 19 (1976): 191–200; 21 (1978): 199–210.

Cross, Frank Moore. "Prose and Poetry in the Mythic and Epic Texts from Ugarit." *Harvard Theological Review* 67 (1974): 1–15.

Cross, Frank Moore, and Freedman, David Noel. *Studies in Ancient Yahwistic Poetry*. Society of Biblical Literature Dissertation Series, 21. Missoula, Mont.: Scholars, 1975.

Culley, Robert C. *Oral Formulaic Language in the Biblical Psalms*. Near and Middle East Series. Toronto: University of Toronto, 1967.

Freedman, David Noel. "Prolegomenon." In *The Forms of Hebrew Poetry, Considered with Special Reference to the Criticism and Interpretation of the Old Testament*, by George Buchanan Gray. The Library of Biblical Studies. New York: Ktav, 1972.

Geller, Stephen A. *Parallelism in Early Biblical Poetry*. Harvard Semitic Monographs, edited by Frank Moore Cross, Jr., 20. Missoula, Mont.: Scholars, 1979.

Gevirtz, Stanley. *Patterns in the Early Poetry of Israel*. Studies in Ancient Oriental Civilization, 32. Chicago: University of Chicago, 1963.

Gray, George Buchanan. *The Forms of Hebrew Poetry, Considered with Special Reference to the Criticism and Interpretation of the Old Testament*. London: Hodder and Stoughton, 1915. Reprint. The Library of Biblical Studies. New York: Ktav, 1972.

Greenstein, Edward L. "Two Variations of Grammatical Parallelism in Canaanite Poetry and Their Psycholinguistic Background." *Journal of Ancient Near Eastern Studies* 6 (1974): 87–105.

Honeyman, A. M. "*Merismus* in Biblical Hebrew." *Journal of Biblical Literature* 71 (1951): 11–18.

Jakobson, Roman. "Grammatical Parallelism and Its Russian Facet." *Language* 42 (1966): 399–429. Treats parallelism of the folk poetry from ancient Canaan, China, Finland, Turkey, and Russia.

Kraft, Charles Franklin. "Some Further Observations Concerning the Strophic Structure of Hebrew Poetry." In *A Stubborn Faith: Papers on Old Testament and Related Subjects Presented to Honor William Andrew Irwin*, edited by Edward C. Hobbs, pp. 62–89. Dallas: Southern Methodist University, 1956.

—————. *The Strophic Structure of Hebrew Poetry, as Illustrated in the First Book of the Psalter*. Chicago: University of Chicago, 1938.

Levin, Samuel R. *Linguistic Structures in Poetry*. The Hague: Mouton, 1962.

Loewenstamm, Samuel E. "The Expanded Colon in Ugaritic and Biblical Verse." *Journal of Semitic Studies* 14 (1969): 176–96.

Lowth, Robert. *Lectures on the Sacred Poetry of the Hebrews*. Translated by G. Gregory. 3d ed. London: Thomas Tegg, 1835.

Lund, Nils Wilhelm. *Chiasmus in the New Testament: A Study in Form-Geschichte*. Chapel Hill: University of North Carolina, 1942. Pp. 3–47, 94–136.

—————. "The Presence of Chiasmus in the Old Testament." *American Journal of Semitic Languages and Literatures* 46 (1929–30): 104–26.

Meek, Theophile James. "The Structure of Hebrew Poetry." *Journal of Religion* 9 (1929): 523–50.

Robinson, T. H. "Hebrew Poetic Form: The English Tradition." *Supplements to Vetus Testamentum* 1 (1953): 128–49.

Subject Index

Author Index

Scripture Index